The Importance of Understanding

BOOKS BY *Lin Yutang*

Kaiming English Books (3 VOLS.)
Kaiming English Grammar
The Little Critic (2 VOLS.)
Confucius Saw Nancy (DRAMA) *and Essays About Nothing*
A Nun of Taishan
A History of the Press and Public Opinion in China
My Country and My People
The Importance of Living
Wisdom of Confucius
Moment in Peking
With Love and Irony
A Leaf in the Storm
Wisdom of China and India
Between Tears and Laughter
The Vigil of a Nation
The Gay Genius
Chinatown Family
Wisdom of Laotse
On the Wisdom of America
Widow, Nun and Courtesan
Famous Chinese Short Stories
Vermilion Gate
Looking Beyond
Lady Wu
The Secret Name
The Chinese Way of Life
From Pagan to Christian

古文小品譯英

THE
IMPORTANCE
OF
UNDERSTANDING

Translations from the Chinese

by LIN YUTANG

THE WORLD PUBLISHING COMPANY

CLEVELAND AND NEW YORK

PUBLISHED BY *The World Publishing Company*

2231 West 110th Street, Cleveland 2, Ohio

PUBLISHED SIMULTANEOUSLY IN CANADA BY

Nelson, Foster & Scott Ltd.

Library of Congress Catalog Card Number: 60-6690

FIRST EDITION

HC 460

▣ CONTENTS

ZEN

EPIGRAMS AND PROVERBS

i

IT WAS ONE OF THOSE EVENINGS. We had invited the Langs and the Targs. My wife knew that Lang was a gourmet and that she could not get away with just a good home-cooked dinner. She produced a pike covered with seaweed and scallop sauce which even I had not tasted in my life. Targ, I knew, was a bibliophile, interested in the bouillabaisse of old editions. What I did not know was that Targ was also a gourmet and Lang also a bibliophile, a collector of medieval scripts. The latter had brought me a 1708 edition of an antique French volume instead of a box of chocolates. When this happens, conversation goes very fast. Targ and Lang started talking about the history of the sauce Béarnaise and *How To Cook a Wolf* by M. F. K. Fisher. And Targ wanted to know if I could borrow or steal a copy of old Giles's *Chinese Biographical Dictionary* which he had read about in one of E. V. Lucas's novels and had been looking for all his life. I do not know what wine we had, but it was not Chablis.

Everybody was relaxed. This was conversation, when every friend in the room knew your heart and none hurt your eyes. After dinner, Targ said he wanted to see my library. I said I had no library but only a den where I worked. I had given away my English books at Singapore, following Yuan Mei's advice on "breaking up libraries." At least I had nothing to enchant a bibliophile with. I had only a very compact and carefully selected collection of Chinese books which followed me everywhere I went. When one travels a lot and has need of one's own Chinese books, the important thing in a book is clear print in compact volumes, rather than rarity of edition. Nevertheless, they are not just a working library but contain authors that I like especially. I have five editions of *Six Chapters of a Floating Life* and four editions of *West-Green Random Notes*. My collection is not the "Hundred Best Books" kind, but contains books that mean much to me personally and that I read and reread for companionship. They are usually of the carefree type which nourishes the soul and relaxes the spirit and, more often than not, celebrates life itself, including the inconsequential wayside flowers. Targ had suggested to me the writing of a book consisting of translations of passages which have meant much to me in the course of reading Chinese literature, and which have inspired or delighted me and are memorable for some reason or other. The suggestion struck a responsive chord in my heart. I have a collection of my favorites, mostly in the form of "literary notebooks," containing essays, sketches, diaries, letters, or just thoughts like Pascal's *Pensées*. Chinese authors rather excel in these things and Chinese literature swarms with them in a bewildering fashion; sometimes they put their thoughts and sketches in some order, and sometimes in no order at all. But they agree in one thing; they write with no eye to posterity and put down these thoughts as a relaxation for themselves or for their most intimate friends. The sentiment, the mood, the thought of the moment is the important thing.

I pulled out an old wood-block edition of *West-Green Random Notes* and said, "The girl Shuangching . . ." and stopped. I started again: "The girl Shuangching — she was married to an illiterate peasant but was a first-class poet herself. . . ." I realized the difficulty of expressing what was involved in such an offhand manner. They looked at the open page of Chinese characters in silence. What a world of language separated us! "This is belles-lettres, an elusive thing, you see," I said. "The style of expression or the poetry of meaning is more important than the matter. The origin of literature is in the mood, the feeling of the moment. When a writer has a sentiment in his breast and feels an itch in his finger, he puts it down, and when he does it beautifully enough for all readers in all ages to share it, it becomes a classic. Aristotle calls it the pleasure of recognition. I would prefer to call it the pleasure of relaxation — both for the writer and the reader."

"What do you mean?" said Targ.

"I mean the reader derives from such writing relaxation for the spirit or nourishment for the soul." I was trying to express the Chinese idea of considering the reading of literature as doing something to a man's spirit. The phrase is *yang shing i ching,* meaning literally to nourish one's original nature and relax one's soul. *Ching* has a very broad meaning: it covers "love," "passion," "sentiment," and feelings of all kinds. Philosophically, it means something close to consciousness, the feeling, responding soul. The English word "sentiment" perhaps comes closest to it; it is a soft word like *ching.* Sentiment is what makes life go, what binds us to this life. But sentiment also adorns life. It is like the fragrance in flowers, the flavor in food, and charm in women. It is what elevates us from a mere animal existence and is the sum total of human life and gives life meaning and delight. Through the enjoyment of writing which embodies *ching,* the heart, the soul, the mind are nourished and strengthened.

I am not sure just how, but I know that the enjoyment of reading of such snapshots of truth and life does nourish one's soul. It frees man from physical bondage, and only the mind remains. The mind recaptures that freedom which it has lost during the hustle and bustle of the day. That is how the soul is strengthened. One condition is absolute relaxation.

There are moments of such absolute relaxation in reading, when the spirit of man is as nearly free as it can be in this life. The poet who writes, "The book in one's half-open hand — midday slumber sweet," gives a picture of such perfect relaxation. He thought he was going to read, but permitted sweet slumber to overcome him. Had he determined either to read, or to sleep, it would have prevented his slumber. There is another picture of perfect relaxation in nature. "At the deserted ferry, the boat has swung across by itself." There is not a soul in sight; the boat, moored at some point, has found its rest in the direction of the tide and established a calm balance. The boat at that moment, by perfect harmony with the forces of wind and water, has, we may say, lost its physical identity. Likewise, when the reader's body has found the perfect posture, his mind becomes free and it becomes strong.

ii

THERE IS A CLOSER CONNECTION between sweet slumber and casual reading than we will admit. In either case, the heartbeat is slower, the tension is gone, and the temperature of the mind is cooler, or should be. The best kind of reading is bedside reading. Of course there are very important people in this world who cannot relax a moment even while they are in bed; they must think of something that will flatter their vanity, increase their body temperature and quicken their heartbeat, and make them even more important. There is also a kind of reading which is intended to excite the soul, either some ghoulish literature or a good suspense novel. This is not the kind of reading I mean. I mean reading which informs the mind and cools the understanding. True wisdom always cools and makes one see things in a better perspective. For whatever one reads, at least the position of the reader is essentially that of a spectator, an observer of life. Even when the reading matter concerns a murder, the reader has the personal comfort of knowing that he is merely an observer at the scene and not in danger of a stab at the back. That is the comfort which the Chinese describe cynically as that of watching a prairie fire across a river, knowing that you are personally safe. There is something in that fact alone. For in that position of an observer, the reader's mind can think calmly and coolly and judge human life better and more clearly and with the warmth of understanding.

I think the word "understanding" is a great word. It asserts the kinship of all mankind, both in its love of truth and beauty, and in its folly and its foibles. Reading of the best kind always gives that understanding of life and of oneself. That is the true purpose of reading. Reading, more than anything else, is a pure act of the mind in the privacy of one's household when the human soul holds communion with some of the wisest men of old, and in holding communion with these wise minds the soul holds communion with itself. The next morning you wake up and see some idiosyncratic behavior or doings of your friend or some member of your household and you smile more understandingly, because you have seen it before and know what some of the wisest minds think of the doings and feelings and struggles of all mankind, from time past till the present hour.

Since I wrote *The Importance of Living,* quite some time ago, I have promised myself that I would one day translate some of the best Chinese writings on this Chinese and peculiarly human outlook and understanding of life which are the sources of my own thinking. I did not know what I was doing when I wrote in that book all that I thought of human life and human subjects from the biggest to the smallest. My readers' reactions always surprised me, as if I had something new to say. It did not seem so to me; I was talking a lot of platitudes, which are called in Chinese "old man's old rubbish" (*laosheng changtan*). Perhaps there is something new and fresh in this Chinese gay acceptance of life with all its tragedy and its pathos but also with all that is good and beautiful in the human heart. Love and pain are here, beauty and ugliness, the transitory nature of our existence and the desire for immortality — the essential conflicts of this human life. Our personal events and happenings are merely episodic, but the tragedy of life (if you want to call it that) is all there, its tragedy, but also its beauty and its humor. True literature always brings out that essential conflict of human imperfections because we are neither angels incapable of evil, nor beasts incapable of higher and nobler aspirations. And so the conflict goes on and we seem to be making progress and we don't. Love will always be with us, and so will pain; moments of joy and moments of suffering; beauty and ugliness; the sinner repents and the great man falls. A touch of sadness and a touch of madness make all the world akin. That is why we resent all great men who are presented to us without moral imperfections, without idiosyncrasies or some form of defect, mental or physical, like Cromwell's wart or President Wilson's hurting toes. There should be some personal weakness somewhere, or some intense love — a form of madness — be it for a woman or aeronautic science, a form of madness which implies absolute devotion to one thing and absent-mindedness or forgetfulness about all other things.

In covering some reading for the preparation of this work, I once more took a mental tour of my old favorites, friends of long ago who have had an invisible influence on me. It was pure joy for me. I was then conscious of something truly fresh and surprising, so different from what one comes across in reading Western literature. Of course I selected only the best, things that have stuck in my mind since my reading them and things that communicate something to me. I refuse to translate anything which does not awake in me an echo of hearty assent. An editor is usually not responsible for the opinions of the authors included, and I am not. But I am also a translator, and felt no obligation to translate any author except those I liked, if not approved. Translation is a very subtle thing; unless you are emotionally in contact with the original author, you cannot do a good job of it. In translating an author, you practically engage to speak for him in a new language, and you cannot do so unless you are speaking for an old friend, so to speak. And your friend, knowing how strange his own expressions must often sound in a foreign language, gives you some freedom in expression, provided that he can trust that you truly understand what he was trying to say, and that it would be the way he would say it in English if he were thinking and writing in English.

It is only necessary to add that the opinions represented here are those of one special class of Chinese — the scholars, writers, and poets — not of successful men of the world usually. Let us say they are the opinions of the best and most educated men with educated values. They are poets and talented women. In this class, there is always a very special conflict which is unknown to the West. The scholars were the ruling class in China, and only in politics could a scholar in ancient China achieve "success." There was always the conflict between such outward success and their poetic vision of life. The latter choice is associated with a simple life, if not stinging poverty, or retirement after a brief official career. It involves also devotion to the simple joys of living — such as seeing famous mountains and having a good, understanding wife, who will not hesitate to pull out a hair ornament in order to pawn it for the wine needed to entertain an old friend who has suddenly dropped in — and other devotions· to art, books, and friendly conversations in which news of official promotions at the court are tabooed. Political life always has shady aspects, and success implies a careful compromise between what one would and would not do. Somewhere a limit must be drawn. One must entertain and be entertained to get along at all, and there is no evil in that. But one can also be lost in such a round of entertainments and getting to "know the right person." The poet's values and the "social"· values are often confused.

In China, there was always a positive outlook in the best of the scholars, to serve and help the country, expressed as "loyalty to the king," but all depended upon whether there was a good king *ad hoc* to serve. Practically no upright and great poet-scholar who stood for his honest opinion lived without a period of being "demoted" to some remote semibarbarian district for espousing unwelcome views of current politics. Su Tungpo was an outstanding example: he was sent as far as the island of Hainan, in the South China Sea. There was Chu Suiliang, who fought against the megalomaniac Empress Wu and was exiled as far as modern Vietnam where he died. In·the nineteenth century, Lin Tseh-shu, who fought the narcotics trade and started the Opium War with England, was exiled to Chinese Turkestan where he died. Han Yu, Liu Tsungyuan, and many other writers had similar fates even if they were not sent as far as that. Han Yu was sent to what is now Swatow, where, at that time, there were plenty of crocodiles. Confucius himself at one time toyed with the idea of "taking a raft and floating out to the seas" to live "among the Nine Barbarian tribes."

This conflict between the practical and the poetic vision of life was always there, and will come up in these selections from time to time, especially in the section "Fools to This World." This conflict was looked upon as being one between "joining the world" and "leaving the world." Very often it was a conflict between outward success and poverty, between one's responsibilities to the world and the saving of one's own soul. Of course one wanted to help and serve the country, but there had to be a good king, and good kings were few and far between. Many stuck to their principles and chose poverty and earned their immortal fame that way. This curious conflict is sadly but well expressed by one Ming scholar, Chu Shihsze, who lost his job because of his honesty and was forced to retire. In a letter to a friend he said, "Thanks to my political enemy, I have been set free to come back to my farm. I can lie in a shallow stream pillowing my head on a rock and do what I like. I am only afraid of public opinion. So long as public opinion is distorted, I can enjoy this freedom of the fairies. For God's sake, leave it alone."

iii

Strictly speaking, there should be no order in a book of this kind which is designed for casual dipping. Most Chinese anthologies or selections do not bother about order. Each piece should stand by itself, to be dipped into when the reader thumbing through the pages finds a word or a line which arrests his attention.

Too much order hurts the mood of relaxation in reading a book. There is, however, some kind of order or grouping in this book; for instance, descriptions of travel, or "after tea and wine" wit, or readings on Zen are grouped together so that the reader knows roughly where to go for what he wants to read at that particular moment.

Briefly, in my mind as editor-translator, there is a classification, strictly in Chinese terms, which goes somewhat as follows: First what expresses sentiment, then what describes scenes, followed by what pleases the senses, what titillates the understanding, what frees the spirit, and what nourishes the mind. These are all submerged in an arrangement better suited to English readers, as presented in the Contents. Briefly, the sections are presented in the following order: How some of the best poets and writers saw the problem of human life with its implied conflicts; their thoughts on love and death; what they felt and called beautiful in nature and the seasons; how they managed to compromise and make adjustments in human society, beginning with "The Half-and-Half Song" (selection 34), which I think is the soundest philosophy of living, provided one has learned the tact of "going around" (selection 35). Next come a few selections on women and those pieces which show how the writers thought they should order their home and daily living; how they beautified existence by art and literature; how they talked and joked "after tea and wine" ("after dinner" in English); how some bared their teeth in wit and satire; how some who were eccentric poets and artists became "fools to this world," were regarded as "odd" by others, and often chose the epithets of "folly" or even "the idiot," "the crazy one" for themselves, signing themselves in this way solemnly on their best paintings — a note of protest and a note of defiance to the gods;

how some of the best philosophized and thought about this whole mess of human life and how they went back to the simple life of contentment, religious (Zen) or otherwise. Finally I have gathered together some independent short lines or pithy paragraphs, containing thoughts or epigrams, and some proverbs.

Chinese literature consists of belles-lettres almost entirely. Drama and the novel came much later. Briefly, the artistic short story appeared in the ninth century, the drama began to come into its own in the thirteenth, and the first important development of the novel came as late as the fifteenth. Most of these creative forms of writing remained outside the pale of legitimate literature. All the time all their life, the Chinese writers were writing essays, essays, and essays, if not poems. They did this par excellence. It was the unburdening of a thought at the time. I believe I have culled some of the best and I have presented them in English dress with considerable excitement on my own part, and hope that I may be able to communicate some of that excitement to my readers so that they share that joy.

NEEDLESS TO SAY, all translations are by myself (except for the selections from the *Lankavatra* and *Surangama Sutras*). In the present highly unsatisfactory state of spelling Chinese names, I have spelled them with the maximum simplicity, such as is used in current newspapers (e.g., "Chen" instead of "Ch'ên,²" and "Shueh" instead of "Hsüeh⁴"). For the students of Chinese who wish to be absolutely sure of the originals, a list of such names in Chinese characters is provided at the back of the book.

人生

HUMAN LIFE

1 回 A Chinese Fantasia:
The Song of Life

» *I have collected and translated here a group of poems by different Chinese poets of different ages, bearing on the central theme, The Song of Life. However infinite the variations and however separated the poets are in time and space, the burden of their song seems to be the same. It expresses a point of view.*

LIU CHIENFU:

Oh, heard you of that old immortal quest?
What of the virgins* sent by king's behest?
No drink immortal yet has Yenti† made,
And Laotse closed his eyes like all the rest.

LIU CHIFU:

Soon withers the *p'u*, flimsy, tasseled reed.
A leaky craft borne on with the rapids' speed.
The fragile willows bend and beckon and ask:
Oh, proud man, what is the hurry indeed?

For ages men the Chang-an road‡ passed,
And like the grass that yearly grows — were blast.
Each time I came upon this bank I found
Myself and this maple older than the last.

---

* Five hundred virgins were sent by Tsin Shih-huang to the China Seas to obtain the elixir of immortality.
† The Chinese god of medicine.
‡ Chang-an was capital of Tang Period, and Chang-an Road means path to official glory.

TANG YIN:

> The winter follows autumn and the summer, spring;
> No sooner cock crows than the bells of vesper ring.
> Mark how thy neighbors one by one depart
> And creep to stop a hole where crickets sing.

PO CHUYI:

> But yesterday he came to my sickbed;
> Today I saw with tears his coffin laid.
> O see ye and take this lesson well to heart.
> Bring out the *pipa*,* quaff the liquor red!

TENG CHINGYANG:

> We are but passing guests from who knows where.
> Say not thy home is here, thy home is there.
> It suits me well wherever I may be;
> The flowers bloom here, there, and everywhere.

CHUEHWEN:

> What rich, golden farms below a hill!
> A newcomer harvests crops that others till.
> O rejoice not, newcomer, at your turn —
> One waits behind — a new newcomer still!

SHAO YUNG:

> Oh, when shall issues not new issues create?
> And plotter and plotted 'gainst their strife abate?
> Look each behind and each his footsteps mind;
> New grudges shouldn't old grudges complicate.

* A guitarlike instrument, sometimes translated as a lute.

CHEN CHIJU:

> Let history be, since it is long gone by.
> What prophet can the Future Knot untie?
> Let's talk of present who in present live;
> Ask not the questions Wherefrom, Whereto, and Why.

CHAO PINGWEN:

> Arise and take thy cane and bring thy pot,
> Hunt out the hill and dale's secluded spot.
> I hear the cuckoos calling on the hills.
> Business? What business? Oh, tarry not!

SHIN YU-AN:

> One drunk is a free dispenser of his smiles,
> Forgotten all injustice, all men's guiles.
> Of late have I just come to realize,
> Spurn bookish wisdom and your ambition's wiles.

TAO HUNGCHING: *

> O tell me, friend, what thy hill lodge has got?
> Why, clouds around the passes, quite a lot!
> They are just for my own enjoyment, but
> To make thee presents — unfortunately not!

ANONYMOUS:

> A lonely hut on a shaded mountain bend;
> He lives this side and clouds at the other end.
> The clouds depart at dawn on their daily rounds
> And say, "Thou lucky monk, no duties t'attend!"

* This man is counted as one of the Taoist "fairies" and is reported to have ascended bodily to heaven. He lived from A.D. 452 to 536.

ANONYMOUS:

> A thousand acres of clouds before this nook;
> God has the sea and I an angler's hook.
> I stretch a sleepy leg in the emperor's bed;*
> Who cares whose names stand in the Service Book?

CHANG CHUNSHOU:

> He casts his nets midstream his haul to take;
> She drops her line and waits her catch to make.
> When all the day's catch is 'changed again for wine,
> They row the boat homeward in showers' wake.

ANONYMOUS:

> From fishing home, I leave the boat untied.
> Just right for sleep — the moon o'er the river wide.
> Though it be driven in a night's rainstorm,
> It will be found somewhere by the waterside.

> No need to shut the door of a mud hut small;
> I slowly leave the lichen-covered hall.
> If guests arrive, the boy will look for me
> In yonder woods, or by the waterfall.

CHEN CHIJU:

> A hut between the hill and lake on the lea;
> Its gate beneath a pine tree's canopy;
> Plain couch, settee, and four walls lined with books —
> Who owns and waters the garden? Chen Meitse.

* This poem celebrates the poet Yen Tseling, who was a childhood friend of Han Kuangwu before he became emperor (A.D. 25–57). He refused office but once slept with the emperor and in his sleep put his leg across the emperor's belly. (See selection 86.)

Discard thy long gown, set thy bare feet free!
A fishing basket and wines of quality!
A supper of carp and I seek the friendly couch,
When someone calls, "Oh, the moon is up already!"

FU KUNGMOU:

O come with me, my friend, and wine thy sorrow!
To match it, the moon's golden liquid borrow!
Then pass the fragrant cup for a tête-à-tête;
Old Father Heaven will take care of the morrow!

SU TUNGPO: *

O the clear moon's speckless, silvery night!
When filling thy cup, be sure to fill it quite!
Strive not for frothy fame or bubble wealth:
 A passing dream —
  A flashing flint —
   A shadow's flight!

O what is knowledge, fine and superfine?
To innocent and simple joys resign!
When I go home, I'll carry on my back
 · A load of clouds —
  A sweet-toned *chin*† —
   A pot of wine.

TUNG CHUNGFENG:

I love my bamboo hut, by water included,
Where rockery o'er stone steps protruded;

* This is the single one poem that I love best in all Chinese poetry.
† A string instrument.

A quiet, peaceful study, small but fine:
Which is so cozy —
So delightful —
So secluded!

No marble halls, no vermilion towers
Are quite so good as my secluded bowers.
The lawn embroidered so with buttercups
Greets me in rain —
Or in shine —
Or in showers.

A short, low wall, with windows hid by trees;
A tiny, little pond myself to please;
And there upon its shady, rocky banks:
A pretty maid —
A little moon —
A little breeze!

And how about a quiet life leading?
From balcony watch the fish in water feeding,
And earn from moon and flowers a leisure life:
Have friendly chats —
Some incense —
And some reading?

For household use, some furniture decrepit.
'Tis enough! the hills and water so exquisite!
When guests arrive, to make it just perfect:
Put on the kettle —
Brew the tea —
And sip it!

O sweep thy yard, but spare the mossy spots!
Let petals bedeck thy steps with purple dots

As in a painting. What's more wonderful:
    Some pine trees —
       And bamboos —
          And apricots!

Let bloom in order pear and peach and cherry!
The morrow lies in the gods' lap — why worry?
Who knows but what and when our fortune is?
    And so be wise —
       Be content —
          Be merry!

When friend arrives that thou hast so admired,
As by some idle nothing in common inspired,
Ask him to stay for a good, carefree half-day:
    And drink when happy —
       Sing when drunk —
          Sleep when tired.

A quiet home, far from the hustling crowd;
Let no trivialities thy mind becloud.
Gay and contented, being disenchanted,
    And not be fussy —
       Nor selfish —
          Nor be proud.

Obey God's will, and wait on Heaven's pleasure.
Thy purity of heart alone do treasure.
Enough the library and the court of flowers
    To lead a life of peace —
       And contentment —
          And leisure.

2 回 Quiet Dream Shadows

From

YUMENGYING

Chang Chao
died after 1698

« *This short volume contains a scholar's reflections on life, distinguished by a rare sensitivity and couched in a very charming style. The word "shadows" in its title suggests the reflections of objects in water, moving glimpses of the real world, as reflections in our thoughts and dreams are. Each one of the epigrams shows an original, individual insight. There were many such collections of epigrams and esthetic appreciations in the late sixteenth and seventeenth centuries, such as those by Chen Chiju and Tu Chihshui, similar in character to this one, but not quite as well done. Chang Chao was not a moralist and wrote what pleased him, with beauty and with joy. (See also selection 7.) Another unique feature of this book is the delightful comments by his friends; one comments on the other, so that we are led into the thoughts and discussions of the group and their opinions. It is a symposium of truncated dialogues in which Chang Chao says a line, and the others may offer comments also of one line if they feel they have something to say. These comments are often light, playful, and intimate, as in a private conversation, and some of them are quite good. They enliven the epigrams and are as necessary as the calyxes to flowers and the greens to a bouquet.*

A great many of these epigrams were translated by me in The Importance of Living. I feel that I should make a new and full translation of this book, including the comments. I have omitted about one tenth, those that make references to ancient Chinese subjects and convey little meaning to the Western reader with-

out long explanations. Of the friends' comments, I have omitted those that are less interesting. The regrouping is mine. The author is referred to in the comments as "Shintsai," his literary name. The book must have been written before 1693, the year of Mao Pichiang's death, because it contains Mao's comments.

1. Human Life

PASSION holds up the bottom of the universe, and the poet gives it a new dress.

Yujo: All human life begins with love between man and woman, from which the other human relationships such as between father and son and between brothers follow.

LOVE is not true love without a form of madness. A literary artist must have zest in life to enter into nature's spirit.

Yunshih: Here speaks a born lover and artist.

Tienshih: Shintsai really understands the zest of life besides being a literary artist.

[Miss] Hueichu: I think I know the passion of love, but I have not the zest combined with talent.

Yutang: She is the only woman commentator. As it is polite in Chinese society to give only first names, only these are given here. Included are two brothers and a nephew of the author. Hanchen is often humorous and Yungching is always down to earth. Some like Yunshih and Chiuyuan were authors in their own right.

IT IS AGAINST the will of God to eat delicate food hastily, to pass gorgeous scenery hurriedly, to express deep sentiments superficially, to pass a beautiful day steeped in food and drinks, and to enjoy your wealth sunk in luxuries.

Yutang: This is the only paragraph which is not strictly a part of the book by Chang Chao, but which I have taken from The Sequel to Quiet Dream Shadows, by Chu Shi.

ONE SHOULD discipline oneself in the spirit of autumn and live with others in the spirit of spring.

ONLY THOSE who take leisurely what the people of the world are busy about can be busy about what the people of the world take leisurely.

OF ALL THINGS one enjoys leisure most, not because one does nothing. Leisure confers upon one the freedom to read, to travel, to make friends, to drink, and to write. Where is there a greater pleasure than this?

> Hoshan: Then you are really busy.
>
> Huei-an: The proverb says, "Steal leisure from business." It can be stolen methodically.
>
> Jochin: Those five things make leisure really worth while.

I THINK it is better to have an understanding wife than a pretty concubine, and better to have peace of mind than wealth.

> [Nephew] Chupo: There is no limit to desires. How can one expect to have a pretty concubine without first having an understanding wife? And how can one have peace of mind without plenty of money?
>
> Yu-an: He means a choice of alternatives. And there are indeed people with plenty of money but no peace of mind.

THE PERFECT LIFE: to live in a world of peace in a lake district where the magistrate is good and honest, and to have an understanding wife and bright children.

> Shiaolin: It would be a pity to have a vulgarian enjoy all this.
>
> Hanchen: Here is a black-faced Laotse thinking of becoming a devil.*
>
> Taikuan: Yes, and rather like imagining eating a juicy steak before a butcher's shop window!
>
> Liyuan: An understanding wife, yes, but also a long life. Otherwise the blessing is not complete.

BLESSED ARE those who have time for reading, money to help others, the learning and ability to write, who are not bothered with gossip and disputes, and who have learned friends frank with advice.

* He means Mephistopheles.

Shengtsao: We can take care of those things which depend on ourselves, but not those which depend on others.

Tanlu: Shintsai has them all.

Shuichiao: I would be satisfied with half of these five.

Yungching: I thought the successful men never wanted friends with frank advice. Shintsai asks for them instead!

THOSE WHO despise money end up by sponging on their friends; those who mix up freely with all sorts of people will eventually hurt themselves.

Shengtsao: What a profound warning!

Tsaomin: For myself, I do not regret it one way or the other.

Tsefa: It does make a difference, though, whether you hurt others or only yourself.

Hanchen: Nowadays people do not welcome being sponged upon. So it is better to be careful.

A SMALL INJUSTICE can be drowned by a cup of wine; a great injustice can be drowned only by the sword.

Shingyuan: So you drown all sorrows by holding a cup of wine with a sword in sight.

Yu-an: I do not think the Blessed Lord would easily give such a sword to men. It might raise more trouble than it can settle.

Huei-an: O, Lungchuan [famous wine] and Tai-o [famous sword], trust me! I can handle both!

A GREAT LOVER loves women, but one who loves women is not necessarily a great lover. A beautiful woman often has a tragic life, but not all those who have tragic lives are beautiful. A good poet can always drink, but being a great drinker does not make one a poet.

Chupo: Passion which is based on sex must after all be distinguished from true love. Tragedy sometimes comes from being a great beauty, but sometimes has no connection with it, but is just fate.

Chiushih: There are poets who cannot drink.

GREEN HILLS come with blue waters which borrow their blueness from the hills; good wine produces beautiful poems, which draw sustenance from the spirits.

Shengshu: Green hills and blue waters make it possible to enjoy wine and poetry. So everything goes back to the hills and waters.

DRINK BY ALL MEANS, but do not make drunken scenes; have women by all means, but do not destroy your health; work for money by all means, but do not let it blot out your conscience; get mad about something, but do not go beyond reason.

Chungchiang: There are some who go to excess and seem the more genuinely great for it.

IF THERE WERE no books, then nothing need be said about it, but since there are books, they must be read; if there were no wine, then nothing need be said, but since there is, it must be drunk; since there are famous mountains, they must be visited; since there are flowers and the moon, they must be enjoyed; and since there are poets and beauties they must be loved and protected.

[*Younger brother*] *Mushan:* Easier said than done. There is the famous Yellow Mountain right in our district. But how many have visited it?

IF ONE HAS to praise someone, rather do it by word of mouth than by pen; if there are persons that must be castigated, also do it by word of mouth rather than in writing.

Pajen: You have no control over it sometimes.

Chupo: The first half of the sentence helps one's integrity, the second half one's character.

Yu-an: It not only helps character, but saves one from getting into trouble.

Tienshih: There are writers today who find no other use for their pen except writing eulogies. Shintsai is not aware of the circumstances which force them to do it. He lives mentally in the Golden Age.

Yunshih: An ancient inscription on a pen says: "The little hairbrush. You can get out when dipped in water, but when you get into writing, you may be crushed." There are eulogies with tongue-in-cheek sarcasms and apparent denunciations which cover real praise. But the best thing is not to commit it to paper at all.

Yutang: A scholar was often asked to write obituaries and memorial tributes by relatives of the deceased. Technically, in China, such eulogies were called "flattering the grave."

ONE CAN FORGET everything except the thought of fame, and learn to be cool toward everything except three cups of wine.

Chupo: Now I hear someone who is feeling hot behind the ears and who wants to get up at dawn and practice fencing.

Tanlu: I can't drink, but I cannot forget the thought of fame.

Yunshih: It is not a bad occupation, this thought about fame. Tanlu is sincere.

OF ALL THINGS in the universe, those that move men most deeply are the moon in heaven, the *chin* in music, the cuckoo among birds, and the willow among plants.

WHEN YOU READ the *Shuihu* and come to the passage where Luta smashes into the ranks of Chenkuanshi or where Wusung kills the tiger with his bare hands, you feel good. By that I mean something like what Li Po felt when he made the queen hold the inkstone for him when he was commanded to write a poem. A man must have such moments of supreme satisfaction in his life. Then he will not have lived in vain. If he cannot, he can hope to make up for it by writing a fine book.

Chupo: Such moments of supreme satisfaction have to happen naturally. They cannot be striven for.

[*Younger brother*] *Mushan:* If elder brother could kill the Ungrateful Wolf [in a story], it would be one of those moments.

IN POSSESSION of a lively imagination, one can live in the cities and feel like one is in the mountains, and following one's fancies with the clouds, one can convert the dark continent of the south into fairy isles. A great wrong has been committed on the plane tree by the necromancers who regard it as bringing bad luck, saying that when a plane tree grows in the yard, its owner will live abroad. . . . Most superstitions are like that.

Hanchen: Those who love the plane tree are often poor. But that is because the Lord does not want us to have all the blessings at the same time. It is true, however, that in autumn its bare-knuckled and knobbed branches are difficult to look at.

THERE ARE HILLS and waters on the earth, in paintings, in dreams, and in one's imagination. The beauty of such hills and waters on the earth is in their grace and variety; that in paintings, richness of ink and freedom of the brush; that in dreams, their changeful-ness; and that in one's imagination, good composition.

Shingyuan: The writing of this book has grace and variety also.

Jihchieh: In literature, the changes and surprises are even more exciting and difficult to describe.

Hanchen: But please not those changes of expression on the face (in snobbery, etc.)!

Shiangtsu: But sometimes when one meets hardships, the hills seem blocked and the waters come to a dead end, as in my case.

BE A GOLDFISH among the fish and a swallow among the birds. These are like Taoist fairies who go through life like the witty Tungfang Manching, safe from harm from those in power.

Hanchen: The goldfish escapes from harm because its flesh is bitter to the taste. Once there was a man who paid a high price for a beautiful variety and sent it as a present to a magistrate. Later the magistrate said to him, "The beautiful fish you sent me seemed to be perfectly tasteless. I have cooked it and tasted it." There are such people in the world!

SO LIVE that your life may be like a poem. Arrange things so that they look like they are in a painting.

Panchien: There are things that will never look like they are in a painting: pigs, dollar bills, and juvenile delinquents.

Chupo: Poems, on the other hand, would also like to be like real life, and paintings would like to be like things.

Tienwai: It is also possible to say, "So live as to be like a painting, and arrange furniture so that the room looks like a poem."

AN ANCIENT WRITER said, "Life would not be worth living if there were no moon, no flowers, and no beautiful women." I might add:

"It might not be important to be born a man, if there were no pen and paper, and no chess and wine."

Jihchieh: Beware of living in vain!

Tienshih: I am sure that foreigners have no pen and paper and chess and wine, or if they have, these things must be all different. Why, then, are human beings also born there?

Hueilai: Life would not be worth living without great heroes and writers.

THAT I MIGHT BE the *shu* among the trees (which is never cut down because of its worthless timber), the *shu* among the grass (which can foretell events), the sea gull among the birds (which merges with the elements), the *chih* among animals (a kind of deer which attacks the guilty one), the butterfly among insects (which flits among flowers), and the *kun* among fish (which has the freedom of the ocean).

Poshui: I wish to be a rock!

Huei-an: I wish to be a dream!

[Miss] Hueichu: I wish to be the shadow in a dream!

IT WAS FORTUNATE of Chuangtse to dream of being a butterfly, but a misfortune for the butterfly to dream of being Chuangtse.

Chiuyuan: This is unfair to Chuangtse. Only he could have dreamed of being a butterfly.

Kaisze: Are you dreaming of being a dream interpreter?

Hanchen: Chuangtse had that dream because he was deeply associated with the flowers. Others might begin such a dream only, and it would be like a man dreaming of starting a wine dinner, to be rudely waked up by his wife!

THAT ONE MIGHT control one's dreams! Then one could go anywhere one likes, conjure up the spirits of the past, and set out on a world trip without waiting for the sons and daughters to be married off first.

Chiuyuan: I sometimes think that ghosts have this advantage over men because they can go where they like.

Hanchen: On the other hand, it is possible that ghosts go everywhere in the upper and the nether world and see *nothing* at all!

YOUNG PEOPLE should have the wisdom of the old, and old people should have the heart of the young.

> Hanchen: I do see white-haired old men with one foot in the grave take a concubine the moment they have a better harvest than usual. Don't they also have "the heart of the young?" But the young people who have the wisdom of the old are rare.
>
> Chupo: There are young men who take a concubine at the age of seventeen or eighteen. So they, too, have the wisdom of the old.
>
> Jochin: A man who feels old cannot be a great soul.
>
> Szechih: Living this way, one is not indeed just a plaything of Father Time.

I CANNOT HOPE to be a farmer, but will learn watering flowers; cannot hope to become a woodcutter, but will be contented with pulling out weeds.

> [Monk] Chunjen: Watering and weeding the garden is after all not a bad life. One feels here, however, that the author has a hankering to weed out and cast off a lot of things he does not like.
>
> Szechih: I call myself a "literate farmer." Is that presumptuous?

RECLUSE SCHOLARS often disdain to discuss affairs of the government. But history is full of affairs of the government. Should one stop reading history, too? They cannot have meant it.

> Chupo: Sometimes, these things are affectations. A real recluse scholar can also assume the helm of government if he is asked to.

A MAN MUST NOT be fastidious about other things, but he must be about reading. He must not be greedy, except in buying books. He should not be a confirmed addict, except in the habit of doing good and helping others.

> Shengtsao: One who helps others not as an instinctive habit may be doing so to be talked about.

TO ENJOY literary fame can take the place of passing imperial examinations; to manage to live within one's means can take the place of wealth; to lead a life of leisure can well be the equivalent of a long life.

> *Chinjen:* But if a famous scholar also passes the examinations, is rich and has learned to live simply without being a slave to wealth, and reaches venerable age and enjoys a life of leisure — would not such a man be living the life of a fairy?
>
> *Jushou:* I am afraid that poor scholars like to comfort themselves with this thought. I do not think it is so charming to be poor.
>
> *Tsingli:* It has been said that if a man will sit idly, he can make a day as long as two days and therefore have a life span of a hundred forty when he lives to seventy.

RANDOM READING and browsing are better than not being acquainted with books at all; it is all right to be detached, but not to be ignorant of the trend of the times.

> *Chupo:* There is a distinction between resisting conventions and fashions of thought, and being ignorant of them.
>
> *Yutang:* Chupo, the nephew of Chang Chao, is one of the most frequent commentators and one of the best. He assisted his uncle in editorship of a very big *Chaotai Tsungshu* (Library of Contemporary Authors) which is well known today.

THERE ARE THOSE who have the beauties of forests and hills before their eyes, but do not appreciate them — the fishermen, woodcutters, peasants, and the black and the yellow [Buddhist and Taoist monks] — and others who have gardens, terraces, and women, but often fail to enjoy them for lack of time or of culture — the rich merchants and high officials.

> [*Younger brother*] *Mushan:* There are those who have good food and cannot enjoy it — the cooks — and those who are in daily touch with rare editions and fine bindings but cannot read them — the moths and book dealers.

TO SIT ALONE at night and invite the moon to tell it one's sorrows; to sleep alone at night and call to the crickets and pour out one's regrets.

Kungchih: Shintsai really knows the heart of a lonely traveler abroad.

AN OFFICIAL's reputation comes from public opinion, but that of his close associates and of beggars of office should be discounted. The reputation of women should come from real knowledge; the views of fans and superficial critics cannot be trusted.

Yungching: Sometimes when an official runs into a barrage of opposition, we may be sure that there is something in that man.

Jochin: This is not always true. When the close associates are not making a point for their personal friends or when the beggars are not trying to secure favors, they can be just also.

Chiuyuan: Confucius had something to say on this: "It is best to be liked by the good men of the village and hated by the bad."

A TRUE LOVER does not change with the years; a good drinker does not change with the seasons; a lover of books does not stop reading because of business.

BUILD ONE'S CHARACTER on the foundation of the moral teachings of the Sung Neo-Confucianists [twelfth century]; but go through life in the spirit of the Chin romanticists [third and fourth centuries].

Paochen: A real Confucianist can be quite romantic.

Yungching: That would make a double-strength saint.

Yunshih: Some puritans [Neo-Confucianists] are romantic, and some are not. Romanticists are sometimes Puritans at heart and others not at all. There is a very fine difference.

IT IS EASIER to be a hero than a sage, and easier to be a writer than a real genius.

Chupo: A hero usually is not a sage, but a sage is always a true hero. The same is true of writers and geniuses.

Yutang: A genius (in Chinese, *tsaitse*) is usually associated with a striking personality, out of which his literary creations naturally overflow. Such a one was Su Tungpo. In another sense, I find *tsaitse* is best translated by the word "poet"—a genius, poor and needing someone to look after him.

IN SELF-CONTENTMENT, a brilliant man takes his ease with birds and flowers; careless of popular fame, he regards himself as being served by the hilltop clouds.

> *Hanchen:* Su Tungpo says: "At such a time, one seems to be thinking of something, and yet is thinking of nothing."
>
> *Yutang:* Tungpo said this when he was officially under detention in a district overlooking the wide Yangtse River, in A.D. 1080. (See selection 37.)

IT IS EASIER to stand pain than to stand an itch; the bitter taste is easier to bear than sour.

> *Yutang:* Tungpo first said this about an itch.

2. Personal Character

WHAT IS A GOOD MAN? Simply one whose life is useful to the world. And a bad man is simply one whose life is harmful to others.

> *Hanchen:* There are, however, those who are harmful and yet enjoy a good reputation, and who manage to profit by a show of unselfishness. These are the worst of all.

THOSE BEYOND GOOD and evil are sages. Those who have more good than bad in them are distinguished persons. Common men have more evil than good, and the scum and riffraff of society have no good at all. Fairies and buddhas have only good and no evil.

> *Chingjo:* An ancient one said, "One should do good, of course, but there are times when one should not."
>
> *Yutang:* The man who said that was one who made that comment when he was led to the execution ground for his upright opposition to a bad government (second century).

SOME MEN AND WOMEN left a name for posterity because they were victims of some adverse circumstance. One can say that they were most unfortunate, but I doubt that one should express regret for them.

> *Hanchen:* True enough. On the other hand, it would hardly be

right to break the leg of a sparrow and then bind it up mercifully.

BE CLEAN AND POOR rather than be filthy rich; accept death cheerily when it comes rather than be worried about life.

Yehjen: I prefer to be filthy rich.

Chupo: My wish is to be clean and rich. But that is hard to come by. Am I wishing too much?

IT IS NOT BAD to be a ghost. One who was penniless has a lot of paper money burnt for his benefit and one who was pushed around all his life is worshiped by people on their knees after his death.

Yehjen: Then why do we speak of a poor scholar as a "poor devil?"

Kangchou: When the poor devil dies, he, too, is honored.

RATHER LEAD a poor but leisurely life than be a success and lead a busy one. But better be simple though rich, than be poor and proud.

Shih-an: A man who is rich and at the same time has leisure can afford to be simple.

Shihliu: No. First learn to be simple though rich. Then of course you have leisure galore.

Chupo: To lead a simple and leisurely life makes wealth and position endure.

THE ANCIENTS PRAISED those who were proud though poor, and not snobbish though rich. Now in modern days it is difficult to find the poor who are not snobbish and the rich who are not haughty.

Lei-an: We notice that as far back as in the Warring Kingdoms [fifth to third centuries B.C.] there were people who were poor but proud.

Chupo: The most unbearable are those who grovel before some and are haughty toward others.

SCHOLARS OFTEN JEER at the rich. Then when they praise a piece of composition, why do they compare it to gold, jade and gems, and brocade?

Hanchen: The rich deserve contempt only when they are uncultured or stingy. We do not object to their pearls and jade.

Chupo: It has nothing to do with riches or poverty. It is just a question whether one is educated or not.

Yunshih: What Chupo says is fair.

Jochin: We just want the rich to have respect for learning and culture. They can do a great deal of good when they can see the point.

BLACK CAN BESMIRCH white and a bad odor wipe out a fragrance easily, but not vice versa. This is what happens when a gentleman is confronted by a cad or a sneak.

[*Younger brother*] *Mushan:* Men after all prefer white and the fragrant to black and what stinks. So in the long run, the gentleman must win.

Yungching: Nowadays it is not at all unusual to find a skunk fighting another skunk.

REMIND A GENTLEMAN of shame and threaten a sneak with pain. It always works.

Chupo: Sometimes, though, a gentleman can awaken a sneak with a sense of shame, and a sneak can make a heroic sacrifice for his country by enduring pain.

Yutang: What a wise remark! This is rare perception.

NOTHING IS MORE BOOTLESS than to give money to the monks, and nothing quite such a waste of time as writing eulogies on the occasion of someone's birthday.

Chientang: If one is paid for such writing, why not?

Yutang: In ancient China, there was a continuous demand for eulogies on the occasion of a funeral notice or for a memorial volume for some dead relative. It was a most embarrassing situation for a scholar, for only praise, not a true biographical sketch, was wanted. The same is true of eulogies on birthdays, which as pieces of writing were a complete waste of time.

I WOULD RATHER be criticized by the rabble than despised by a gentleman, and rather fail at the imperial examinations than be unknown to great scholars.

Jochin: Not to be criticized by the common herd is to be one of them, and a man despised by a gentleman cannot be a "fine scholar."

A MAN MUST HAVE pride in his character [literally "in his bones"], but not in his heart. Not to have pride in character is to be with the common herd, and to have pride in one's heart does not belong to a gentleman.

> Tienwai: Here is a moral truth expressed beautifully by a gifted writer.

NO MAN CAN KNOW everything. The best and highest kind of man knows something, but is sure that there is something he does not know and seeks it. Next come those who know one point of view, but admit another point of view when told. Next come those who will not accept it when told, and the lowest are those who know one side of a question and hate to have people tell them the other side.

> Shingyuan: It takes an intelligent man to listen.
> Yungching: This is really the wisdom of the sages, expressed in a casual conversational style.

A MILITARY MAN who does not talk lightly of war is also a cultured man; a cultured man who does not rest with his smug opinions has something of the conqueror's spirit.

> Szechih: A really cultured man is never smug.

A LITERARY MAN discussing wars and battles is mostly an armchair strategist; a military man who discusses literature relies mostly on rumors picked up from hearsay.

> Chiehnan: Nowadays, when a military man discusses wars and battles, it is also mostly armchair strategy, and when a literary man discusses literature, it is also mostly based on rumors picked up from hearsay.

A SAGE speaks for the universe.

> Yutang: This is what is called "the grand manner" in writing.

IS IT VERY DIFFICULT for Heaven [God] to bring peace to the world? I do not think so. All He needs to do will be to send into this world about two dozen great, upright men — one to be the king, one to be prime minister, one to be crown prince, and the rest to be provincial governors.

> Chiuyuan: It is difficult to be God and satisfy everybody. The proverb says, "Do not be the sky of April."
>
> Yunshih: A very true statement, but a strange, striking way of putting it.
>
> Yutang: Or for God just to strike a tyrant dead with a thunderbolt and save millions from sufferings, starvation, and death. Who will answer the question of why God did not do it?

I THINK BUDDHISM and Taoism are most useful and should not be destroyed. For when we visit the famous mountains, it is often difficult to find a good resting place for the tired feet, or have meals and refreshments except at the temples, or to rush into shelter in case of rain. Sometimes a journey takes several days, and one cannot stop in the open overnight without fear of tigers and leopards. . . . But even in cities, it is necessary to have temples, for a stopover in long journeys, for rest in a short one, for having tea in summer, ginger soup in winter, and for a rest for the carriers. This is a practical consideration, and has nothing to do with the theory of retribution.

> Yutang: What a curious defense for the existence of Buddhism and Taoism!
>
> Chupo: This is a good way of taking care of these people. But I shouldn't allow them to say mass for the dead at people's homes. Let them have prayers and services, golden idols with copper bodies, and have fine buildings. Let them even marry and have children and eat meat, if they like.

3. Women and Friends

TO LOVE A BEAUTIFUL WOMAN with the sentiment of loving flowers increases the keenness of admiration; to love flowers with the sentiment of loving women increases one's tenderness in protecting them.

> *Pichiang:* Only in this spirit can true appreciation and true tenderness be shown.
>
> *Yutang:* We all know Mao Pichiang's tenderness toward Miss Shiaowan.
>
> *Chupo:* What luck for flowers and women to meet such a lover!

WOMEN ARE FLOWERS that can talk, and flowers are women which give off fragrance. Rather enjoy talk than fragrance.

> *Wuchien:* A correction here. Queen Feiyen's breath was like orchid, Queen Hoteh had a fragrant body odor, and Shueh Yaoying's flesh and skin were said to emit a certain perfume. It is not only flowers that smell well.

GIRLS BETWEEN FOURTEEN and twenty-five of whatever locality usually have a charming accent, but when you see their faces, there is a great difference between the ugly and the beautiful.

> *Hanchen:* There is some truth in the saying that the bamboo screen is the courtesan's means of attraction.
>
> *Chupo:* When one has an ugly maid, it is not a bad idea to insist on talking with her across a door, or if there are a number of them, listen to them whispering in the next room.
>
> *Yungching:* But if there is a pretty one with a coarse masculine voice, what are you going to do?

FOR A WOMAN to have the expression of a flower, the voice of a bird, the soul of the moon, the posture of the willow, bones of jade and a skin of snow, the charm of an autumn lake and the heart of poetry — that would indeed be perfect.

AVOID SEEING THE WILTING of flowers, the decline of the moon, and the death of young women. One should wait to see the flowers in bloom after planting them, see the full moon after waiting days for it, and complete writing a book after starting it, and should see to it that a beautiful woman is happy and gay. Otherwise, all the labors are in vain.

Chikung: I doubt this statement. Do you want to see a beautiful woman grow old until she has a wrinkled face and a toothless mouth?

A SCHOLAR'S INKSTONE should be exquisite, but so should a businessman's. A concubine for pleasure should be beautiful, but so should also a concubine for continuing the family line.

> *Hanchen:* An exquisite inkstone takes ink better and that is all there is to it. But a pretty concubine invites jealousy. What are you going to do about it?
> *Chupo:* Jealousy is in women, whether the concubine is pretty or not.

IT IS GOOD TO LOOK at a lady at her morning toilet after she has powdered her face.

> *Tanshin:* What would be the time to look at a lady's evening toilet? What is Shintsai's opinion?
> *Pingchih:* Hush! Hush!
> *Tienshih:* For evening toilet, the time should be when the lady is slightly drunk. But at that time one's eyes are blurred, too.

THERE IS AN ANCIENT SAYING that women who can read and write are apt to have loose morals. My opinion is that this is not the fault of education, but that when an educated woman has loose morals, the public gets to know about it more quickly.

> *Chupo:* That is why famous scholars should also be particularly careful about their conduct.
> *Jochin:* The chaste become more chaste with education. The licentious will be licentious without education.

WHEN A SCHOLAR MEETS another scholar, usually there is a feeling of mutual sympathy, but when one beauty meets another, the sense of tenderness toward beauty is always lacking. May I be born a beautiful woman in the next life and change all that!

> *Hoshan:* There is an old popular verse which says, "Old Pao laughs at Kuo for his clumsy sleeves during a dance; when Pao is asked to dance during dinner, his sleeves are even more unmanageable." Then what?

Fanshiu: Wait till Shintsai is born a woman and see!

Shiangke: Remember the ancient remark of a woman about another woman: "Even I fall in love with her."

Yungching: Don't forget, Shintsai, when you come back!

I PROPOSE TO HOLD a grand temple gathering for sacrifices to all the famous beauties and all the great poets of the past, with absolutely free intermingling of the men and women. When I find a first-class monk of real learning, I am going to do it.

Tienshih: Wait another twenty or thirty years so that I can be counted among the honored spirits.

[*Monk*] *Chungchou:* I am a first-class monk. Hurry up and do it. Their spirits are waiting to be liberated from their netherworld troubles.

Hanchen: The invitation is ready, but no date has been fixed. The souls of the ancient beauties and poets will be getting impatient. Also I am afraid that there will be a number of souls who consider themselves beauties and poets and will come uninvited. The temple cook will never be able to provide meals for such a crowd. What do you think, Shintsai?

[*Monk*] *Yuanfeng:* Shintsai is my client. Brother Chungchou is trying to take him away from me.

Yutang: What monks! It is difficult to bear in mind that monks are also human.

A SCHOLAR MUST have bosom friends. By a bosom friend I do not mean necessarily one who has sworn a pledge of friendship for life and death, but one who has faith in you against rumors, although separated by a thousand miles, and tries every means to explain it away, who will assume the responsibility and make a decision for you, or in case of need make a financial settlement, even without letting you know or worrying whether by so doing he is laying himself open to criticism. This is what I call a bosom friend.

A CLOUD BECOMES multicolored when it reflects the sun, and a mountain current becomes a fall when it passes over a cliff. Things become different from what they associate with. That is why friend-ship is so valued.

Chupo: The character of the multicolored cloud and the water-fall depends on the sun and the cliff. That is why friends must be chosen carefully.

A REMARKABLE BOOK is one which says something never said before; a bosom friend is one who will confide in you all his heartfelt feelings.

Yunshih: This book can be said to say things never said before and reveals heartfelt feelings.

ONE DOES NOT LIVE in vain if there is one in this world who truly understands oneself.

TO TALK WITH A LEARNED FRIEND is like reading a remarkable book; with a romantic friend, like reading good prose and poetry; with an upright friend, like reading the classics; with a humorous friend, like reading fiction.

Shengshu: These various kinds of books will also enjoy having such readers, I am sure.

Chupo: Such a statement comes from one who really appreciates books and friends.

IT IS NECESSARY to have good friends when living in the country. One can get tired of the peasants who talk only of the crops and the weather. Among friends, those who write poetry are the best; next, those good at conversation; next those who paint; next those who can sing; and lastly, those who can play wine games.

Hanchen: Those who talk fantastic drivel should be the last.

Jihchieh: Among the guests in a rich man's house, those who talk fantastic drivel usually rank among the first.

Yungching: Poets always can talk fantastic drivel.

Yunshih: I like this. It gets better and better.

DRINK A TOAST to cavalier friends during the Lantern Festival [fifteenth of January], to handsome friends during the Dragon Boat Festival [fifth day of fifth moon], to charming friends on the Double Seventh [the seventh of seventh moon], to friends of mild disposition during the Harvest Moon [fifteenth of eighth moon], and to romantic friends on the Double Ninth [ninth day of ninth moon].

> Yutang: Cavalier (hao) friends suggest those who are adventurous in spirit, with contempt for conventions and social restrictions; the Dragon Boat festival at the beginning of summer is asso- ciated with the boat race, involving a general turning out of all men and women; friends of a mild disposition (tan) are those who are quiet and contented, with simple tastes; romantic (yi) friends are those inclined to live away from society, and the Double Ninth is associated with mountain climbing.

> Chushien: Where do you classify me?

> Wuchen: You are somewhere between the cavalier and the charming friend.

> Mingyu: In Yangchow, there are plenty of handsome friends, less cavalier friends, and still less charming friends. As for mild friends and romantic friends, they simply do not exist.*

> Chupo: There are always such friends to be found. What I appreciate most is the author's thought of toasting them on such occasions.

> Tienshih: On New Year's Eve, we should toast our less fortunate friends.

> Yenku: Toast me any time of the year.

> Chinyung: I have a suggestion. Drink a toast to the lanterns at the Lantern Festival, to the colored ribbons on the racing boats during Dragon Boat, to the Pair of Lovers in the sky on the Double Seventh, to the moon during the Harvest Moon, and to chrysanthemums on the Double Ninth. Then all the friends will come by themselves, attracted by the sentiments.

IT IS EASIER to find real understanding among friends than among one's wife and mistresses. Between a king and his ministers, such a close understanding is even more rare.

> Mingyu: It is more difficult to find understanding in one's wife than in one's mistress, and doubly difficult in a wife with a mistress in the home.

> Chupo: Such understanding is rare also between brothers.

> Hanchen: On the other hand, the gods and spirits seem to under- stand us better.

* Yangchow was the center of luxury.

SOME OF THE GREATEST joys of life are: to discuss literature with a friend, to compose tête-à-tête together a poem by providing alternate lines, to sit at the palace examinations, and to be sent abroad as a diplomat to a dependency.

> *Lijen:* In a tête-à-tête, one may have no time for discussing literature or writing joint poems.
>
> *Choutze:* To be sent abroad as a diplomat is not easy.
>
> *Sungping:* There is no harm in dreaming.
>
> *Chupo:* To have friends alone with you and at the same time discuss literature or write poems may be too much of a good thing.
>
> *Chichang:* Even the gods will be envious.
>
> *Yutang:* Chinese poems often go by couplets. In writing "alternate lines" friends generally take a subject such as a scene in snow. The rhyme is agreed upon. One person begins a couplet for the other to complete. The other completes it and starts the first line of another couplet. This can go on when fancy is free and get better and better, until their "intestines run dry."

4. Nature

SPRING IS the natural disposition of Heaven [the creator]; autumn is one of its varying moods.

> *Chiangchung:* Men also share the natural disposition of spring, and sometimes also the varying moods of autumn.
>
> *Tienwai:* This goes to the very heart of the universe and of the human spirit.

THE ANCIENT PEOPLE regarded the winter as the "extra" period of rest of the other three seasons. I think the summer may also be considered to have three "extras" or rest periods: the summer morn is the "extra" of the night, the evening talks are the "extra" of the day's activities, and the siesta is an "extra" period for rest from seeing people. It is indeed true as the poet says, "I love the lifelong summer day."

PROSE AND POETRY are best when they have the spirit of autumn; drama and love ditties are best when they reflect the mood of spring.

Hanchen: Autumn is the tragic mood, but the expression of sadness should come naturally.

Yutang: The contrast is briefly between sobriety and expansiveness, between balance and overflowing life. It would be wrong to call it a contrast between affirmation and negation. It is not that simple.

THIS THING CALLED RAIN can make the days short and the nights long.

A RAINY DAY in spring is suitable for reading; a rainy day in summer for playing chess; a rainy day in autumn for going over things in the trunks or in the attic; and that in winter for a good drink.

Shingyuan: Among rains in the four seasons, that in autumn is most difficult to bear. But irrespective of season, the sound of rain is always good for a drink.

A SPRING RAIN is like an imperial edict conferring an honor, a summer rain like a writ of pardon, and an autumn rain like a dirge.

Chupo: One can have too much of writs of pardon.

A SPRING WIND is like wine, a summer wind like tea, autumn wind is like smoke, and [winter wind?] like ginger or mustard.

THE CLOUD IS EVER-CHANGEFUL, sometimes piled up like high cliffs, sometimes translucent like water, and sometimes it resembles human beings or beasts or fish or insects. That is why clouds are most difficult to paint. The so-called paintings of clouds that I have seen are sheer tours de force.

Chupo: There are front and back and inside and outside among the layers of clouds. One side may be facing the sun and is bright, while the other is dark. It is true that there has never been a painter famous for painting clouds.

ONE HATES THE NEW MOON for its declining early and the third-quarter moon for its coming up late.

Tungtang: I can regulate my sleeping hours in accordance with its coming up and decline.

Sungping: Rather the thing to look out for are the clouds which may obscure it.

Chingjo: It is the nature of the universe to go in cycles. Please do not hate its slowness in coming up or its decline.

THIS IS WHAT the moonlight does: it makes a conversation on Shan [Zen] seem more spiritual and ethereal, a talk about swordsmanship seem more romantic, a discussion of poetry more charming, and a woman more enchanting.

Shihtan: In contrast, imagine sitting at a formal dinner on a hot day, passing the examinations in cold snow, and facing a puritanical scholar on a dark, rainy day!

ONE DOES NOT LIVE in vain to have heard the bird songs in spring, the cicada's song in summer, the insects' chirp in autumn, and the sound of crunching snow in winter, and furthermore, to have heard the sound of chess in daytime, the sound of flute in moonlight, the sound of winds whistling through the pines, and the sound of rippling, lapping water. As for the noise of fighting youths and scolding wives, it were better to be born deaf.

Chupo: One who has lived away from home for long yearns for the sound of one's children reciting their lessons.

Yu-an: Now I understand it is sometimes better to be deaf.

THE SOUND OF GEESE makes one think of Nanking, that of creaking oars reminds one of the Kiangsu lake district; the sound of rapids makes one feel like being in Chekiang, and the sound of bells on horses' necks suggests travel on the road to Chang-an [in the northwest].

Chinjen: Namo Kuanshihyin Bodhisattva Mahasattva! [Means "hallelujah!"]

Yungching: And when all noises of the world stop?

ALL SOUNDS ARE BETTER listened to from a distance, but that of the string instrument *chin* is an exception.

Mingyu: All such sounds of the pine forest, a waterfall, a flute, surfs, sound of reading, and temple bells and singing of litany should be listened to from a distance. But the nuances of *chin* notes, of singing, and of falling snow can be appreciated only when heard close by.

Tienshih: All colors can be looked at close by, but the mountain-sides are best seen from a distance.

THERE IS A DIFFERENCE when listening to the *chin* under a pine tree, to a flute under the moonlight, to a waterfall along a stream, and a Buddhist service up in the mountains.

Chupo: This difference is difficult to describe.

Yungching: But it is important to know the difference.

THE BEST BIRD SONGS are those of the thrush, and next to them those of the oriole and the blackbird. But the latter two have never been cage birds. Perhaps they have the soul of high-minded scholars — they can be heard, but not kept.

Hanchen: Parakeets have been kept. But there are times when one could do without them.

Yunshih: "The oriole has now become familiar with us, and when it departs, it makes four or five cries," says a poem. This seems to indicate a feeling on the part of the bird. The poet must have kept it.

THERE ARE FOUR KINDS of noise made by water: in a cataract, in a spring, over rapids, and in ditches. Three kinds of noise made by the winds: those of "pine surfs" (whistle of winds over pine forests as heard from a distance), of autumn leaves, and of waves. Two kinds of noise made by rains: that of drops on plane leaves and lotus leaves, and of rain water coming down drainpipes into bamboo pails.

THE EYE CANNOT SEE ITSELF, the nose does not smell itself, the tongue cannot taste itself, the hand cannot clasp itself. Only the ear can hear itself.

[*Younger brother*] *Mushan:* It is the mind that hears it.

Chupo: The mind can have confidence in itself.

Shih-an: An ancient saying says, "The eye and the eyebrow never get acquainted with each other, because they are too close."

IT SHOWS THE HEART of Buddha (misericordia) to worry about clouds with the moon, about moths with books, about winds and rains with flowers, and to sympathize with beautiful women and brilliant poets about their harsh fate.

Tanshin: In that case, one has not a moment's peace of mind.

Sungping: A gentleman has deeper worries.

Chiaosan: To sympathize with the harsh fate of beautiful women and brilliant poets — this makes one want to cry.

Chupo: The beauties and the poets will never thank you enough.

Hanchen: After reading this, I begin to worry about fog with the crabs.

Chupo again: Hanchen is really worrying about himself not having crabs.

Huei-an: These are all farfetched, like the man of Chi who worried that some day the sky might fall down.

IT IS ABSOLUTELY necessary for flowers to have butterflies, for hills to have springs, for rocks to be accompanied by moss, for water to have water cress in it, for tall trees to have creepers, and for a man to have hobbies.

Shihlu: It is true that "all things that have come to stay originate with someone's hobby."

SEE FLOWERS in the company of beautiful women; drink under the moon with charming friends; take a stroll in snow with high-minded persons.

Tanshin: The flower itself is a beauty, the moon is a charming spirit, and snow itself is the incarnation of purity of heart. So one can enjoy them just as if they were a beauty, a charming spirit, and a pure-hearted saint even when alone.

Hanchen: Except that to gorge oneself with rich food at such moments would be contradictory in spirit. One should not dream of riding on a stork and visiting Yangchow [being a fairy and enjoying worldly luxury at the same time].

Chupo: To have these material conditions and such good company

SNOW reminds one of a great high-minded scholar; the flower reminds me of a beautiful woman; wine brings up memory of great cavaliers; the moon makes one think of friends; a beautiful landscape makes one think of some good verse or prose.

Chupo: What a passionate soul!

BE THE DAY LILY among grass. Do not be the cuckoo among the birds.

> *Yutang:* The day lily is called "forget-sorrow" and the cuckoo's song is so sad it is said to cry tears of blood. (Originally the cuckoo was a boy who died when he found his stepbrother dead on the mountains from persecution by his stepmother. In mercy God transformed him into a cuckoo and he is still crying for his brother. The sound *koo-koo* means in Chinese "elder brother").

FLOWERS which are both pretty and have a good smell are the plum, the chrysanthemum, the [Chinese] orchid, the narcissus, the *Chloranthus inconspicua,* the banksia rose, the rose, and the winter sweet. The others are all for the eye. Among those whose leaves as well as flowers are good to look at, the begonia ranks first, the lotus comes next, and then follow the cherry apple, the *Rubus commersonii* [of the rose family], the red poppy, and the narcissus. The amaranth and the *Musa uranoscopus* [of the banana family] have prettier leaves than flowers. The crape myrtle and the magnolia have nothing to recommend themselves either in leaves or in flowers.

> *Chupo:* That which wins the first place among them all by means of its leaf alone is the bamboo.

THE FOLLOWING FLOWERS create each a mood: the plum flower goes with poetry [which alone of all flowers blooms in pink against a background of snow], the orchid with seclusion [flowering on mountain cliffs content with being unseen], the chrysanthemum with the rustic flavor, the lotus with simplicity of heart, the cherry apple with glamour, the peony with success [power and wealth], the banana and the bamboo with gentlemanly charm, the begonia with seductive beauty, the pine tree with retirement, the plane tree with absence of worry, and the willow with sentimentality.

> *Chinyung:* These have all their talent (as in scholars) and their glamour (as in women).

MOST FLOWERS that are pretty have no smell, and those that are a composite do not bear fruit. How rare is a perfect talent! The lotus, however, combines both.

> *Jihchieh:* From its root and leaf to its flowers and seeds, the lotus serves a useful purpose.
> *Kuanyu:* The lotus bloom does not last long. Where one's talent is perfect, one's luck isn't.
> *Tanlu:* For me, it would be perfect if the litchi had pretty flowers and the peony bore good fruit.
> *Chinyung:* The perfect talent always invites jealousy. That is why the lotus is honored with the name of a "gentleman."
> *Yutang:* The lotus grows out of mud, but is uncontaminated by it.

ONE CAN USE the pine flower for measurement, its seeds for perfume, its branches for a duster to drive away insects, its big shade for cover, and the wind whistling through it as music. Thus a man living in the country with a hundred pine trees benefits from them in many ways.

> *Yushan:* But don't forget the large ants that are found near it.
> *Hanchen:* Why not imagine yourself the king of ants?
> *Tienwai:* One can lie under tall pines and imagine oneself in an undersea crystal palace with the surfs surging overhead.

THE BAMBOO SHOOT is unique among vegetarian food, and so are the following, each in its class: the litchi among fruit, the crab among shellfish, wine among drinks, the moon in the firmament, the West Lake [Hangchow] among hills and waters, and the Sung *tze* [poems of irregular lines written to music] and the *chu* [songs for the opera] in literature.

EVEN AUTUMN INSECTS and spring birds can make melodious songs to please the ear. How can we who write make just noises like the mooing of a cow or the cackling of a crow?

> Yungching: The cackle of a crow and the mooing of a cow, however, are often taken for poetry.

THE CICADA is the retired gentleman among the insects, and the bee is an efficient administrator.

> Chingchiu: The mosquito is the jailor among insects, and the fly the hobo.

A FLY RESTS on a man's face, and a mosquito sucks man's blood. What do these insects take man for?

> Kangchou: They are just monks who beg for alms.
>
> [Monk] Chunjen: It's a secret.
>
> Chupo: This is the essence of Chuangtse's philosophy [that everything is relative and has its own standards].
>
> Huei-an: What do they think? Just good meat and drink. They may even think that we smell like mutton and relish it.
>
> Yunshih: There are beings that collect around your face and suck your blood. They are flies and mosquitos and yet they are not. But they do suck your blood. What do they consider us people?

THE SPIDER is the racial enemy of the butterfly, while the donkey is a satellite of the horse.

> Shingyuan: This is like the conversation of the Chin romantics.
>
> Chiaoshan: I never heard of such talk since the beginning of the world!

ALL BABIES and the young of animals are lovely, except the donkey colt.

> Liaosze: All things that have grown old are unattractive, except the old plum tree and the old pine.
>
> Yungching: That depends. There are donkey lovers who think the baby donkey pretty.

THE HORSE is a public servant, the cow a retired scholar. The deer belongs to fairyland, the pig to this world.

Chachun: Once under General Tien Tan, the cow was used in
battle by having its tail set on fire to rush the enemy lines, but
I have never heard of a retired horse. When Emperor Wu
set his cavalry horses free to pasture, this was what is usually
called "compulsory retirement."

IN HUMAN BEINGS, the female is more beautiful than the male.
Among the birds, the male is prettier than the female. Among the
beasts, there is no difference.

Chachun: This is not quite true. Sometimes a man is handsomer
than a woman.

Sungtse: Chachun happens to say so at the moment. I don't
think this is his considered opinion.

5. The House and Home

ONE NEED not be too particular about the pen and ink when
doing copy work, but should be particular when writing for things
to be framed up. Also one can have a random collection of books
for reading, but should insist on good, adequate reference works.
Likewise, what landscape one sees in passing in travel is not too
important, but that of the place where you are going to build a
house and settle down is of prime importance.

Pichiang: Women with whom one has casual affairs need not be
especially beautiful, but the mistress one is going to live with
at home must be.

Yutang: He has already immortalized Miss Shiaowan. Mao Pichiang
lived from 1611 to 1693.

Yunching: There is a sense of relative importance shown in
Pichiang's statement.

A BUSY MAN must plan to have his garden next to his house, but a
man of leisure can afford to have it at some distance away.

Chupo: A real man of leisure would make the garden his home.

THE ESSENTIAL THING in a garden with terraces is plan and composition, and not ornamental details. I have often seen homes which
expended a great deal of effort on such carvings and ornamenta-

tions. These are difficult to keep in good condition and costly in repairs. Better have a simpler taste.

> [Younger brother] Mushan: It occurred to me that house gardens and crooks have something in common; garden homes achieve their effect by deceptive curving corridors, and crooks and cheats play the same game of hide-and-seek with the law.

PLANTING FLOWERS invites the butterflies, and in the same way rocks invite clouds, the pine invites winds, a water pond invites duckweed, a terrace may be said to invite the moon, bananas invite the rain, and willows invite cicadas.

> Yutang: The word used is "invite," as to a party. Each is attracted by what is appropriate to it and is shown by it to best advantage.
> Chiuyo: A library attracts friends.
> Lienfeng: Brewing of wine attracts me.
> Kentsai: Where can we find such a host?
> [Miss] Hueichu: Shintsai is one.
> Yungching: Making an anthology of poetry invites criticism.
> Tienshih: A grasping nature "invites" riches.

DIFFERENT TYPES of rocks should be selected for different places: "primitive" ones should be placed with the plum tree, rugged, heavy ones near pines, slender slabs near bamboos, and delicate varieties in a flowerpot or tray.

IN PLANTING TREES, so much depends on in how many years you want to see the results. For immediate results, choose bananas; planning for one year, choose bamboos, for ten years, willows, and for a hundred years, pine trees.

> Shingyuan: Planning for a thousand years, write books.
> Chupo: For a hundred generations, plant "virtue."

THERE ARE ten kinds of worries or things to look out for: (1) Moths in book bags. (2) Mosquitoes on summer nights. (3) A leaky terrace. (4) Dry chrysanthemum leaves. (5) Big ants near pines.

(6) Too many fallen leaves of bamboos. (7) Too quick wilting of lotus flowers. (8) Snakes near creepers. (9) Thorns on a trellis of flowers. (10) Being poisoned from eating porcupines.

> *Ti-an:* There are no big ants near pines on the Yellow Mountain.
> *Tienwai:* I have two worries or regrets: first, that brilliant men have no character, and secondly that beautiful women often have tragic lives.
> *Yutang:* Chang Tai (1597–1689) gives a formula for cooking porcupines and eating them without harm.

IT IS WONDERFUL to see from the outside a man writing characters on window paper from the inside.

LATTICEWORK is all right, but it should consist of fine lines and spaces, and not made with big ones. It would not look nice in windows.

THE VASES used for arranging flowers should be chosen so that their size and shape agree with the flowers but their dark or light shades of color contrast with them.

> *Chupo:* With such a regard for beauty, the flowers may be willing to part from their branches without regret. They will be satisfied with the new home.
> *Mitsao:* The contrast in shade is for the purpose of making the vase and flowers look unified in effect.

CERTAIN THINGS must be provided in the home: good pens and ink-stone, although the owner himself is not a calligraphist; a home book of medical recipes, although not a doctor; and a chessboard although he may not play.

> *Hanchen:* And a good cellar, although the owner may not drink.

A MAN LIVING in the city must make scrolls of painting serve for a natural landscape, have flower arrangements in pots serve for a garden, and have books serve for his friends.

TO AMUSE ONESELF, play the *chin*, to amuse oneself with a friend, play chess, and to have general entertainment, play *matiao* [a game of cards, ancestor of mah-jongg].

> *Shuansheng:* Rather enjoy a small party than a big one.

MUSICAL INSTRUMENTS that are good to listen to and to look at playing are the *chin* and the *shiao* [a flute]; those good to listen to, but not to look at playing are the *sheng* [small reed organ held close to the mouth] and the *kuan* [oboelike instrument, but simpler].

> *Shengshu:* What is beautiful to look at but not to hear is the scolding and screaming from a beautiful young wife.

THE QUALITY OF THINGS made, vessels, utensils, and toys, has steadily improved in these years, while their prices have steadily gone down. It must be that the artisans are becoming poorer.

> *Chupo:* It must be due to poverty. The artisans have no choice but to put more work into it and sell a product for less.

WHEN A GOOD MIRROR meets an ugly owner, a good inkstone meets a vulgar person, and a good sword finds itself in the hands of a common general, there is nothing these things can do about it.

6. Reading and Literature

ALL LITERARY MASTERPIECES of the ancients and moderns were written with blood and tears.

> *Ching-ai:* Even this book of enjoyment of life shows tears. Looked at more closely, sometimes they are tears of blood.
>
> *Hanchen:* Bad literature is probably written all with blood and no tears.*

LITERATURE is landscape on the desk; landscape is literature on the earth.

> *Shengshu:* One necessary qualification for each. Writing must have sinuous grace before it can be compared with landscape,

* All sex and violence.

and a landscape must have pleasant turns and surprises before it can be compared with writing.

A GOOD READER regards many things as books to read wherever he goes; a good landscape, chess and wine, and flowers and the moon are all books to be read. A good traveler also sees a landscape [a picture] in everything: in history, in poems and wining parties, and in flowers and the moon.

> Hoshan: This well describes the secret of a good reader and good traveler.

> Hanchen: Lying in bed at night, one can conjure up any number of beautiful scenes from real life and literature.

> Huei-an: Books, hills, and water — they are all one and the same thing.

GENERALLY reading is a pleasure. But reading history, more often than not, makes one gripped with sadness or anger. But even that feeling of sadness or anger is a luxury.

> Chupo: The best is when you forget yourself entirely, and are even unaware that you are happy or maddened.

WINTER is good for reading the classics, for one's mind is more collected. Summer is good for reading history, for one has plenty of time. The autumn is good for reading the ancient philosophers, because of the great diversity of thought and ideas. Finally, spring is suitable for reading modern authors, for in spring one's spirit expands.

> Pinu: This Quiet Dream Shadows is good for reading for all seasons.

THE CLASSICS should be read by oneself while alone (for reflection). History should be read together with friends (for discussion of opinions).

> Chingchou: Female friends will do also.

THE BENEFIT of reading varies directly with one's experience in life. It is like looking at the moon. A young reader may be compared to one seeing the moon through a single crack, a middle-aged reader seems to see it from an enclosed courtyard, and an old man seems to see it from an open terrace, with a complete view of the entire field.

> Chupo: My uncle's reflections upon life seem to be made from the crystal palace in the moon itself, looking down upon this world of human life as one sees to the bottom of a clear lake.
> Yuwan: In my opinion, there is the same difference in one's understanding of religion.

IT IS not only through reading that we make friends with ancient authors; even in looking at their manuscripts, we have the same feeling.

NEXT TO THE AUTHOR of a good book is the man who makes a good commentary on it.

> Chiaoshan: Writing commentaries is not an easy task. One has to bring out the author's meaning and implications even in his most common remarks.
> Chupo: I do not think it is difficult. All one needs is the proper time and leisure to do it, plus peace of mind.

TO ASK a famous scholar to be tutor for your children, to discuss official promotions and examinations at a mountain retreat, and to ask a famous writer to be the ghost for your compositions—these things are utterly wrong.

> Kangchou: Often the famous scholar is invited just because the man hears of his name, without knowing more about him.
> Jihchieh: And there are so-called "famous writers" nowadays.

ONE CAN ADMIRE and try to imitate the writing of great thinkers, but not that of a famous writer. One can fail and yet not make too bad a mistake in the first case, but the result may be disastrous in the second.

> Chiuchiao: I beg to differ. What I hate most are the great thinkers.
> Jihchieh: That is because he does not know what they are talking about.

Chupo: Many there are today who have written a few books and consider themselves forthwith great thinkers.

MONKS NEED NOT abstain from wine, but only from being vulgar; red skirts [women] need not master literature, but they should have good taste.

Chikung: I can imagine what will happen when a wine-drinking monk meets an illiterate red skirt.

ONE WHO CAN READ the wordless book of life should be able to write striking lines; one who understands the truth which is difficult to express by words is qualified to grasp the highest Shan wisdom.

THE DIFFICULTY is not in reading books, but in applying the truths to life, and the greater difficulty is in remembering them.

Shuwu: Shintsai seems to place remembering above applying them. There are those who can remember them, and cannot apply.

Chupo: It is indeed difficult to remember, but also to apply.

Yutang: You both misunderstand Shintsai. He means "to remember to apply them."

AMONG THE CLASSICS of fiction, the Shuihu [about a band of rebels in times of a bad government] is a book of anger, the Shiyuchi [a religious allegory and story of adventure] is a book of spiritual awakening, and the Chinpingmei [Hsimen Ching and His Six Wives], a book of sorrow.

Hanchen: Some say that the Chinpingmei is pornography. It is like those who eat "pork à la Tungpo" and imagine they can talk about Su Tungpo.

Jihchieh: This Quiet Dream Shadows is a book of enjoyment.

Chikung: I should rather say that it is a book of life's flavors.

THERE ARE FACES that are ugly but interesting, and others that are pretty but dull. There are, too, books that are not well written, but utterly fascinating, and others that are well written, but extremely dull. This is difficult to explain to superficial critics.

Jochin: After all, a charming book must have something in it, and a fascinating one cannot be too badly written.

Shuehping: But when it is "well written" but dull, we can say it is badly written.

IT IS MORE PROFITABLE to reread some old books than to read new ones, just as it is better to repair and add to an old temple than to build one entirely new.

Chupo: This statement comes from one who really has read a great deal and read well, and has reread some old books.

THE SECRET of composition lies in this: Try to express difficult points clearly and avoid the obvious and superficial. Commonplace subjects must be illuminated with fresh thoughts, and commonplace themes must be shown to have deeper implications. As to amplifications, tightening up, weeding out overwriting and common, overused expressions, these are matters of revision.

FIRST STUDY the classics, then history. Then one has a deeper central point of view. Then one can go back to the classics again, when one will not be satisfied with merely beautiful phrases.

THE ANCIENT PEOPLE say: "A man becomes a better poet after he has tasted poverty." That is because from poverty and hardships, one gains depth and experience. People who are rich and well-to-do do not taste all aspects of life, and they can only write about the winds and the clouds, and the moon and the dew. As a substitute for personal experience, they might go about and watch the sufferings of the common people, especially in times of war and famine, and in that way acquire a vicarious experience of life.

Huei-an: But there are many poor people and few good poets. The circumstances do not account for everything.

3 🔲 What Can I Do About It?

Prefaces I and II to

THE WESTERN CHAMBER

Chin Shengtan
c. 1609 - 1661

« *Chin was a great commentator on Wang Shihfu's play The Western Chamber. He was among the first to regard fiction and drama as literature on a par with the classics. The two prefaces were entitled "Lamentation over the Ancients" and "A Gift to Posterity" respectively. I have tried to preserve the conscious repetition of certain phrases as a characteristic of Chin's style.*

i

SOMEONE MAY ASK ME why I have undertaken to make a commentary on *The Western Chamber* and publish it. I can only say, "I hardly know myself. I just had to do it."

Ages have passed since life began in the universe, and months and years have whizzed by and vanished like a lightning flash or dissolving clouds, or a passing hurricane or flowing water. In this month and year, there is this temporary me which, too, shall pass away like a lightning flash or dissolving clouds, or a passing hurricane or flowing water. However, fortunately there is for the present this me, which gives rise to the question, How is this present me going to employ its time? I have thought about doing something, but the thought also occurs to me that I do not know whether I shall be able to do it, and even if I do it, that something which I shall have accomplished will also pass away like a lightning flash or

75

dissolving clouds, or a passing hurricane or flowing water. Now if I wish to do something and know beforehand that that which I do will pass away, will not then what I do be in vain? Thus one lands in the hopeless dilemma between wishing to do something by the present me and knowing that what I do shall pass away presently. What indeed can I do about it?

Did not the ancients also know this? Countless ancient people stood and sat at this spot where I am standing or sitting now. Did they not know secretly that one day they would be gone and someone else would be here to take their place? They knew that they could do nothing about it, accepted it, and kept quiet.

I therefore cannot help a feeling of dissatisfaction with the thoughtlessness of the universe. I never begged to come into this life. I should have been either given this life to live forever, or not at all. For no reason I came into this life. For no reason that which came into this life became me, and for no reason the me which came into this life is not made to live forever, and is furthermore endowed with a feeling and a consciousness to regret it. Alas! I do not know where the immortals live and whether they can come back to life. But even if I knew where they lived and they could come back to life, would they not join me in this lamentation over the universe?

I suspect that the ancients knew this well, and furthermore, being more intelligent than myself, they knew that the universe was not really thoughtless, but that the universe, too, could do nothing about it. For if there was to be no life, there would not be this universe; but since there is this universe, there has to be life. That is perfectly true, but it would be unfair to say that because the universe gives life, therefore it made a decision to bring this particular me into life. For the universe simply gives life to all creation and is unaware of whom or what it has created, and the creatures cannot know each what or who it is. If one is sure that that which lives today is me, then it is equally sure that that which will be born tomorrow will be not-me. At the same time, the not-me which will be born tomorrow will regard itself as veritably me. This should puzzle the universe itself, and we cannot know who is to blame.

Now if the universe never deliberately brought me to life but gave life to something which happens to be me, then all I can do will be just to follow along. Since the universe never considered giving life to this me, then all this me can do will be to let it pass like a lightning flash or dissolving clouds, or a passing hurricane or flowing water. And as one can do nothing about one's coming and going, one can also do nothing about this short interval when the temporary me exists except to find temporary diversions to occupy one's time where real diversions are difficult to find. One way would be to till a farm and live in retirement, like Chuko Liang before he was called to power. Another way would be to live like Chuko Liang after he was called to power, and attend to a thousand duties and responsibilities to the neglect of one's meals until one died. Both ways would do. Another way would be to suffer from hunger and cold and pray for a better future life; another, to be married to a princess and be a power at court, and live in a riot of luxuries and entertainments, with swarms of servants; another, to eat one bowl of meager congee a day and sleep under a tree in snow and ice, and give 48,000 sermons on salvation and save life in countless numbers like the sand of the Ganges. All these would do as occupations to fill the interval of time.

Then one thinks as follows. It is true enough that that which was born before me was not-me, and that which will be born after me will also be not-me. Therefore that which exists now and is regarded as me may not be really me. If that which is me is not really me, then I should not bother to wonder what to do about it, but equally there is no reason why I should not wonder what to do about it. One may still hope that the me is real and therefore I should not waste its time. On the other hand, if one knows that the me is not really me, why should one not let it waste, and waste completely, its time? For it is the not-me which wastes its own time, and not me who wastes it. Then one may further completely waste time by thinking that this time should not be wasted, but should be carefully harnessed and utilized to some good purpose. But even then, it may be the not-me which completely wastes its own time by thinking not to waste it. One may go so far as to concentrate one's energies to create something worth while which may last to eternity and thus completely waste the completely wasted time. However, the complete wasting of the completely wasted time will be done by not-me and not by me. If so, one can very well, too, let me waste the time of the not-me. I can squander the energies of not-me for my own pleasure. I can regard the left hand of not-me as my left hand and tap the belly of not-me, or regard the right hand of not-me as my own right hand and finger the beard of not-me. One can do all these things. When the not-me writes a poem, I can sing it. When the not-me sings, I can listen. When the not-me listens, I can dance for joy. And when the not-me dances for joy, I can rejoice over my immortal fame.

Now we do not know what the objects are which are before me and which we call an inkstone, a pen, a piece of paper, but since they go by those names, we will call these things by their usual names. We do not know what is a hand or a thought, but we, too, will call the hand and the thought by these names. We call this place by the window "here" and this present time "today." And so they stand for "here" and "today" for me. As I write, a bee flies into my window and an ant crawls along the balcony. The ant and the bee are enjoying their present temporary life even as I am enjoying my temporary existence. When I become an "ancient one," so too will the ant and the bee become an "ancient bee" and an "ancient ant." What mystery and what joy that I should be living today at this hour by this place before this window with pen, inkstone, and paper spread before me, while my mind thinks and my hand writes in the company of the present bee and the present ant!* My readers born after me will never know that there is an ant and a bee at this moment when I am writing. But if the readers after me cannot know about this ant and this bee when I am writing, then such readers do not really

* This is Zen.

know about me. But I know about my readers in the future. They who will read this piece of composition as a temporary occupation or even without thought of a temporary occupation will be doing so because they don't know what to do about it, seeing that life passes like a lightning flash or dissolving clouds, or a passing hurricane or flowing water.

I have therefore come to realize that wasting one's time is one way of occupying it, not wasting time is also another way of occupying it, and not to mind going on wasting time even knowing that it is a waste of time is also another way of occupying it. I have so labored on this book because I want these commentaries to be superb, and I want them to be superb because I have dared. I have dared because I have well understood life. I have well understood life, and therefore I can do what I naturally want to do. To do what I naturally want to do is also a way of occupying time. I have no time to consider whether my future readers know or do not know about me. Alas! in the same way, I wish to lament over the ancients who were more intelligent than myself, but I cannot know who they were! I have therefore labored over the commentary and published it as a form of lamentation over the ancients. This lamentation over the ancients is not really for the ancients, but just another way of occupying time.

ii

WE CALL THOSE before us the ancients and those born after us posterity or future generations. Are they not alike? In a sense they are. The ancients never saw me and the future generations also shall never see me. They are then alike in the sense that both have no personal relations with me. But in another sense, there is a difference. I never saw the ancients but think of them every day, but I do not think of the future generations. It is clear then that, as the ancients never thought of me and I do not think of the future generations, so as I think of the ancients every day of my life, the future generations, too, will think of me. In the case of the ancients, we can truly say that there is no personal relationship, but in the case of the future generations, they may think of me and remember me although they have not seen me. That they have not seen me personally is not their fault. If then they do think often of me, they must have a feeling about me, and there is established a kind of personal relationship. Therefore I owe them a present.

The problem is how to do it and in what form can I give a present? I am sure the future generations will want to read, and wanting to read, they shall need light. I wish to be the light for the readers. Unfortunately, there are already the sun and the moon, and I cannot transform myself into oil for lamplight. What can I do?

I am sure the future generations will want to read, and wanting to read, they must have friends. These friends come and go, and sometimes do not come, and do not leave. Perhaps one likes a passage, and he reads and lets the others hear it. Perhaps one doubts the ideas of a passage, and he reads it and discusses it with them. Then all of them read it together and discuss it together. Then they all sit together and do *not* read and laugh and have a good time. I wish to be their friend and read and enjoy and discuss a passage with them. Unfortunately, they are not yet born, and when they are born, I shall have gone. What can I do?

I am sure that since the future generations like reading and friendship, they must also like the high mountains, the great rivers, and exotic flowers and trees. For these are the originals of what one finds in reading. When one reads, one feels like visiting the high mountains and great rivers and exotic flowers and trees. And when one visits the high mountains and great rivers and exotic flowers and trees, one feels as if one were enjoying reading. Then the same readers will like, besides reading and friends, also good tea and incense and delicious wines and tonics. In their hours of rest, they will need these things to stimulate their spirits, refresh their bodies, recuperate their minds, and restore their vigor. I wish to be transformed into all these things as a present. Unfortunately, even though I may succeed in these transformations before they are born, they may not be aware that these things represent me, being my transformations. What can I do?

I am sure also that future readers will also want a sweetheart who will stand by their side on a frosty morning or on a rainy night to keep them company and get up and go to bed at the same time. I wish to be transformed into such a sweetheart, to keep them company on a frosty morning or on a rainy night. Unfortunately, I have no control over these transformations and do not know myself what I shall be transformed into, perhaps a rat's liver or the thigh of a cricket. What can I do?

Therefore I have thought of a way. Choose some thing in this world which has the power to survive in the future.* Choose some thing in this world which has the power to survive in the future, but is unknown or not fully understood today. Choose some thing in this world which has the power to survive in the future, and is unknown or not fully understood today, but which I can interpret and clarify to a nicety. Now that some thing which has the power to survive in the future must be a book. That some thing which has the power to survive in the future but is unknown or not fully understood today among books must be *The Western Chamber*. That some thing in this world which has the power to survive and is unknown or not fully understood today, but which I can interpret and clarify to a nicety, must be *The Western Chamber* with my commentaries. I have made these commentaries because I feel I owe something to the future generations and do not know how else to give them a present. I cannot say whether my comments agree with the ideas of the author or not. If they do, regard this edition of *The Western Chamber* as the one which is for the first time understood. If not, consider *The Western Chamber* which is already known as one book, and consider this

---

* Note here the precise but carefully repeated phrases which remind one of a lawyer's English. It seems repetitious, but is deliberately so— a style which grows out of the fact that there is no relative pronoun in the Chinese language.

edition as another book altogether, being the ideas and thoughts of Shengtan (myself). In making these comments, my motive is really not to go to all the trouble for the sake of the ancient author, but because I feel I have an obligation to the future readers and wish to do something about it.

4 ▣ Friendly Chats

Preface to

SHUIHUCHUAN

Chin Shengtan
c. 1609 - 1661

« *The Shuihuchuan is a novel celebrating the exploits of a band of rebels in times of misgovernment, and has been translated by Pearl Buck as* All Men Are Brothers. *Shih Nai-an (c. 1350) is the author of the book, but many people, myself included, are inclined to the opinion that the Preface was written by Chin Shengtan, the editor and great commentator of the current version. Certainly the style is recognizably that of Chin. (See selection 3.)*

A MAN SHOULD NOT MARRY after thirty if he is not already married, and should not enter the government service if he is not already in the service. At fifty, he should not start to raise a family, and at sixty should not travel abroad. This is because there is a time for everything; done out of season and time, there may be more disadvantages than advantages. One wakes up at dawn completely refreshed, washes his face and puts on the headdress, has his breakfast, chews willow branches [for brightening his teeth], and attends to various things. Before he knows it he asks is it noon, and is told it is long past noon. As the morning goes, so goes the afternoon, and as one day passes, so pass the 36,000 days of one's life. If one is going to be upset by this thought, how can one ever enjoy life? I often wonder at a statement that such and such a person is so many years old. By this one means an accumulation of years. But where have the years accumulated? Can one lay hold of them and count them? This shows that the *me* of the past has long vanished. Moreover, when I have completed this sentence, the preceding sentence has already vanished. That is the tragedy.

Now everybody agrees that what we enjoy most in life is friendship, and what we enjoy most in friendship is the leisurely conversation. But how rare such things are! Some days it is cold and windy and some days it rains; sometimes you are laid up in bed with an illness and sometimes you go to call on a friend and he is not at home. You feel like a prisoner. I have but a few small farms, planted with glutinous rice [for making wine]. I cannot drink myself, but I want my friends to drink when they come. My house faces a broad river with a bank of tall trees where my friends can loiter or squat or sit down as they like. I have only four old maids for attending to the kitchen and serving the guests; as for the dozen houseboys, they do the job of running errands and sending invitations. In their leisure hours, I make them weave mats and make broomsticks, for the purpose of keeping the room fit to receive my friends. When all of them come to see me, there is a total of sixteen persons, but it is rare that they all come and, except for rainy, windy days, it is equally rare that none of them turns up. As a rule, six or seven friends gather at my place. They do not make it a rule to drink when they are here; they may do so or not just as they like, for what they enjoy are not the drinks, but the conversation. My friends do not talk politics, and this not only to avoid trouble, but also because there is no point in discussing hearsays of the doings at the court. Such gossip is often pure rumor and to discuss it would be a waste of time. Nor do we discuss other people's mistakes, for people have no mistakes and we should not malign them. We do not talk to impress others, nor are others impressed. We do wish people to understand what we are talking about, but after all people will not understand. For we discuss the mysteries of this gift of life, and people are usually too busy to be interested in such questions.

Since my friends live mostly a detached way of life, we are often able to canvass the ways of human nature as we see it around us. But nobody records them after the day is over. Sometimes we think it may be useful to put these talks down in a book for posterity, but we have never come to it, for the following reasons: first, none of us is interested in leaving a name and each is therefore too lazy to do so; secondly, to talk is a pleasure, but to write it down takes an effort; thirdly, when we die, no one will be able to read it; and fourthly, we will regret next year what we write this year. This *Shuihuchuan*, in seventy-one chapters, is written mostly after my friends have left and in the lamplight. I would say half of it is written on days of storm and rain when none of them visits me. The story has so long occupied my mind that it has become a habit of mine to develop it without having actually taken a pen in hand to write it. The ideas will come sometimes when I am standing by the hedge at twilight, or when I am in bed at night, or watching things, or fumbling at my girdle while lost in thought. Some readers may ask, Why do I write this one since I have just said that we do not want to take the trouble to write books. But this is an exception, for it does not add to my reputation if it becomes popular* and can do no harm if it does not, and secondly, it is a play of the mind and imagination when I have nothing better to do. Besides, it does not take a scholar to read a novel, and lastly, such blemishes as there are will not be taken seriously as in other forms of writing.

Alas! human life is limited. How do I know what readers of a future generation will think of this book? I am satisfied if my friends of today like it when I show it to them. I have no idea whether I myself in my future reincarnation shall like it, or even whether my future self shall have the chance to read it at all. So why should I let this consideration weigh with me?

---

* Shih Nai-an was the first of the great Chinese novelists. In the fourteenth century when he lived, the novel was not yet recognized as a serious form of literature.

5 ▣ Dreams, Interesting and Otherwise

Preface to

HUAYANG ESSAYS

Shih Chenlin
1693 - c. 1779

« *Among the books I love most are West-Green Random Notes
and the Huayang Essays of the same author. I love them for
their wayward charm and their beauty of language. Shih Chenlin
was not too well known, being loved by a small circle of con-
noisseurs, for he lived a retired life, too happy to be concerned
much with the prominent society of his days. He took his chinshih degree in 1737, which entitled him to a smooth career in
officialdom, but preferred to go home and teach and settle down
as a country squire, a master of himself. He was rewarded by
living to the grand old age of eighty-six. There is an idea among
Chinese circles that when a genius produces something, the
gods are jealous. The wood blocks for West-Green Random
Notes were destroyed by fire in his lifetime. A century later when
Wang Tao, a scholar refugee living in Hong Kong, reprinted his
Huayang Essays, again the wood blocks were destroyed by fire.
This Preface is dated 1767. Too bad he shows no evidence of
having read The Red Chamber Dream (unanimously considered
the greatest novel in all Chinese literature) which was at that
time just beginning to be circulated in hand-written copies in
Peking. He was there. What he would have said about this
novel!*

OUR LIFE IS LIKE A PLAY as we stomp about the stage,
laughing with joy or shouting in a rage. It is like a dream in which
we write and talk like somnambulists. After all, there are only four

things which are the contents of literature: ideas, human reactions, events, and scenes. There are curious ideas, interesting events, fascinating human reactions, and arresting scenes. The curious interest in all these is the center and fountain of all life and literature. Would it not be a sin against this curious heaven and curious earth to go on dreaming uninteresting dreams and acting in dull plays? But we do: we make meaningless bows to witless persons, eat tasteless food, and engage in helpless conversations. Now this may be a little unkind to say of the gentlemen, but that very scene of their doing so is interesting and curious.

I was born late and never saw the ancients, and with my limitations of knowledge have never read the "extraordinary books." I write both poetry and prose just as I feel, unable, I am afraid, to reveal what is of curious interest in ideas or events, or human reactions or scenes. They deserve the snorting of humans and the laughter of ghosts. There are tears in these. Who will cry over them?

Sometimes the winds are rough and Liehtse [reputed to be able to ride the winds] would find no interest in them. Sometimes the moon is dark and Li Po would find no interest in inviting it for company. Sometimes the flowers are withered and Chuangtse's butterflies would find no interest in flitting about. And sometimes the locust tree is dried up and the ants would find no interest in its southern bough.* There are tears in these. Again who will cry over them?

Ink-Farmer is an interesting person. He lives in an interesting garden, wields an interesting pen, writes interesting verse, makes interesting friends, but loves the uninteresting me. He is going to spend his most interesting money to publish my uninteresting book. It reminds me of Wu Chensheng who published my *West-Green Random Notes* over my protests. Another friend, Tsao Chenting, kept a stock of copies. But the God of Fire thought it

---

* A reference to "Southern Bough Record," a Rip van Winkle type of short story, depicting what a man saw in his dream of a visit to the kingdom of the ants, with its king and queen and nobles and their pompous vanity.

a most uninteresting book and destroyed it. There was then no need for humans to snort or ghosts to laugh. There are tears in these. Again who will cry over them?

But Ink-Farmer said with a sigh, "I do not think it is so bad after all to dream of being a young man or a pretty lady, nor so deplorable to dream of being a young man and find oneself a middle-aged person, or of being a pretty lady and find oneself a clown. What is deadening would be to spend one's time fighting over uninteresting pennies and amassing uninteresting small gains. Will there still be tears left in these dreams? And again who will cry over them?

Let's go and visit the blessed spot of the Huayang Caves, No. 8.

Written at Liuyiyuan of Pearl Lake
[in Anhwei] after the Double Ninth, 1767.

6 ▣ Beginning of Knowledge
and of Sorrow

Preface to

WEST-GREEN RANDOM NOTES

Shih Chenlin
1693 - c. 1779

« *This book of random notes is my favorite. I promise myself*
that someday I will tell the story of the girl Shuangching
(mentioned in the preface in this book). Selection 13 gives
a good sample of the author's style.

WHEN I WAS A CHILD, I was frightened by the sudden
alternations of light and darkness and was told that it was night
and day. I was mystified by the sudden appearance and disappear-
ance of beings and was told that it was birth and death. People told
me to distinguish the stars and said, "That one is the Sieve, and
that one the Dipper." I learned to distinguish the birds and was
told this one was a raven and that a magpie. This was how my
knowledge began.

When I grew older, I gradually lost the wonder at the sudden
alternations of light and darkness and appearance and disappear-
ance of beings. Sometimes in the maze of confusions I let my
spirit soar upward to space. Looking down at the sudden changes
of light and birth and death of things, I felt a twinge of sorrow. I
remember that once in my childhood, I was going to feed a hen.
Someone told me that its young chicks were there. I crawled over

and saw two chicks hiding from under the wings of their mother and peeping at me. I was seized with a sense of sorrow and forgot about the feeding. This was how my sorrows began.

Once I was crawling along the garden walls and found an object. I was going to eat it like a piece of pastry. People laughed at me and said it was a piece of rock. On this rock stood one word, "West," and another word, "Green," and I was forced to learn these two words. This was how my reading began.

It is a piece of rock, hollow at the center, still facing me on my desk, where I am writing these *Random Notes*.

Composed in a dream,
December 12, 1737.

7 回 The Seven Remedies

Chang Chao
died after 1698

« Chang Chao is the author of Quiet Dream Shadows (selection
2). He was editor of the famous Yutsu Shinchih, a collection of
unusual sketches of men and events, and was coeditor with Yang
Fuchi of the very big Library of Contemporary Authors (Chao-
tai Tsungshu), and with Wang Cho of the Sandalwood Table
Library (Tanchi Tsungshu), which has to do with the unusual
and the recherché in writing. It was in this last collection that I
discovered this delightful masterpiece.

He wrote a very pure style. The form of this sketch could, in
other hands than his, degenerate into an elaborate descriptive
poem of the fu type, which I detest. The fu is always over-
wrought, consisting of parallel balanced constructions, and the
effect is always a kind of pompous, stilted prose with a pretense
at poetry. "The Seven Remedies" is highly descriptive and high-
flown, but remains good prose.

THE OWNER OF SEEDY GARDEN was suffering from a state
of hypochondria. He looked depressed and could not concentrate,
morose and silent and absent-minded, like one crying without
tears or like who has tasted something bitter and will not speak
about it. One might regard him as a fitting company for the crying
geese or the mournful cuckoo. His was a case which no medicine
and no acupuncture could cure.

Someone who was a good talker visited him and sympathized
with his condition. He said to him, "You look ghastly and heart-
broken. Allow me to plant and grow for you the drown-sorrow

flower and the worry-not grass. You sit down quietly and let me talk. Will you let me?"

"Certainly," replied the Owner.

"The most important thing is the ability to loosen and get rid of something which is worrying you and forget your sorrow. I will get together some romantic friends who are good at games and come and keep you company. We will cover a table with tapestry and have white and black chips. We will play with the best-made cards of Peach-bend and lovely, lustrous dice of Chuanchu Alley, with beautiful white silver for stakes and plenty of copper cash. It will make your hands feel good just to clutch and feel these things. We can play *matiao** or pigsty, or throw dice for the hunt [name of a game] and see who gets the prizes of A and B. Or we can play the three leopards or the game of official promotion,† with differences in the size of the leopards and played by any number. Then you will laugh and scream at the turning of the dice and everybody will roll up his sleeves and shout to help the dice come right. And as the dice come out, victory is claimed for one and defeat for another in short succession. The winner will throw up his hat and the loser will vow for a recoup. Such is the joy of gambling. Perhaps it may cure you."

"No," replied the host. "Gambling is against the law and especially forbidden by my father. I cannot go against the king's law or Father's order and be put in a cangue or quaff poison. Besides, I am afraid of noise. I have always hated gamblers especially and tried to avoid them. This I certainly cannot do."

"Well, then, imagine a beautiful spring day when you feel the first breath of spring come over a velvety lawn. I will pick for you the best thoroughbreds and you will ride on a first-class steed and carry a bow of the finest quality like the famous Fanju, and arrows of the ancient make of the Shushens, and we will go out toward the eastern countryside. There we will set up a cloth

---

* Antecedent of mah-jongg, which came into popularity about the year 1600.
† Similar to modern dice games, where one takes so many steps according to the number thrown up by the dice.

screen for target and measure the distance and test the strength of the bow and arrows and have an archery match.* We will have a fine company and shall have no need of drums or bells, and shall not wear helmets. The bow bends into a crescent and the arrow goes forth like a shooting star, and one feels good and happy as on a holiday. Then the arrows continue to whistle in the air. The one who hits the target will be so pleased with himself, while the others' hands itch to have their turn. We may not be as good as the ancients, but will have something to boast about among our group. Then we put the bows and arrows in their sheaths and jump on a horse and prance and wheel about with a whip in hand. We'll feel like flying eagles or winged spirits coursing through space, the horses' hoofs barely touching the ground and their forms moving like shadows. This is the joy of riding and shooting. Perhaps this will cure your malady?"

"No, sir," replied the host. "I am too weak to stand up fully dressed and as gentle as a virgin. Why, I haven't the strength to tie up a chicken. I am not like those beef-eating husky boys. My heart palpitates just to look at people racing. Why, I do not think I can even carry a heavy bow. My constitution will not permit me to do so."

"Perhaps I may suggest something else in that case. The country is in peace and the government is anxious to get all the good men into the service. Anyone who shows talent is shown the greatest encouragement and one can look forward to an easy and smooth official career. Why don't you take a journey to the capital and perhaps see the prime minister! Ah, you will be given an official tally† and have your official parasol shining in the sun in some region. Now you will be sitting upon a high terrace, governor of a city, and as magistrate you will plan and provide, sign documents and collect

---

* The passage here is full of literary references to classical literature, such as the name of famous bows, etc.
† This consists of a piece of metal which is broken in half, one half given to officials serving in distant districts or frontier regions, especially to military commanders. When an important message is to be sent, this half is sent as identification to match the other half at the court.

taxes. Your smile will be welcome like the spring wind by the people, and a scowl will send the underlings into a scurry. And when you come out from your office, you will have plenty of leisure and get together a number of young scholars and teachers and discuss literature and composition. You will have your black ink and your red ink, with which to grade the candidates and decide on their respective merits. Sometimes you will go out to the country with your official flags and inquire into the farmers' conditions. You will walk along rice fields and pass hills and dales and find out if the people have complaints, or if there are some good scholars living in retirement. And after a few years of this, your good records will be appreciated and you will be promoted. Here is an official career which may cure you and make you feel satisfied."

"Oh, no," replied the host. "People are made differently; some have talent and some have not. I shan't pretend that I have any administrative ability, and even if I had, I wouldn't make it my ambition. Look at what happened to so many officials. Some got into trouble because of permitting bandits or because of the escape of convicts. Some were dismissed on account of faulty administration of justice and some because of accounts in money or grains. And many are subjected to official criticism of one kind or another. You don't mean to ask me to follow in their footsteps."

"That may be true. Let me suggest something else. The ancients said that there are three forms of immortality, through action, through character, or through words. Why don't you, then, invite a group of like-minded persons interested in writing and have matches in literary composition? We'll then have at our disposal the best kind of writing brushes of Chungshan, fine-grained inkstones, the most beautiful paper for writing verse made by Shieh Tao, and the rare ink cakes made by Tingkuei.* We will have the best quality of imported incense and drink exquisite *yuchien*

---

* Tingkuei was a maker of ink unequaled in quality, and Miss Shieh Tao invented the making of special paper, colored pink usually, of the letter-paper size. Shieh Tao was a famous courtesan (A.D. 768–831.)

tea. Subjects will be given out for versification and the class of
rhyme words shall be determined by lot, and each will occupy a
special desk by himself and match his composition against the
others. For the *fu* a person can take as long as he likes, even ten
years, to bring it into perfection, or in the other case, the compe-
tition will be to see who completes a poem in the shortest space
of time. And the competitors will sit there and rack their brains
for their most ingenious lines, and cut and fashion their composition to perfection like jade or embroidery, and weigh and consider
the choice of words to a nicety and brighten up or tone down certain passages to the proper effect. Or we may write poems out of
certain prescribed words, or set to certain well-known melodies.
And there will be manuscripts of all kinds piled up on the desk,
some reflecting the joys in the company of flowers and birds, and
some sad enough to draw tears from ghosts. Sometimes a line is so
perfect that you cannot substitute or add another word without
spoiling the effect. Such is the joy of literary composition. Can
you perhaps get cured by this kind of occupation?"

"I'm afraid not," replied the host. "There is no limit to literary
scholarship and one's energy is limited. One works hard to produce
a good piece of writing and in the end who will read it? Sometimes
one is pleased with one's own writing when it is just completed.
The very next day, he cannot stand it. I'll be so ashamed to show
it to the real writers. No, I can write only rotten stuff. I shan't
want to have my burlap compared with other people's silk
materials."

"Wine is the best dispeller of sorrow. Its name is Uncle Joy and
it has been compared to liquid jade. I know you love to drink;
you used to enjoy wine games. Though I can't say that you have a
potbelly, you have a special capacity for liquor. I shall buy for you
wines from the best cellar and you shall drink the most fancy
concoctions like bamboo green, from great jars and goblets, and
leave the world to run by itself. As for wines, you shall have
famous vintages from Wuchow and Tsinyu, or wines made with
the spring water of Huishan, or the Shangtang brand of Luchow.

There will be wines of Soochow and of Chiutse, or the litchi red from Wutsu district, or autumn-dew white wine from Haining We shall have a full collection of the best, all at your disposal! And you shall sample each and pick the best, and enjoy a drink with luscious crabs and taste their creamy softness, and there shall be turtle and goose claws and sturgeon and scallop and all delicacies of the land and sea, with all greasiness removed and aroma preserved. And when the dinner is finished, start drinking again with ivory trays. The wine games shall be refined and the punishments not too severe, while the friends shall be simple and tireless. Such is the joy of drinking. This ought to cure you of your headaches."

"I am sorry," said the host. "My craving for wine is no longer what it used to be since last summer. With a goblet in hand, I often hesitate whether to take it or not. If I take too much, I feel pain in the chest. I do not think I can avail myself of this remedy."

"I know what ails you," said the other man. "You sit all day confined to the house and brood over some secret sorrow. You have not allowed yourself to go out and see the inspiring sights of mountaintops. No wonder you sit huddled up like a wooden idol and feel like having porcupine bristles all over your chest. May I order for you a carriage for a distant journey and go out with paddles which ride the air? There are more famous mountains than I can count on my fingers. Briefly, there are the five sacred mountains of Hengshan, Changshan, Taishan, Huashan, and Sungshan, with the last named in the center and the Taishan leading in rank. Besides, there are the Wuyi, Wutang, Tienmu, Tienchu, Niushou, Omei, Shiungerh, Chichu, Chiuhua, Kungtung, Chunyu, Yentang, Tientai, Lungmen, Kueiku, Chiuyi, Shiherh, Pakung, Tienmuh, Huchiu, Wolung, Niuchu, Paotu, Peiyo, Huangshan, Pichi, Chinshu, Liangfu, Shuanglung, Maku, Tulu, Peiku, Chinshan, Chiaoshan, Chungnan, Kuangfu, and others too many to mention. Why don't you ascend the high peaks and halloa from the top of your voice and have a big cry to ease the ache in your chest, giving an outlet to your pent-up distress?"

"No," replied the host again. "There are proper times for travel and the necessary conditions must be there to enjoy them. I am sure a trip will give me a temporary relief, but I doubt it will have any permanent value. Think of some other remedy for me."

"It seems that all the pleasures of the world cannot please you and all the joys of human life will not liberate you from your sorrows. I propose to go and look for the immortal fairies and spirits in the Ten Continents and the Three Isles. I shall ask for the appearance of the Eight Immortals of Huainan and the Four Old Men of Shangshan, and bring you the magic concoctions of Yaochih and the rare herbs of Fenglai, with baskets of green arrowroot and fairy peaches and whole hampers of Chiao pears and smoked dates. A slight taste of these magic fruit or a smell of their aroma will restore your complexion and give you energy and a youthful look. You will tread harmlessly through the cemeteries and ancient graveyards, open up the graves, take the divine pills, and drink celestial nectar. A teaspoonful of that medicine and a new vitality will glow through your body, and you will have turned back from a dire sickness to the road of steady recovery and be saved from the clutches of death. And you live again happily with your beloved wife."

Before the speaker had finished, the host clapped his hands in laughter and his whole countenance changed. A new light shone in his eyes. His sickness was gone before he knew it.

8 ▣ The Past and Future

"AT THE ORCHID PAVILION"

Wang Shichih
A.D. 321 - 379

« *This piece by Wang Shichih, the "Prince of Calligraphists," has an unusual and most distinguished history. The original manuscript was regarded as so priceless that it was said to have been buried with the great founder of the Tang Dynasty, Tang Taitsung. Many rubbings from the stone inscription of the script through the succeeding centuries provide a history of the gradual partial erosion of the carving in stone, and students date these rubbings according to the condition of a particular stroke in a given character. The earliest we have now is the Tingwu rubbing of the eleventh century, the stone itself having been lost during a northern invasion. The peculiarity of this precious script is that Wang himself later made a clean copy of it, but failed to recapture the beauty and absolute spontaneity of the first draft. So it was the first draft, with its deletions and insertions, which was inscribed in stone.*

THIS IS THE NINTH YEAR of Yungho (A.D. 353), *kueichou* in the cycle. We met in late spring at the Orchid Pavilion in Shanyin to celebrate the Water Festival.

All the scholar friends are gathered, and there is a goodly mixture of old and young. In the background lie high peaks and deep forests, while a clear, gurgling brook catches the light to the right and to the left. We then arrange ourselves, sitting on its bank, drinking in succession from the goblet as it floats down the stream. No music is provided, but with drinking and with song, our hearts

98

are gay and at ease. It is a clear spring day with a mild, caressing breeze. The vast universe, throbbing with life, lies spread before us, entertaining the eye and pleasing the spirit and all the senses. It is perfect.

Now when men come together, they let their thoughts travel to the past and the present. Some enjoy a quiet conversation indoors and others play about outdoors, occupied with what they love. The forms of amusement differ according to temperaments, but when each has found what he wants he is happy and never feels old. Then as time passes on and one is tired of his pursuits, it seems that what fascinated him not so long ago has become a mere memory. What a thought! Besides, whether individually we live a long life or not, we all return to nothingness. The ancients regarded death as the great question. Is it not sad to think of it?

I often thought that the people of the past lived and felt exactly as we of today. Whenever I read their writings I felt this way and was seized with its pathos. It is cool comfort to say that life and death are different phases of the same thing and that a long span of life or a short one does not matter. Alas! The people of the future will look upon us as we look upon those who have gone before us. Hence I have recorded here those present and what they said. Ages may pass and times may change, but the human sentiments will be the same. I know that future readers who set their eyes upon these words will be affected in the same way.

9 回 The Universe a Lodging House

From

"A NIGHT FEAST"

Li Po

A.D. 701 - 762

THE UNIVERSE IS A LODGING HOUSE for the myriad things, and time itself is a traveling guest of the centuries. This floating life is like a dream. How often can one enjoy oneself? It is for this reason that the ancient people held candles to celebrate the night.

10 回 Human Contradictions

Preface to

AUTUMN AWAKE POEMS

Wang Kaiyun
1832 - 1916

« Wang Kaiyun was known as one of the best poets in the modern generation.

ON THE SECOND DAY after the full moon, August, *Mouwu* (1858) I felt tired and lay down to rest in bed and fell asleep. Later I felt cold in the room and waked up. At first I thought it was early in the night. I listened, but the whole household was quiet. Throwing on a gown, I left the room and saw the light of the stars in the courtyard while the Great Dipper shimmered in the distance. A cassia tree was covered with dew and a few bamboos, pointing upward toward the moon, rocked gently. The side door stood half-open while the white garden wall seemed coated with silver, contrasting with the moss-covered areas which stretched into the shade. . . .

The thought comes to me that the essence of a mirror, while permitting reflections, is independent of them, and that of a river, while it flows continuously, is something which stays in its place. But the continuous reflections and the continuous flow do something to the mirror and the river respectively, although the changes in the course of time are hardly perceptible at the moment. We have heard of the water which bores through rocks in Chi and the bronze mirror in Wu which was polished smooth by wind blasts.

The candlelight which burns oil singes the wick and a writing brush wears out in the course of time. Such are the imperceptible changes. A bamboo grows up in ten days from a shoot while a cypress takes a hundred years to reach a great height. Some things change faster than others. To some people the hundred years of a life span seem short, while others congratulate themselves on reaching old age, forgetting the days that are numbered. Such views have about as much validity as the summer insect's opinion of winter or the large bat's fear of snow. This thought has occupied my mind for the past year, but with the exception of such moments, we go on living and feel quite happy about it. We see things differently at different moments and after waking up, dream away again. Let me be alert and seek the mental quiet behind the phenomena of things. . . .

Soon I heard the maid getting up and my wife was awake. Noises returned to the courtyard, as if we had all returned from some faraway land. So must we disturb and disrupt the essence of eternity with our daily home affairs, and even the recluses hiding out in the mountains sometimes yearn for activity of some kind. Thus, even granting that man can by diligent practice acquire the immortality of the fairies, it is for the exceptional few only, and not for us to maintain such a norm of life. We are faced with these contradictions, discussing the immortal life in the mortal world and hoping to become one day a recluse while living in the cities. What about the fine resolutions to resign one's post and go home?* I do not think that we should lightly mock at those who are carrying on in power and glory or those who take to the woods and seek after the Golden Age. Both kinds have their satisfactions and their frustrations. One day, the man with a public responsibility may think of retirement and another day one who lives in retirement may yet long for public activity. That is why Tsesze advises on "living according to one's station in life." . . .

For in this dream life of a hundred years, the poetic tragic spirit

* The writer occupied a post under President Yuan Shihkai.

is yet outside the normal seven human sentiments [of joy, anger, sorrow, happiness, love, hate, and desire]. Therefore I have concentrated on the eternal truths, and dipped pen in ink to express these thoughts. I call them *Autumn Awake Poems*." . . .

11 📖 The Wear and Tear of Life

From

"ON LEVELING ALL THINGS"

Chuangtse
c. 335 - c. 275 B.C.

« *Chuangtse was, in my opinion, China's greatest philosopher. For this statement, I refer to my reasons given in* From Pagan to Christian, *p. 130. (See introductory note, selection 78.)*

GREAT WISDOM IS GENEROUS; petty wisdom is contentious. Great speech is impassioned, small speech cantankerous.

For whether the soul is locked in sleep or whether in waking hours the body moves, we are striving and struggling with the immediate circumstances. Some are easygoing and leisurely, some are deep and cunning, and some are secretive. Now we are frightened over petty fears, now dismayed over some great terror. Now the mind flies forth like a swift arrow, to be the arbiter of right and wrong. Now it stays behind as if sworn to an oath, to hold on to what it has secured. Then, as under autumn and winter's blight, comes gradual decay, and submerged in its own occupations, it keeps on running its course, never to return. Finally, worn out and imprisoned, it is choked up like an old drain, and the failing mind shall not see light again.

Joy and anger, sorrow and happiness, worries and regrets, indecision and fears come upon us by turns, with ever-changing moods, like music from the hollows, or like mushrooms from damp. Day and night they alternate within us, but we cannot tell whence they spring. Alas! Alas! could we for a moment lay our finger upon their very Cause?

But for these emotions I should not be. Yet but for me, there would be no one to feel them. So far we can go; but we do not know by whose order they come into play. It would seem there was a soul; but the clue to its existence is wanting. That it functions is credible enough, though we cannot see its form. Perhaps it has inner reality without outward form.

Take the human body with all its hundred bones, nine external cavities, and six internal organs, all complete. Which part of it should I love best? Do you not cherish all equally, or have you a preference? Do these organs serve as servants of someone else? Since servants cannot govern themselves, do they serve as master and servants by turn? Surely there is some soul which controls them all.

But whether or not we ascertain what is the true nature of this soul, it matters but little to the soul itself. For once coming into this material shape, it runs its course until it is exhausted. To be harassed by the wear and tear of life, and to be driven along without possibility of arresting one's course — is not this pitiful indeed? To labor without cease all life, and then, without living to enjoy the fruit, worn out with labor, to depart, one knows not whither — is not this a just cause for grief?

Men say there is no death — of what avail? The body decomposes, and the mind goes with it. Is this not a great cause for sorrow? Can the world be so dull as not to see this? Or is it I alone who am dull, and others not so?

12 ▣ The Butterfly's Dream

From

"ON LEVELING ALL THINGS"

Chuangtse

C. 335 - C. 275 B.C.

ONCE UPON A TIME, I, Chuang Chou, dreamt that I was a butterfly, fluttering hither and thither, to all intents and purposes a butterfly. I was conscious only of my happiness as a butterfly, unaware that I was Chou. Soon I awaked, and there I was, veritably myself again. Now I do not know whether I was then a man dreaming that I was a butterfly, or whether I am now a butterfly, dreaming that I am a man. Between a man and a butterfly, there is necessarily a distinction. The transition is called "the transformation of material things."

« For further selections and notes about Chuangtse see selections 75, 78, 92, and 93.

13 ▣ The Ambition-Mind and the Profit-Mind

From

WEST-GREEN RANDOM NOTES

Shih Chenlin
1693 - c. 1779

« *This whole essay develops the idea of how national and personal affairs are born of the mind and influenced by the mind. The Chinese word shin denotes both the heart and the mind as a single concept. In this sense, the word "mind" here is used to cover ambitions, plans, hopes, longings, desires, both pure and impure, as well as thought and ideas. The essay presents the novel idea that the world is moved by the "mind," in the metaphysical sense somewhat similar to Schopenhauer's idea of the world as "will." (See note on the author, selection 5.)*

MY FRIEND TSAO CHENTING made a painting, which is entitled "Discussing the Mind on a Snowy Night by a Small Window." He brought it to Tsishiashan (where I live) and I wrote a verse on it. In addition, I wrote the following note:

> When the ambition-mind burns,
> One's chest grows wings.
> When the profit-mind stings,
> One's bowels grow thorns.

The ambition-mind, or love of a good name, governs us from birth to death. A child smiles when he is praised and cries when he is scolded, and an old man lying on his deathbed and drawing his last breath still thinks of leaving a good name. Likewise, the profit-mind, or the love of possessions, also governs us from birth to death. A child is happy when he is given something and cries when it is taken away from him, and an old man lying on his deathbed and drawing his last breath still thinks of his worldly possessions. Now when these hopes and ambitions for a good name or accomplishments are frustrated or suppressed, the accumulated force of such longings goes upward and affects changes in the firmaments, causing thunder, rains, hail and snow, and disturbance among the feathery tribe.* And when the struggles and hopes for wealth and worldly gains are frustrated or suppressed, the accumulated force goes downward and affects changes in the rivers and vegetation and soil and water and in the scaly tribe. Therefore, those who are not dead to the ambition for success die of success, and those who are not dead to the struggle for wealth die of money-making. The sages tried to bring peace to the world by changing the minds of men in the direction of regulating these two primary forces. It must be noted, however, that loyalty, integrity, and virtuous conduct in the realm of morals, and poetry, prose, painting, and calligraphy in the realm of arts, also stem from the desire for a good name. Similarly, to retire from the world and live in a region of beautiful landscape and till a farm or be a woodcutter or a fisherman — these also come from the man's desire for what he considers to be of profit to him. This opposite set of desires and ambitions also goes forth and causes changes in the times, bringing the sweet rain and balmy winds and rich harvests and clement weather. When the ambition-minds and profit-minds of the millions are frustrated and ready to cause upsets in the seasons and are confronted with the other mind, they melt away. When one's mind burns with the fire of worldly ambition for glory and power,

---

* A common Chinese concept that the universe comes from certain forces, such as the *yin* and *yang*, and this balance is often disturbed by what men do. Thus an emperor often took the blame of misgovernment upon himself on the appearance of a sun's eclipse or any great seasonal disturbances.

this other mind cools it. When a ruler's mind is cold and indifferent to the people's sufferings, this other mind kindles it and stirs it into flame again. It is difficult to estimate what the mind can do.

I have been looking for some simple-hearted friends among the people of the world, but found most of them smothered under the wings of ambition or suffering from the penalties and irritations of their wealth. I sought refuge in the deep mountains and enjoyed the moon and the wild flowers.* I could not see a soul and decided to settle down there. Sometimes I would be thinking of a friend and, luckily enough, the friend I was thinking of would appear and join me. Looking down from the mountaintop, we saw the human world below, and the busy activities of the myriad beings appeared like those of larvae or beetles after a spring rain. What we have here is also a kind of ambition-mind and profit-mind that goes beyond the worldly ambitions and profits.

When Chenting showed me his painting, I said, "This expresses a thought long in my mind. But who are those people discussing the mind?" And this was Chenting's reply:

Take the understanding of the summer clouds, for example. One's mind may love them, admiring their splendor at sunset as they break out in gold and orange and change into a thousand forms. With such a person who has a sympathetic understanding and love for the summer clouds, I would discuss the mind of the clouds. Or one may think of snow in summer and if there is another person who is thinking of the same thing, he would be the person with whom to discuss the mind and heart of the snow. Or if one thinks of the moon on a rainy night and another person has the same thought, he would be the person with whom to discuss the mind and heart of the moon. I dreamt of being a butterfly and may be born as a phoenix in some future generation, and the same thing may happen to another person. Now on this month and day, there is a Tsao Chenting and there is a Shih Chenlin sitting

* The author, Shih Chenlin, practiced what he preached. (See introductory note, selection 5.)

here in Tsishiashan talking of the butterfly and the phoenix. I am sure that a thousand years, or perhaps ten thousand years from now, there will be another Tsao Chenting and another Shih Chen-lin talking about butterflies and phoenixes at the same place. These would all come from the butterfly-mind, the phoenix-mind, the friendship-mind, and the landscape-mind. Whether such persons belong to the same generation or not, or whether they come at the right time or not, is inconsequential.

The mind of God is merciful. He is concerned lest men should die of the ambition-mind and the profit-mind, and lest we should neglect to direct the love of a good name toward righteousness and the love of possessions toward true riches. You cannot discuss this with those who are going to die of the struggle for fame and wealth. Nor can people understand when you speak of being dead to the ambitions for fame and worldly possessions. In the primordial time, before the universe was, I am sure there were the same manifestations of the mind as today and this must be also true of the time when the universe was formed from nebulae, except we have no way of seeing it. How can you be sure that Tsao Chenting and Shih Chenlin were not there before the universe was, although we cannot remember it? We cannot be sure, however, that there may not be other beings who remember, clearly and vividly, how many times Tsao Chenting and Shih Chenlin were born and came and went out of this world. Only those who know this can discuss with us our two minds.

Be that as it may, everybody in this world, from the most enlightened to the illiterate peasants and children, has in him this mind of understanding and love which is usually hidden, silenced and lost in formlessness. It is apart from life and death and apart from ambition and profit. But it is there: one mind affects another, the conscious affects the unconscious, and the unconscious affects the conscious. One cannot help discussing this mind-essence, and yet does not know how to express it. It cannot talk of itself and no one can talk for it. It cannot be communicated to those who are in it, nor to those who are outside it. Thus are accumulated the millions of minds and hearts and souls of the past and present which break out into laughter in time of sorrow and into sorrow in time of laughter, and wake up from drunkenness to sobriety and vice versa. All this mass of feelings and desires and human hopes is there, more than can ever be recorded in all the tomes of history or expressed in songs. Yet it is all in me. Therefore, from the primordial beginning to the endless future, only I can apprehend this mind and only I can dismiss it from consciousness.

There is still another consideration. The myriads of minds change and grow bright or dim like the wax and wane of the moon or the change in the brightness of the day from noon to sunset. In its plenitude of power, this mind reaches the utmost limits of space. In its finest realization, it emerges as a great intellectual or artistic genius. In its deepest realization, it emerges as love. As talent or as love, this mind penetrates and illumines by its gift of understanding or imaginative sympathy where the sun and the moon fail. Sometimes you see a successful man take an interest in some scholar, being attracted by his talent, or a swordsman who risks danger to help a friend, or a woman who cares for a man because of his looks. That sympathetic understanding or love is limited to those who have an attractive talent or looks, or who enjoy one's friendship. I, Tsao Chenting, swear before God that whenever there is a true talent, I will help him if I am born as an official, even though I may suffer for it, and I will help him if I am born a swordsman, even if he is not my friend or even hostilely disposed toward me, and if I am born a woman, I will not be ashamed of him, though this genius may be shocking in appearance. And I swear in the name of Man that I will help him even though it may cost my own name or fortune. It is my wish to see that all the suppressed talents in the heart and mind of the millions may blossom and find successful expression.

14 ▣ On Zest in Life

Preface to

HWEISHIN COLLECTION OF POEMS OF
CHEN CHENGFU

Yuan Chunglang
c. 1600

« Yuan Chunglang was leader of a literary school in the late Ming
Dynasty known as the Kung-an School. (See selection 67.)

I FIND THAT ZEST is a rare gift in life. Zest is like hues on
the mountains, taste in water, brilliance in flowers, and charm in
women. It is appreciated only by those who have understanding,
and is difficult to explain in words. True enough, it is common
nowadays to find people who affect a taste in certain diversions.
Some cultivate a love for painting, calligraphy, and antiques, and
others are fascinated by the mystics and the recluses and the life
of a hermit. Still others are like the people of Soochow who make
a hobby of tea and incense, turning it almost into a cult. These
are superficial, and have nothing to do with real zest and understanding of the flavor in living.

This zest for living is more born in us than cultivated. Children
have most of it. They have probably never heard of the word "zest,"
but they show it everywhere. They find it hard to look solemn;
they wink, they grimace, they mumble to themselves, they jump
and skip and hop and romp. That is why childhood is the happiest
period of a man's life, and why Mencius spoke of "recovering the
heart of a child" and Laotse referred to it as a model of man's

original nature. The peasants who live near the mountains and forests do not make a cult of these things; in their life of freedom and absence of social conventions, they enjoy the beauties of nature all as a part of their living. The more degenerate men become, the harder they find it to enjoy life. Some are fascinated by merely sensual enjoyments and call it "fun," and find their pleasure in meats and wines and sex and riotous living and defiance of social customs, saying they are thus liberating themselves. Often as one progresses in life, his official rank becomes higher and his social status grows bigger; his body and mind are fettered with a thousand cares and sober duties. Then knowledge, learning, and life experience stop up even his pores and seep down to his hardened joints. The more he knows, the more befuddled he becomes, and the more removed he is from understanding this zest in living.

長恨

LOVE AND DEATH

15 ▣ On Love

"ON HEROES AND WOMEN"

Chou Chuan
c. 1600

It is often said that "the great heroes of history met their match in women." By this people mean that the love of a woman is a dangerous thing and that such episodes somehow take away from our idea of a "hero." One must keep away from the snares and temptations of women. And so forth.

I beg to differ. I think what makes heroes heroes is that they have love in a greater measure than others and are capable of greater devotion to something, with their heart and soul in it. Only those who can make great sacrifices can love truly. All the universe comes from love. Where the heart dictates, a man guides his life by it. It is not confined to any one thing, but runs through all human affairs, beginning with the love of woman. Love and devotion can be just as well applied to a national cause, to friendship, to the business in hand. Therefore the *Book of Songs* [edited by Confucius] did not regard the love between man and woman as sin, and the *Book of Changes* spoke of marriage as fulfilling "the heart of the universe." We can run through the great names of history in our mind and find that not one of them did not have a great love. There was Shiang Yu. What a warrior and what a man! When he found himself surrounded by the enemy and the end was near, he got up in his tent, wrote some verse, and sang with his sweetheart, and they wept together before killing themselves with a sword. And his enemy, too, who became the First Emperor of Han, had an unsuspected tenderness. Assuredly he was a great warrior

117

who scolded his generals like boys. He then became emperor, but before his death, he said to his queen, "Dance for me, dear, the folk dance of our home country and I shall sing for you our folk songs." Thus an emperor died.

I therefore say that it takes a man with a great heart to have a great love affair. I have noticed that those who made good as scholars and writers loved certain things to the exclusion of everything else. And when a crisis arose, these people acted with decision and firmness and showed a strength of character above the others. When the country called, they responded. There is no mystery about it. They had a big *heart*, and merely transferred that great love from one thing to something else. Therefore, as I say, love is not confined to any one thing. Only those who make some great sacrifice can love truly.

« *I am sure that the heart can shake a throne. It is the wholeness of love that accomplishes great things in this universe. Here we are dealing with a vital force that cold philosophers in their gray plaster walls little know. One thinks of Nelson and Napoleon. The greatest emperor in all China's history, whose reign is conceded by all to be the best, was Tang Taitsung (reigned, A.D. 627–649) the real founder of the great Tang Dynasty. I like the episode of his love for his twelve-year-old princess, nicknamed "Bizon." When the little girl died, he was unconsoled and lost his appetite for a whole month. He explained to his servants who urged him to eat, "I love this child so much. I can't get over it. I don't know why." Is it not our weakness that makes our strength?*

16 ▣ The Mortal Thoughts of a Nun

From a Popular Drama

Anonymous
before 1700

A YOUNG NUN AM I, sixteen years of age;
My head was shaven in my young maidenhood.

For my father, he loves the Buddhist sutras,
And my mother, she loves the Buddhist priests.

Morning and night, morning and night,
I burn incense and I pray, for I
Was born a sickly child, full of ills.
So they sent me here into this monastery.

Amitabha! Amitabha!
Unceasingly I pray.
Oh, tired am I of the humming of the drums and the tinkling of
    the bells;
Tired am I of the droning of the prayers and the crooning of the
    priors;
The chatter and the clatter of unintelligible charms,
The clamor and the clangor of interminable chants,
The mumbling and the murmuring of monotonous psalms.
Prajnaparamita, Mayura-sutra,
    Saddharmapundarika —
        Oh, how I hate them all!

While I say Mitabha,
    I sigh for my beau.

While I chant saparah,
    My heart cries, "Oh!"
While I sing tarata,
    My heart palpitates so!

Ah, let me take a stroll,
Let me take a stroll!

(*She comes to the Hall of the Five Hundred Lohans, where are clay figures of the Buddhist saints, known for their distinctive facial expressions.*)

    Ah, here are the Lohan,
What a bunch of silly, amorous souls!
    Every one a bearded man!
How each his eyes at me rolls!

Look at the one hugging his knees!
    His lips are mumbling my name so!
And the one with his cheek in hand,
    As though thinking of me so!
That one has a pair of dreamy eyes,
    Dreaming dreams of me so!

    But the Lohan in sackcloth!
What is he after,
    With his hellish, heathenish laughter?
With his roaring, rollicking laughter,
    Laughing at me so!
            — Laughing at me, for
When beauty is past and youth is lost,
    Who will marry an old crone?
When beauty is faded and youth is jaded,
    Who will marry an old, shriveled cocoon?

The one holding a dragon,
    He is cynical;

The one riding a tiger,
      He is quizzical;
And that long-browed handsome giant,
      He seems pitiful,
For what will become of me when my beauty is gone?

These candles of the altar,
      They are not for my bridal chamber.
These long incense containers,
      They are not for my bridal parlor.
And the straw prayer cushions,
      They cannot serve as quilt or cover.

   Oh, God!
Whence comes this burning, suffocating ardor?
      Whence comes this strange, infernal, unearthly ardor?
I'll tear these monkish robes!
      I'll bury all the Buddhist sutras;
I'll drown the wooden fish,
      And leave all the monastic putras!

I'll leave the drums,
      I'll leave the bells,
            And the chants,
                  And the yells,
And all the interminable, exasperating, religious chatter!

I'll go downhill, and find me a young and handsome lover —
Let him scold me, beat me!
      Kick or ill-treat me!
I will *not* become a buddha!
I will *not* mumble mita, prajna, para!

17 ▣ The Death of a Queen

From

HISTORY OF HAN (HANSHU)

Pan Ku
A.D. 32 - 92

WHEN THE EMPRESS MADAME LI* was seriously ill, His
Majesty went to see her. She covered up her face with her bed
quilt, and said, "I thank Your Majesty for the honor. But I have
been ill for a long time and I have been so emaciated that I am
unfit to receive you. My only wish is that you take care of my
brothers and the princes of my blood after my death."

"You are very ill, and I am not sure that you will be able to
recover," replied the emperor. "Do let me see you and tell me
what you want me to do for your brothers. Isn't this simpler?"

"But I dare not. It is not fit that I should see you in my condition with my face so ravaged by disease."

"Please let me see you. I will give you a thousand taels and give
your brothers high posts," pleaded the emperor.

"That is in your power. But please do not insist," replied
Madame Li.

The emperor continued to plead. The empress then turned her
face toward the other side and did not speak any more, and her
breathing was hard. The emperor was displeased and left.

When the emperor was gone, her sisters said to her, "Why

* In Chinese usage and by necessity, women and ladies in a household where there were a number of wives or concubines were addressed
by their maiden name. In the case here, Madame Li was the empress
of great emperor Han Wuti (reigned, 140–87 B.C.), who conquered
Turkestan.

didn't you let him see you just for the sake of your brothers? As if you hated him!"

"I did what I did exactly for the sake of my brothers," replied Madame Li. "You must understand men. I rose to this position because of my looks, and he still thinks of me because he has in his mind what he saw of me when I was young and beautiful. If I should let him see me now, he would be so disgusted that really the chances of my brothers receiving his favors would be impaired."

When Madame Li died, the emperor gave her a lavish funeral. Later, he made her elder brother, Li Kuangli, a general and Duke of Haishi, and made Li Yennien Vice-Commander of the Guards.

The emperor could not stop thinking of her. There was a magician of Tsi, who claimed that he could conjure the souls of the departed. A room was therefore prepared with bed curtains, and candles were burned during the night and wines and meats were laid out on the table. The emperor was made to sit in another room in the distance. He saw a beautiful woman resembling Madame Li come in and sit on the bed and walk about. But he was not permitted to get closer. He was greatly touched and wrote a verse:

Is it you?
But is it you indeed?
You came.
But when you came, your movements were so stately and slow.

The court musicians were ordered to set this to music.

18 ▣ To a Beauty

From

"SHIENCHING FU"

Tao Yuanming
A.D. 372 - 427

« *This is the only love poem by Tao Yuanming, one of the greatest poets in Chinese literature (see note, selection 33). Tao was
a poet of nature, whom Po Chuyi and Su Tungpo desperately
admired. It is amusing to find that there are Chinese puritans
who called this poem the only "blemish in a white jade." This
translation of mine is not literal, and entailed a great deal of
compression to get at the gist and essence of the poem.*

YOU WHO ARE BLESSED, incomparable, unsurpassed,
So carelessly perfect in beauty and grace,
So chaste and ethereal in thought and demeanor,
     In all your ways.

You were sitting, unaware of not being alone,
Pensively fingering the strings — the while
Your white arms and silk sleeves trail the *chin*, and on
     Your lips a smile.

The melody stopped and you glanced at the view
Of lengthening evening shadows on the plains.
You could not have known, for you never knew
     A man in chains.

O happy one, if I could tell you all my longing,
The envious thought of all the things that you own,

The humblest objects close to you that belong
     To you alone.

I would be the rouge that kisses your lips,
The collar that brushes your fragrant hair,
The girdle that embraces your gentle waist,
Your shoes that follow your steps everywhere.

I would be the fan that wafts your whispers,
Your shadows that follow in your every move,
The candles that shine upon your beauteous face,
The bird that you feed and returns your love —
     Then I would live!

Yet were I any one of these things, I would fear
To be the forgotten dove, the castaway fan,
The shadows in darkness, the candles at dawn —
     I live in vain!

19 In Memory of a Woman

From

SIX CHAPTERS OF A FLOATING LIFE

Shen Fu
1763 - c. 1808

« *Six Chapters of a Floating Life is one of the most beloved little
volumes, recording for the most part the author's home life with
his wife. Faithful and written simply and without exaggerations,
it is one of the tenderest tributes to a woman. I choose here the
beginning and the end.*

A. The Wedding Night

THIS WAS ON JULY 16 in the year 1775. In the winter of
this year one of my girl cousins was going to get married and I
again accompanied my mother to her maiden home. Yun was of
the same age as myself, but ten months older, and as we had been
accustomed to calling each other "elder sister" and "younger
brother" from childhood, I continued to call her "Sister Su."

At this time the guests in the house all wore bright dresses, but
Yun alone was clad in a dress of quiet color, and had on a new
pair of shoes. I noticed that the embroidery on her shoes was very
fine, and learned that it was her own work, so that I began to realize
that she was gifted at other things, too, besides reading and writing.

Of a slender figure, she had drooping shoulders, and a rather long
neck, slim but not to the point of being skinny. Her eyebrows were
arched and in her eyes there was a look of quick intelligence and

soft refinement. The only defect was that her two front teeth were slightly inclined forward, which was not a mark of good omen. There was an air of tenderness about her which completely fascinated me.

That night, when I came home from my relatives' place in the country, whither I had accompanied my female cousin the bride, it was already midnight, and I felt very hungry and asked for something to eat. A maidservant gave me some dried dates, which were too sweet for me. Yun secretly pulled me by the sleeve into her room, and I saw that she had hidden away a bowl of warm congee and some dishes to go with it. I was beginning to take up the chopsticks and eat it with great gusto when Yun's cousin Yuheng called out: "Sister Su, come quickly!" Yun quickly shut the door and said: "I am very tired and going to bed." Yuheng forced the door open and seeing the situation, said with a malicious smile at Yun, "So, that's it! A while ago I asked for congee and you said there was no more, but you really meant to keep it for your future husband." Yun was greatly embarrassed and everybody laughed at her, including the servants. On my part, I rushed away home with an old servant in a state of excitement.

Since the affair of the congee happened, she always avoided me when I went to her home afterward, and I knew that she was only trying to avoid being made a subject of ridicule.

On the twenty-second of January in 1780, I saw her on our wedding night, and found that she had the same slender figure as before. When her bridal veil was lifted, we looked at each other and smiled. After the drinking of the customary twin cups between groom and bride, we sat down together at dinner and I secretly held her hand under the table, which was warm and small, and my heart was palpitating. I asked her to eat and learned that she had been keeping fast for several years already. I found that the time when she began her fast coincided with my smallpox illness, and said to her laughingly: "Now that my face is clean and smooth without pockmarks, my dear sister, will you break your fast?" Yun looked at me with a smile and nodded her head.

This was on the twenty-second, my wedding night. On the twenty-fourth, my own sister was going to get married, and as there was to be a national mourning and no music was to be allowed on the twenty-third, we gave my sister a send-off dinner on the night of the twenty-second, and Yun was present at table. I was playing the finger-guessing game with the bridesmaids in the bridal chamber and being a loser all the time, fell asleep drunk like a fish. When I woke up the next morning, Yun had not quite finished her morning toilet.

That day, we were kept busy entertaining guests and toward evening, music was played. After midnight, on the morning of the twenty-fourth, I, as the bride's brother, sent my sister away and came back toward three o'clock. The room was then pervaded with quietness, bathed in the silent glow of the candle lights. I went in and saw Yun's woman servant taking a nap behind the bed, while Yun had taken off her bridal costume, but had not yet gone to bed. Her beautiful white neck was bent before the bright candles, and she was absorbed reading a book. I patted her on the shoulder and said: "Sister, why are you still working so hard? You must be quite tired with the full day we've had."

Quickly Yun turned her head and stood up saying: "I was going to bed when I opened the bookcase and saw this book and have not been able to leave it since. Now my sleepiness is all gone. I have heard of the name of *The Western Chamber* for a long time, but today I see it for the first time. It is really the work of a genius, only I feel that its style is a little bit too biting."

"Only geniuses can write a biting style," I smiled and said.

The woman servant asked us to go to bed and left us and shut the door. I began to sit down by her side and we joked together like old friends after a long separation. I touched her breast in fun and felt that her heart was palpitating too. "Why is Sister's heart palpitating like that?" I bent down and whispered in her ear. Yun looked back at me with a smile and our souls were carried away in a mist of passion. Then we went to bed, when all too soon the dawn came.

As a bride, Yun was very quiet at first. She was never sullen or displeased, and when people spoke to her, she merely smiled. She was respectful toward her superiors and kindly toward those under her. Whatever she did was done well, and it was difficult to find fault with her. When she saw the gray dawn shining through the window, she would get up and dress herself as if she had been commanded to do so. "Why?" I asked. "You don't have to be afraid of gossip, like the days when you gave me that warm congee." "I was made a laughingstock on account of that bowl of congee," she replied, "but now I am not afraid of people's talk; I only fear that our parents might think their daughter-in-law lazy."

Although I wanted her to lie in bed longer, I could not help admiring her virtue, and so got up myself, too, at the same time with her. And so every day we rubbed shoulders together and clung to each other like an object and its shadow, and the love between us was something that surpassed the language of words.

B. The Deathwatch

HER ILLNESS BECAME WORSE and worse every day. I wanted to send for a doctor, but Yun stopped me saying:

"You know my illness started in consequence of deep grief over my mother's death following upon Kehchang's running away; then it was aggravated through my passion for Han and finally made worse by my chagrin at this recent affair. Besides, I was often too cautious and afraid of making mistakes. I have tried my best to be a good daughter-in-law, and have failed, and have consequently developed dizziness and palpitation of the heart. The illness is now deep in my system and no doctor will be of any avail, and you may just as well spare yourself the expense. As I look back upon the twenty-three years of our married life, I know that you have loved me and been most considerate to me, in spite of all my faults. I am happy to die with a husband and understanding friend like you and I have no regrets. Yes, I have been as happy as a fairy at times, with my warm cotton clothing and frugal but full meals and the

happy home we had. Do you remember how we used to enjoy ourselves amongst springs and rocks, as at the Tsanglang Pavilion and
the Shiaoshuanglou? But who are we to enjoy the good luck of a
fairy, for which only those are worthy who have lived a virtuous
life from incarnation to incarnation? We had, therefore, offended
God by trying to snatch a happiness that was above our lot; hence
our various earthly troubles. It all comes of your too great love, bestowed upon one who is ill-fated and unworthy of this happiness."

After a while she spoke again amidst sobs, "Everyone has to die
once. My only regret is, we have to part halfway from each other
forever, and I am not able to be your wife until the end of your
days and see with my own eyes the wedding of Fengsen." After saying this, tears rolled down her eyes as big as peas. I tried to comfort
her by saying, "You have been ill for eight years, and this is not
the first time that you are in a critical condition. Why do you
suddenly say such heartbreaking words?"

"I have been dreaming lately," she said, "of my parents who
have sent a boat to welcome me home. Whenever I close my
eyes, I feel my body is so light, so light, like one walking among the
clouds. It seems that my spirit has already departed and only my
body remains."

"This is the effect of your extreme weakness," I said. "If you will
take some tonic and rest yourself properly, I am sure you will get
well."

Then Yun sighed again and said, "If there were the slightest ray
of hope, I would not have told you all these things. But now death
is approaching and it is high time I spoke my mind. I know you
have displeased your parents all on my account; therefore when I
die, your parents' attitude will change round, and you yourself
will feel more at ease toward your parents. You know they are
already very old, and when I die, you should return to them as
soon as possible. If you cannot bring my remains back to the native
district for burial, you can temporarily keep my coffin here and
then see to its removal afterward. I hope you will find another
one who is both beautiful and good to take my place and serve our

parents and bring up my children, and then I shall die content."
At this point, I broke down completely and fell to weeping as if my
bowels had been cut through.

"Even if you should leave me halfway like this," I said, "I shall
never marry again. Besides, 'it is difficult to be water for one who
has seen the great seas, and difficult to be clouds for one who has
seen the Yangtse Gorges.'" Then Yun held my hand and was
going to say something again, but she could only mumble the
words "Next incarnation!" half audibly again and again. Suddenly
she began to feel short of breath, her chin was set, her eyes stared
wide open, and however I called her name, she could not utter a
single word. Two lines of tears began to roll down her face. After a
while, her breath became weaker, her tears gradually dried up and
her spirit departed from this life for ever. This was on the thirtieth
of the third moon, 1803. A solitary lamp was shining then in the
room, and a sense of utter forlornness overcame me. In my heart
opened a wound that shall be healed nevermore!

My friend Hu Kengtang kindly helped me with ten dollars, and
together with this and what I could obtain by selling what I had
in the house, I saw to her proper burial.

Alas! Yun was a woman with the heart and talent of a man.
From the time she was married into my home, I had been forced
to run about abroad for a living, while she was left without sufficient money, and she never said a word of complaint. When I
could stay at home, our sole occupation was the discussion of
books and literature. She died in poverty and sickness without
being able to see her own children, and who was to blame but
myself? . . .

According to custom, the spirit of the deceased is supposed to
return to the house on a certain day after his death, and people
used to arrange the room exactly as the deceased had left it, putting
his old clothes on the bed and his old shoes by the bedside for the
returning spirit to take a farewell look. We called this in Soochow
"closing the spirit's eyes." People also used to invite Taoist monks
to recite incantations, calling to the spirit to visit the deathbed and

then sending it away. This was called "welcoming the spirit." At Yangchow the custom was to prepare wine and dishes and leave them in the dead man's chamber, while the whole family would run away, in order to "avoid the spirit." It often happened that things were stolen while the house was thus deserted. On this day, my landlord, who was staying with me, left the house, and my neighbors urged me to leave the offerings at home and get away also. To this I gave a cold, indifferent reply, for I was hoping to see the spirit of Yun again. There was a certain Chang Yumen of the same district who warned me saying, "One may be very well possessed by the evil spirit, when one's mind dwells on the uncanny. I should not advise you to try it, for I rather believe in the existence of ghosts."

"This is the very reason I am going to stay — because I believe that ghosts do exist," I replied.

"To encounter the spirit of the deceased on its return home has an evil influence on living men," Chang replied. "Even if your wife's spirit should return, she is living in a world different from ours. I am afraid you won't be able to see her form, but will, on the other hand, be affected by her evil influence."

I was so madly in love with her that I did not care. "I don't care a bit about it," I said to him. "If you are so concerned about me, why not stay on and keep me company?"

"I'll stay outside the door. If you should see anything strange, just call for me."

I then went in with a lamp in my hand and saw the room was exactly as she had left it, only my beloved was not there, and tears welled up in my eyes in spite of myself. I was afraid then that with my wet eyes, I should not be able to see her form clearly, and I held back my tears and sat on the bed, waiting for her appearance with wide-open eyes. Softly I touched her old dress and smelled the odor of her body which still remained, and was so affected by it that I fainted off. Then I thought to myself how could I let myself doze off since I was waiting for the return of her spirit? I opened my eyes and looked around and saw the two candle lights burning low on the table as small as little peas. It gave me goose flesh and I shuddered all over. Then I rubbed my hands and my forehead and looked carefully and saw the pair of candle lights leap higher and higher till they were over a foot long and the papered wooden frame of the ceiling was going to catch fire. The sudden glow of the lights illuminated the whole room and enabled me to look around clearly, when suddenly they grew small and dark as before. At this time I was in a state of excitement and wanted to call in my companion, when I thought that her gentle female spirit might be scared away by the presence of another living man. Secretly and in a quiet tone, I called her name and prayed to her, but the whole room was buried in silence and I could not see a thing. Then the candle lights grew bright again, but did not shoot high up as before. I went out and told Yumen about it, and he thought me very brave, but did not know that I was merely in love.

20 ◪ In Memory of a Child

"SACRIFICIAL PRAYER TO AH CHEN"

Shen Chunlieh
? - 1624

« *I think this is one of the most tender things I ever read, especially toward the end.*

ON THE TWENTY-THIRD OF DECEMBER of the year 1619, Shen Chunlieh's eldest daughter, Ah Chen, died of smallpox which failed to appear, and was buried on the northern mounds. Her mother, Madame Po, recited Buddhist sutras daily in her favor, and urged the writing of a sacrificial prayer for her, but he did not have the heart to take up a pen and do it. On the twenty-first day of her death, he prepared for her a sacrifice of cooked food, and composed a piece to weep over her, which was burned on the scene of her childhood games, and is as follows:

Alas! great is my sorrow! Your name is Ah Chen, written with the components Ping and Chen, because you were born in the year Pingchen (1616). When you were born, I was not truly pleased, for I was a man over thirty, and you came not a boy but a girl. But before you were one year old, you were already adorable. When one nodded to you, you opened your mouth and laughed. During this period, Chouma [amah] was taking care of you, and she woke up ten times a night, and never took off her girdle while going to bed. When you were hungry, you sought for milk from your mama, and when you were well filled, you went to bed with Chouma. And Chouma suffered many misunderstandings on your account. She moved you from a wet place to a dry place, and went to great troubles to lighten a small suffering. If she paid you too much attention, your mother would reprimand her, and if she paid too little attention, you would cry.

Last year, I was unlucky. On account of the examinations, I had to tear myself away from you. I failed in the examinations and Chouma died. When I came back, you pulled at my sleeves and asked for toys. With you by my side, my sorrow was relieved. You grew more teeth and you daily grew in wisdom. You called "Dada" and "Mama" and your pronunciation was perfect. You often knocked at the door and asked "Who is it?" When my nephew came, you called him "Koko" [elder brother]. He took away your toys in play and you ran away and protested. When your maternal uncle came, you pulled at his gown. You called out "Mama" and you laughed in a silvery voice. When your paternal uncle came, you played the host. Lifting the cup, you said, "Ching!" and we roared with laughter. Your grandpa went to the country, and you yourself went to Soochow. For a year you had not seen him, and we asked you if you knew grandpa, and you said, "Yes. White cap and white beard." You had never seen your maternal grandpa, and when we asked you, "Whence comes this guest?" you said "Peking!" Your maternal grandma was very fond of you and regarded you like her own. Several times she took you to Soochow with her. You asked for toys at midnight and asked for fruit at day's dawn. Your own parents asked you to come home, but you refused, saying "Grandma would think of me."

This year in June, you had boils, and I went to Soochow specially to take you home. I touched your affected spots, and your face showed pain. But you did not cry, thinking it was not right. Every time you took a fruit or sweetmeat, you looked at people's faces, and if we did not approve, you would not put it in your mouth. Sometimes you touched things and accidentally spoiled them, and one just looked at you, and your hand would shrink back. Your mama was too strict with you, and she often admonished you, for fear that when you grew up, you would form such habits. I did not agree, and told her in private, "Let the baby alone. What does she know at this young age?" When you were at Soochow, and mama and I were coming home, we asked you if you would come or stay. And your heart lay both ways, and you hesitated to reply. Then you came home, and we were so glad, and we coaxed you and we pulled faces to get your laugh. You carried a toy basket of dates and sat on a low stool to eat porridge. You repeated the "Great Learning," and you bowed to Buddha. You played at guessing games, and you romped about the house. You clapped your hands and thought yourself very clever.

But within a fortnight, the day of your death came. Was it Heaven's will or was it your fate? Even the fairies do not know. Before you died, we sent for a doctor. Some said it was a cold, and some said it was smallpox. It could not be a cold, and it might be smallpox, and we still wonder what you died of. You were clever at speech, but you were silent then. You only panted and stared at us. We wept around you and you wept, too.

Alas! great is my sorrow! According to conventions, why should one weep at a daughter's death. According to my age, I am in my prime and poor and alone. You were very intelligent, and I was satisfied with you, although a girl. But who knew that the gods would be so cruel to me? Ten days before you, your younger sister, Ah Shun, died of the same disease in three days. You know her well, and now that you have no company there, you must stick together with your sister. You can already walk about, but your sister can hardly stand steadily. You should take her by the hand and go about together and must be good to each other and never quarrel. If you meet your amah [Chouma], you could ask her, saying, "Pa had a wife by the name of Ku and a mammy by the name of Min." Ask her to take you to them, and they will surely take care of you. You can stay there for the present, and you should be near Ku. Sister is small and you should lead her, and you are small and Ku should protect you. Sometime later, I will find a propitious ground and bury you three in the same grave.

I am thinking of you now, and it is hard to forget you. If you should hear my prayer, come to see me in my dreams. If fate decrees that you must yet live an earthly life, then come again into your mama's womb. I am offering Buddhist sacrifices and prayers, and I have soup here for you, and I am burning paper money for your use. When you see the Judge of the Lower World, hold your hands together and plead to him, "I am young, and I am innocent. I was born in a poor family and I was contented with scanty meals. I never wasted a single grain of rice, and I was never willfully careless of my clothing and my shoes. Whatever thou commandest, I am only a young child. If evil spirits ever bully me, may thou protect me!" You should just put it that way, and you should not cry or make too much noise. For remember you are in a strange underworld, and it is not like it is at home with our own people. Now I am composing this, but you do not yet know how to read. I will only cry, "Ah Chen, your father is here." I can but cry for you and call your name.

21 回 A Great Love Letter

Tsui Inging

« Written in about A.D. 798, this is one of the most loved love letters in Chinese literature, both because of the circumstances of its writing and because of the beauty and delicacy of language. Yuan Chen (A.D. 779-931) met Miss Tsui on his way to the capital. He discovered Miss Tsui living with her widowed mother in an annex to the temple where he was stopping. They had a mad love affair. Yuan Chen was not a faithful lover, nor an honorable person. After the affair, he left for the capital, married a rich girl, and excused himself by saying that his friends had complimented him for "having reformed." This was the letter Miss Tsui, daughter of a prime minister, sent him.

I am delighted to receive your letter and touched by your loving remembrance. I am excited and happy to receive the box of hair ornaments and the five inches of rouge. I appreciate these thoughful gifts, but of what use are they to me in your absence? They bring you closer to me, and only because of my longing for you. I am glad that you were well and able to pursue your studies at the capital, and I am only sorry for myself, shut up in this small town. But there is no use grieving about fate. I am prepared to take what it has in store for me. I miss you so much since your departure in autumn, and I try to appear happy and gay when there is company, but when I am alone, I cannot restrain my tears. I dreamed often of you and we were so happy together like old times, and then I woke up, clinging to the half-warm quilt with a sense of desolation. I feel that you are so far away from me.

A year has passed since you were gone. I am grateful beyond

words that in a gay city like Chang-an you have not forgotten your old sweetheart entirely. But I shall always be true to my promise. We were formally introduced by my mother, but under the circumstances I lost my self-control and completely surrendered myself to you. You know that after our first night together, I swore I would never love anyone but you, and we would be true to each other for life. That was our hope and our promise to each other. If you keep your promise, all is well, and I shall be the happiest woman in the world. But if you discard the old for the new and think of our love as a casual affair, I shall love you still, but shall go down to my grave with an eternal regret. It is all up to you and I have nothing further to say.

Take good care of yourself, please. I am sending you a jade ring, which I wore in my childhood, hoping it will serve as a souvenir of our love. Jade is a symbol of integrity, and the circle of the ring signifies continuity. I am also sending a strand of silk threads and a tear-stained bamboo tea roller. These are simple things but they carry the hope that your love will be as spotless as the jade and as continuous as the ring. The tears on the [spotted] bamboo and the skein of threads will be reminders of my love and my tangled feelings for you. My heart is near you, but my body is far away. If thinking would help, I would be hourly by your side. This letter carries with it my ardent longing and my desperate hope that we may meet again. Take good care of yourself, eat well, and don't worry about me.

« *Later, after years, Yuan Chen came back for a visit.
Miss Tsui was already married and refused to see him.*

22 ▣ Taiyu Predicting Her Own Death

From

THE RED CHAMBER DREAM

Tsao Shuehchin
c. 1717 - 1763

« *The following is the famous "Song of Taiyu Burying Flowers"*
in the great novel. The scene is often acted by Mei Lanfang.
From a premonition of her own end from tuberculosis, com-
pounded with a temporary misunderstanding with her lover Pao-
yu, Taiyu took a hoe and basket to gather and bury the fallen
flowers and, as was the custom, wrote a sacrificial song of prayer,
with reference to herself.

FLY, FLY, ye faded and broken dreams
    Of fragrance, for the spring is gone!
Behold the gossamer entwine the screens,
    And wandering catkins kiss the stone.

Here comes the maiden from out her chamber door,
    Whose secret no one shall share.
She gathers the trodden blossoms lingeringly,
    And says to them her votive prayer.

I smell the scent of elm seeds and the willow
    Where once did blush the peach and pear.
When next they bloom in their new-made spring dress,
    She may be gone — no one knows where.

Sweet are the swallows' nests, whose labors of love
    This spring these eaves and girders grace.
Next year they'll come and see the mistress's home —
    To find her gone — without a trace.

The frost and cutting wind in whirling cycle
    Hurtle through the seasons' round.
How but a while ago these flowers did smile
    Then quietly vanished without a sound.

With stifled sobs she picks the wilted blooms,
    And stands transfixed and dazed hourlong,
And sheds her scalding tears which shall be changed
    Into the cuckoo's heartbreak song.

But the cuckoo is silent in the twilight eve,
    And she returns to her lone home.
The flickering lamp casts shadows upon the wall,
    And night rain patters, bed unwarmed.

Oh, ask not why and wherefore she is grieved.
    For loving spring, her heart is torn
That it should have arrived without warning,
    And just as noiselessly is gone.

I heard last night a mournful wail and I knew
    It was the souls of parting flowers,
Harried and reluctant and all in a rush,
    Bidding their last farewell hours.

Oh, that I might take winged flight to heaven,
    With these beauties in my trust!
'Twere better I buried you undefiled,
    Than let them trample you to dust.

Now I take the shovel and bury your scented breath,
    A-wondering when my turn shall be.
Let me be silly and weep atop your grave,
    For next year who will bury me?

Oh, look upon these tender, fragile beauties,
    Of perfumed flesh and bone and hair.
The admirer shan't be there when her time is up,
    And the admired shall no longer care!

23 ▣ Forlorn

From

THE WASHED JADE COLLECTION (SUYU TZE)

Li Yi-an
1081 - after 1141

« *Li Yi-an was the greatest poetess of China. Once her husband asked one of his friends to pick out the best lines that he liked from a number of his poems, having, however, concealed in them some pieces by his wife. The friend picked out, to his dismay, only lines from her pen! The beauty of her words in expressing the ultimate forlornness in separation in this poem can only be suggested in the translation.*

> SO DIM, so dark,
> So dense, so dull,
> So damp, so dank,
> So dead!
> The weather, now warm, now cold,
> Makes it harder
> Than ever to forget!
> How can a few cups of thin wine
> Bring warmth against
> The chilly winds of sunset?
> I recognize the geese flying overhead:
> My old friends,
> Bring not the old memories back!

Let fallen flowers lie where they fall.
        To what purpose
                And for whom should I decorate?
By the window shut,
        Guarding it alone,
                To see the sky has turned so black!
And the drizzle on the kola nut
        Keeps on droning:
                Pit-a-pat, pit-a-pat!
Is this the kind of mood and moment
        To be expressed
                By one word "sad?"

24 ▣ The Story of a Collection of Antiques

"POSTSCRIPT TO A CATALOGUE
ON A COLLECTION OF BRONZE
AND STONE INSCRIPTIONS"

Li Yi-an
1081 - after 1141

« *Li Yi-an and her husband fled down south during the fall of the
Northern Sung Dynasty to the Kin invaders in 1126. She survived her collector husband and had an unhappy second marriage. (See preceding selection.)*

I MARRIED INTO THE CHAO FAMILY in 1101. My father-
in-law [a former premier] was the minister of civil service, but the
family did not live extravagantly. Tehfu (my husband) was at that
time a student at the Imperial University. On the first and
fifteenth of every month, he could leave college. He would pawn
his clothing and with 500 cash* in his pocket go to Shiangkuo
Temple in search of old prints and come home with some fruit.
We would enjoy examining what he had bought while munching
fruit together. Two years later, when he got a post in the government, he started to make as complete as possible a collection of
rubbings or prints from bronze or stone inscriptions and other
ancient scripts. When a print was not available, he would have
a copy made and thus our collection of famous calligraphy and
antiques began. Once a man tried to sell us Hsu Shi's painting of

* One thousand cash equals one "dollar."

"Peony" for 200,000 cash, and Tehfu asked permission to take it home and keep it for a few days and consider. We found no means to buy it and reluctantly returned it to the owner. Tehfu and I were upset about it for days. When he served as magistrate at two posts, he spent his entire salary over the care and preservation of rare editions. Every time we obtained a rare book, we would examine it critically and see about its repair and rebinding, or if it was a painting or antique vessel, we would spend the evening pawing over it and looking for imperfections. Because of this, our collection was considered the best among all the collectors in regard to mounting and care and condition of the scripts. Whenever we found in bookstalls a volume which was complete and had no bad errors, we would purchase it for the purpose of comparison with other texts.

I have a power for memory, and sometimes after supper, sitting quietly in the Homecoming Hall, we would boil a pot of tea and, pointing to the piles of books on the shelves, make a guess as to which line of which page in which volume of a book contained a certain passage and see who was right, the one making the correct guess having the privilege of drinking his cup of tea first. When a guess was correct, we would lift up the cup and break out into a loud laughter, so much so that sometimes the tea was spilled on our dress and we were not able to drink at all. We were then content to live and grow old in this world! Therefore, we held our heads high, although we were living in poverty and sorrow. . . . In time our collection grew bigger and bigger and the books and art objects were piled up on tables and desks and beds, and we enjoyed them with our eyes and with our minds and planned and discussed the collection, tasting a happiness above those enjoying the horse races and music and dance.

In the year 1126, Tehfu was magistrate at Tsechuan when the northern invaders threatened the national capital [Kaifeng]. He had a presentiment that we were not going to be able to keep the collection intact during the ensuing chaos. The following year, we came down south on the occasion of the funeral for his mother.* We realized that a part of the collection had to be sacrificed. First we discarded the heavy, bulky volumes, the less important works of a painter, and vessels that bore no inscriptions. Next we threw out books of which standard editions existed, paintings of no extraordinary merit, and bronze that was too heavy for transportation. Even then, the collection filled fifteen cartloads and was carried in a fleet of boats when we came down the Huai River. We had planned on moving things kept at our old house at Chingchow the following year, but the house, we found later, was burned down with its dozen roomfuls of objects.

In 1129 [when the enemy came down to Nanking], we were living at Chihyang. Tehfu had to go to the temporary capital [then at Nanking]. As he stood on the bank to say good-by, I felt sick at heart and asked, "What shall I do in case of trouble?" He replied from the bank, "Do as the others. If necessary, abandon the food supplies first, then the clothing; the books next, the scrolls after that, and the bronze last of all. But never part with the Sung ware no matter what happens. And take good care of it!" Then he left on horseback.

In August, Tehfu died of an illness. At that time, the imperial court was fleeing to Kiangse. I asked two employees to bring more than 20,000 volumes of books and over 2,000 prints of inscriptions to Hungchow first. In winter of that year, the town fell and all was lost. What we had brought down the river in a fleet of boats was all gone. What was saved were a few small scrolls, the works of Li Po, Tu Fu, Han Yu, and Liu Tsungyuan, the *Shih Shuo*, the *Debate on Iron and Salt* [monopoly], several dozens of rubbings, over a

* Of course they fled for another more imperious reason, the fall of North China. But to ascribe it to the occasion of a mother's funeral is accepted as the correct way of saying it. Likewise, it is highly improbable that her husband, son of a minister, had to "pawn clothing" to buy odd curios, as said at the beginning, but this is also accepted as the poetic way of saying it. It has become the tradition for scholars to say that one's wife took off a gold brooch from her hair to sell it for money with which to buy wine to entertain a friend for the night.

dozen pieces of bronze, and several boxes of *Southern Tang History*, which happened to be with me in my personal luggage. As I could not have gone upriver, I came down south and moved from Taichow, to Wenchow, to Chuchow, to Yuehchow, finally to Hangchow [where the Southern Sung capital was finally established], and had the collection stored at Chengshien. In 1130, rebel troops came to the town and raided it, and all that passed into the ownership of old General Li. About 50 or 60 per cent of what had been saved was again gone. I had still six or seven baskets with me which I brought with me when I moved to Yuehcheng. One night, a burglar came and got away with five baskets. What I have now left are only a few odd volumes of several incomplete books.

I suddenly came upon this Catalogue (compiled by my husband) and the feeling was like that of meeting an old friend. I remember when we were living at Tunglai at our house called "Tsingchihtang," Tehfu was working every day on the volumes, giving each ten volumes a protecting cloth case with silk fastenings. Usually, he checked over two volumes per day and wrote a postscript note on one volume. Among the 2,000 volumes [of prints from stone and bronze], only 502 now bear his signature and notes. The ink is as fresh as the day he wrote them, but the tree over his grave has shot up to a considerable height already. I realize that this is the common fate of things; they come and go, or change ownership or are destroyed. There is nothing surprising in it. I merely write this story down, that collectors may take warning from it.

The fourth year of Shaoshing (1134).

THE SEASONS

25 ▣ Spring Fever

From

THE LITTLE CRITIC (SECOND SERIES)

Lin Yutang

I HAD COME BACK from the trip to Anhwei to find spring in my garden. Her steps had lightly tripped over the lawn, her fingers had caressed the hedgerows, and her breath had touched the willow branches and the young peach trees. Therefore, although I had not seen her coming, I knew she was here. The rose bugs, of the same green as the stem on which they thrived, were again in evidence, earthworms again put in their appearance by throwing up little clusters of mud in the garden beds, and even those poplar branches that I had chopped up into small sections, of one or two feet long lying in a heap in the yard, performed a miracle by putting forth green and merry leaves. Now after three weeks, I could already see the shadows of leaves dancing on the ground on a sunny day, a sight that I had not seen for a long time.

What is happening to the men and animals is a different story. There is sadness all around. Perhaps it isn't sadness, but I have no other word for it. Spring makes you sad and spring makes you sleepy. It shouldn't, I know, and if I were a peasant boy, or if everyone in my household from master to cook had only to look after buffaloes, I am sure we would not feel sad about it. But living in the city in spring is different. Consciously nothing is happening. But the unconscious self, with the heritage of millions of years, tells us that we are deprived of something, missing something.

I think I have found the word now: it is called "spring fever." Everyone is having a spring fever, including Chubby, my dog. I had cured my spring fever by taking a trip to Anhwei and seeing those emerald pools near Yulingkuan. But I had boasted of my trip before my cook and he happened to be from Anhwei and it made him extremely sad. For he is washing dishes and cutting carrots and cleaning kitchen utensils in spring, and that makes him sad. My boy, a tall husky farmer from Kiangpei, is polishing windows and mopping the floor and sticking letters in the letter box and pouring out tea the whole day for me, and that makes *him* sad. Then we have the cook's wife in our household as washwoman — by the way, I like her extremely, because she is fairly good-looking and has all the virtues of a good Chinese girl; she keeps her mouth shut and works the whole day, moving about on her little half-emancipated feet, ironing and ironing and ironing and not saying a word, and she does not giggle but laughs in a natural, quiet way when she laughs, and talks in a low voice when she talks. Perhaps she alone is not feeling sad, for she is grateful that we have spring in the garden already, and there is so much green and so many leaves and so many trees and such good breeze. . . . But her husband, the cook, a handsome dandy, is growing impatient of his work and giving us worse food than usual. He is listless most of the time, and makes his wife wash all the dishes in order that he may go out early. Then Ah Ching, the "boy" — he is really a tall man — came one day to me and said that he wanted leave for an afternoon. A leave from Ah Ching! I was completely surprised. I had told him to take a day off every month, but he had never done so. And now he wants a half-day's leave to "arrange an important matter with a friend from his native district." So *he*, too, has caught the spring fever. . . .

While Ah Ching was taking leave from my home, somebody else was taking leave from office to visit my garden. It was the messenger boy from the K—— Book Company. He had not appeared for a long time, for a grown-up man had been delivering the manuscripts and proofs in the last month or so. Now the boy must take his place and deliver the proofs, or perhaps a single letter, or a copy of a magazine, or even to convey me a good wish. That boy — I know he is living down in the eastern district, where you can see only walls and walls and back doors and refuse cans and cement floors, with not a green leaf around. Yes, green leaves could grow from the crevices of rocks, but could *not* grow from the cracks of cement floors. . . .

There is sadness, too, among the animals. Chubby has been a monk, and so long as spring isn't here, he is a contented dog. I always thought my garden big enough for him to play about, so I never let him out. . . . But now the garden isn't big enough for him, not by a long shot, in spite of all the bones and the delicious leftovers. Of course, it isn't that. I understand him. He wants *her*, no matter blonde or brunette, pretty or ugly, so long as she is a she. But what could I do? Chubby is very sad.

Then a tragedy happened to our little household of pigeons. There is really only a couple. There were six or seven of them when I took over the house, but all left and only this sweet couple remained. They had tried to raise a family in the loft of my garage, but always had no luck. Two or three times, the young was hatched and then it would learn to fly before it could walk and would fall dead. I didn't like that look in the parents' eye, twinkling and twinkling, and they standing silently on the opposite roof to contemplate the funeral. This last time, it looked as if they were going to be successful, for the young one was growing bigger every day, and had even come out to the loft window and gazed at the outside world and could already flap its wings.

But one day, our whole household was thrown into a flurry by the announcement by the rickshaw boy that the young pigeon was dead. How had he died? The rickshaw boy had seen him just roll on the ground and die. It called for a Sherlock Holmes brain like mine.

Mysteriously, I felt over the body of the dead young pigeon.

The pouch under the neck, which used to be full of food, was evidently empty. Two eggs were lying in the nest. The mother pigeon had been hatching again.

"Have you seen the father pigeon lately?" I opened the query.

"Not for a few days already," said the rickshaw boy.

"When did you see him last?"

"Last Wednesday."

"Hm — hm!" I said.

"Have you seen the mother about?" I asked again.

"She didn't leave the nest much."

"Hm — hm!" I said.

It was evident there had been desertion. The spring fever had done it. It was death from starvation beyond the shadow of a doubt. The mother pigeon could not leave the nest, and she could not find food for the young one.

"Like all husbands," I muttered.

Now with her husband deserting her, and her young one dead, the mother pigeon would not even sit on the eggs. The family has been broken up. Sitting for a while at the opposite roof corner, and taking a last look at her former happy home (where her two eggs still lay), she flew away — I don't know where. Perhaps she will never trust a male pigeon again.

26 〇 Summer Heat

From

ANALECTS FORTNIGHTLY

(Miss) Yao Ying
(contemporary)

« *Miss Yao Ying is a contemporary writer whose regular contributions, "Nanking Correspondence," in the Chinese humor magazine* Analects Fortnightly *were greatly admired for their perfection of style and humor.*

WHEN SUMMER ARRIVED, the first important question was: Where to go? My friends have often discussed this question with me. Some are for Mokanshan, because it is so near; some are for Tsingtao, because the beach there is so pleasant, and some are for Kuling — the great and beautiful Kuling, with its cool mountain air, its gorges and mountain pools, besides being within easy reach. When my friends had finished with their opinions, they asked me what I thought. I said: "I have two conditions for a summer resort: first, it must cost me no trouble to get there, and secondly, it must be a *real* resort, a retreat in the mountains where you don't see your friends' faces all over again, don't hear about government officials' names, and don't read newspapers. It must be a real 'retreat.' Otherwise, I would prefer to stew in the heat of Nanking." I wasn't quite explicit, but they understood me.

It is the end of July now, and I am still in Nanking, and I shall still be in Nanking when this article appears. My friends often came to me for explanations. "I have no explanations," I said.

One who was a fine scholar reinforced his quest for reasons by a quotation from Mencius: "Mencius said," he said, " 'If I have no official position, then I have no duty to talk politics; then am I not indeed a free man to go wherever I like?' Now, you are free, what's the idea of your hanging around here and making a fool of yourself?" "I'm not making a fool of myself," I said. "Besides, you left out one little clause from the quotation. Mencius really said, 'Since I have no official position and no duty to talk politics, *and besides, have plenty of dollars,** therefore I am a free man to go wherever I like.' "

As a matter of fact, Mencius was all wrong. If I had an official position and had the duty to talk politics, taking a summer vacation would be easy enough. For instance, if I were in charge of party or military affairs, I could say I had received an urgent telegram from Chiang Kaishek, asking for my presence at Kuling. Or if I were in the Ministry of the Interior or of Railways, I could go to Tsingtao to inspect the municipal government or investigate the railway traffic there, or even go to Mokanshan to urge General Huang Fu to come out of his retirement, or go to the Western Hills in Peiping to investigate the famine conditions in the northwest. . . . I could not only enjoy any summer retreat I wanted but also have all my traveling expenses paid for. That would indeed be a beautiful idea. And now people are criticizing me for making a fool of myself by staying at Nanking. So there you are. Is Mencius right? Or am I right?

Now my remaining at Nanking has not made the slightest difference to its temperature. The thermometer has not gone down because I chose to stay. In fact, it is ominously going up. According to the report of the Observatory, it is the hottest summer in the last sixty years. Strange to say, when it gets too hot, my head swirls with new ideas and my imagination becomes extremely active. When the iceman brought in the ice, I sat there looking at it, and it seemed to me that its top was like snow-capped peaks

* It is known to Chinese readers that Mencius never said this about dollars.

and its bottom like a green meadow, and the little rivulets which trickled down its sides were in fact mountain gorges and waterfalls. I was losing myself in this scenery and shivering with cold, when a whiff of hot, suffocating air almost smothered me. The hot wind reminded me of the tropics and the people living there. They haven't committed suicide because of the heat, so why should I? Besides, they must regard me living in the temperate zone very much as I regard those people in Kuling. And so I felt quite contented, and from that contentment, there was peace in my heart.

I was so exulted with my own thoughts when another whiff of hot winds almost stifled me. Then a visitor called, and his rickshaw coolie was asking for extra pay on account of the heat. I looked at him, drenched through with perspiration and as wet as a drowned cat, and I was comparing my own condition with his and feeling grateful to the creator of the universe who, according to good, honest Christian logic, loved me more than the rickshaw coolie, when for the third time I was almost choked by a breath of suffocating air from the streets.

Then I became very angry, with what I don't know, but intensely angry. I consulted the calendar, and found it was the Day of Great Heat. I realized where I was, for although the Entrance of Autumn was not far off, still there were yet twenty-four days of "Autumn Tiger" [Indian summer] to come. It would be such a long, long time before the Mid-autumn Festival. I wished the Mid-autumn were right here, and the Double Ninth, so that I could roam about under the moonlit sky like Su Tungpo, or climb up the hills and have my hat blown off by high September winds like Meng Chia. I was so annoyed with these thoughts that I sealed up the calendar and told my servants never to show it to my face. Then I looked at the papers and saw a comparative table of the temperatures in the last fortnight, and I learned that from July 1 to July 5, it was already over 90 degrees, and after the fifth, it went up to the hundred naughts, and I was so enraged with the temperature that I burned up the morning paper in revenge, and threw the thermometer into the icebox. After a while, I went to examine it in the icebox, and found the temperature had gone down to 60, and at night it even reached zero, and I shouted with joy. I cried, "How nice! How nice!" in the fashion of Chin Shengtan (the impressionist critic of *The Western Chamber*).

Then I looked around my house, and had nothing but utter contempt for my landlord and for the imbecile who called himself an architect. My bedroom was bathed in sunshine from morn till night, and my parlor, which faces west, had also "plenty of sunshine." Sunshine indeed! If I could only wring that idiot's neck. From four till eight in the afternoon, it is literally like an oven. Even after eight, the temperature within these two rooms is considerably higher than that outside. If this isn't a "hotbed of revolution," I don't know what is. The only good thing is that my friends who know the dangers of falling into the "hotbed" which is my parlor, are now avoiding visits at my home. . . . The more I thought of these things, the more furious I became, until my mother was afraid I was going to go faint with the heat. "You just keep your mind quiet," said she. "When one's mind is quiet, then one feels cool."

Of course, this is age-old Chinese wisdom. But how could I keep my mind quiet? Therefore I thought of a better way. Rather than keep my mind quiet, I would prefer to work hard. I would keep on as usual — I would still get up and have my meals and go to sleep, plant my vegetables, water my flowers, and feed my cat and dog; I would still go out shopping, and call on friends and visit places and read the papers, and contribute articles to the *Analects Fortnightly* and the *Jenchienshih* — I would still do everything I used to do. I would work as usual and forget it. Of course, the more furiously I worked, the more I perspired and panted for breath, but I didn't care. The worst of it would be to take a few more baths a day. Taking a bath in summer is really only a kind of sport, and a very pleasant sport at that.

Since I have revolted against the weather and begun my New Life, I have felt so much better and more at ease. I am at peace with the world now. . . .

27 ▣ Harvest Moon on West Lake

From

DREAM MEMORIES OF WEST LAKE

Chang Tai
1597 - 1689

« *The author was born in a family of high officials, enjoying fabulous luxury. After the Ming Dynasty fell, he lived in reduced circumstances but persisted in his life as author with proud independence. Some of his most charming writings are his recollections of the West Lake of Hangchow. He always writes in a highly individualistic, pithy style.*

THERE IS NOTHING TO SEE during the harvest moon on West Lake [Hangchow]. All you can see are people who come out to see the moon. Briefly, there are five categories of these holidaymakers. First, there are those who come out in the name of looking at the harvest moon, but never even take a look at it: the people who, expensively dressed, sit down at gorgeous dinners with music in brightly illuminated boats or villas, in a confusion of light and noise. Secondly, those who do sit in the moonlight, but never look at it: ladies, daughters of high families, in boats and towers, also handsome boys [homosexuals] who sit in open spaces and giggle and chatter and look at other people. Thirdly, boat parties of famous courtesans and monks with time on their hands who enjoy a little sip and indulge in song and flute and string instruments. They are in the moonlight, too, and indeed look at the moon, but want people to see them looking at the moon. Fourthly, there are the young men, who neither ride, nor go into boats, but after a drink and a good dinner, rush about in their rowdy dress and seek the crowd at Chaoching and Tuanchiao where it is thickest, shouting, singing songs of no known melody, and pretending to be drunk. They look at the moon, look at the people looking at the moon, and also look at those not looking at the moon, but actually see nothing. Lastly, there are those who hire a small boat, provided with a clay stove and a clean table and choice porcelain cups and pots, and who get into the boat with a few friends and their sweethearts; they hide under a tree or row out into the Inner Lake in order to escape from the crowd, and look at the moon without letting people see that they are looking at the moon and even without consciously looking at it.

The local Hangchow people come out on the lake, if they do at all, between eleven in the morning and eight in the evening, as if they had a morbid fear of the moon. But on this night, they all come out in groups, in the hope of getting good tips. The sedan chair carriers line up on the bank. The moment they get into a boat, they tell the boatman to hurry and row across to the Tuanchiao area, and get lost in the crowd. Therefore in that area before the second watch [ten o'clock], the place is filled with noise and music bands in a weird, boiling confusion, like a roaring sea or a landslide, or a nightmare, or like Bedlam let loose, with all the people in it rendered deaf for the moment. Large and small boats are tied up along the bank, and one can see nothing except boats creaking against boats, punting poles knocking punting poles, shoulders rubbing shoulders, and faces looking at faces. Soon the feasting is over, the officials leave, the yamen runners shout to clear the way, the sedan chair carriers scream for fare, the boatmen give warning that the city gates will soon be closed. A grand procession of torches and lanterns, with swarms of retainers, passes on. Those on land also hurry to get into the city before the closing of the gate, and very soon almost the entire crowd is gone.

Only then do we move the boat to Tuanchiao. The rocks have become cool by this time, and we spread a mat on the ground and invite ourselves to a great drink. At this time, the moon looks like a newly polished mirror, the hills appear draped in a new dress, and the face of the lake is like a lady after a fresh make-up. Those who have been hiding themselves under a tree and enjoying a quiet sip come out now also. We exchange names and invite them to join us. There we have charming friends and famous courtesans; cups and chopsticks are in place, and songs and music begin, in the chilly dream world of moonlight. The party breaks up at dawn, and we get into the boat again and move it into the miles of lotus-covered surface, where we catch a nap in an air filled with its fragrance, and have a perfect sleep.

28 ▣ How I Celebrated New Year's Eve

From

THE LITTLE CRITIC (SECOND SERIES)

Lin Yutang

THE OLD CHINESE NEW YEAR, of the lunar calendar, was the greatest festival in the year for the Chinese people, compared with which every other festival seemed lacking in completeness of the holiday spirit. For five days the entire nation dressed in its best clothes, shut up shop, loafed, gambled, beat gongs, let off firecrakers, paid calls, and attended theatrical performances. It was the great day of good luck, when everybody looked forward to a better and more prosperous new year, when everybody had the pleasure of adding one year to his age and was ready with an auspicious luck-bringing word for his neighbors.

The humblest maid had the right not to be scolded on New Year's Day, and strangest of all, even the hard-working women of China loafed and cracked melon seeds and refused to wash or cook a regular meal or even handle the kitchen knife. The justification for this idleness was that to chop meat on New Year's Day was to chop off good luck, and to pour water down the sink was to pour away good luck, and to wash anything was to wash away good luck. Red scrolls were pasted on every door containing the words: Luck, Happiness, Peace, Prosperity, Spring. For it was the festival of the return of spring, of life and growth and prosperity.

And all around, in the home courtyards and in the streets, there was the sound of firecrackers, and the smell of sulfur was in the air. Fathers lost their dignity, grandfathers were more amiable than ever, and children blew whistles and wore masks and played with clay dolls. Country women, dressed in their best, would go three or four miles to a neighboring village to watch a theatrical show, and village dandies indulged in what flirtations they dared. It was the day of emancipation for women, emancipation from the drudgery of cooking and washing, and if the men were hungry, they could fry *nienkao* [hard New Year pudding], or make a bowl of noodles with prepared sauce, or go to the kitchen and steal cold cuts of chicken.

The National Government of China has officially abolished the lunar Yew Year, but the lunar New Year is still with us, and refuses to be abolished.

I am ultramodern. No one can accuse me of being conservative. I am not only for the Gregorian calendar, but am even for the thirteen-month calendar, in which all months have exactly four weeks or twenty-eight days. In other words, I am very scientific in my viewpoint and very logical in my reasoning. It was this scientific pride which was badly wounded when I found my celebration of the official New Year a great failure, as anyone who pretended to celebrate it with any real feeling must have found out for himself.

I didn't want the Old New Year. But the Old New Year came. It came on February 4.

My big Scientific Mind told me not to keep the Old New Year, and I promised him I wouldn't. "I'm not going to let you down," I said, with more good will than self-confidence. For I heard rumblings of the Old New Year's coming as far back as the beginning of January, when one morning I was given for breakfast a bowl of *lapacho*, or congee with lotus seeds and dragon-eyes, which sharply reminded me it was the eighth day of the twelfth moon. A week after that, my servant came to borrow his extra month's pay, which was his due on the New Year's Eve. He got an afternoon's leave and showed me the package of new blue cloth which he was going to send to his wife. On February 1 and

February 2, I had to give tips to the postman, the milkman, the expressman, the errand boys of book companies, etc. I felt all along what was coming.

February 3 came. Still I said to myself, "I'm not going to keep the Old New Year." That morning, my wife told me to change my underwear. I said, "What for?"

"Chouma is going to wash your underwear today. She is not going to wash tomorrow, nor the day after tomorrow, nor the day after the day after tomorrow." Being human, I could not refuse.

That was the beginning of my downfall. After breakfast, my family was going to the bank, for there was a mild sort of bank panic, which came in spite of the fact that by ministerial orders the Old New Year didn't exist. "Y. T.," my wife said, "we are going to hire a car. You might come along and have a haircut." I didn't care for the haircut, but the car was a great temptation. I never liked monkeying about a bank, but I liked a car. I thought I could profitably go to the City Gods' Temple and see what I could get for the children. I knew there must be lanterns at this season, and I did want my youngest child to see what a rotating lantern was like.

I should not have gone to the City Gods' Temple in the first place. Once there at this time of the year, you know what would happen. I found on my way home that I had not only rotating lanterns and rabbit lanterns and several packages of Chinese toys with me, but some twigs of plum blossoms, besides. After coming home I found that someone from my native place had presented me with a pot of narcissus, the narcissus which made my native place nationally famous, and which used to bloom so beautifully and gave out such subtle fragrance on New Year's Day in my childhood. I could not shut my eyes without the entire picture of my childhood coming back to me. Whenever I smelled the narcissus, my thoughts went back to the red scrolls, the New Year's Eve feast, the firecrackers, the red candles, and the Fukien oranges and the early morning calls and that black satin gown which I was allowed to wear once every year.

At lunch, the smell of the narcissus made me think of one kind of Fukien *nienkao,* rice pudding made with turnips, which I used to have for the New Year in my childhood.

"This year, no one has sent us any turnip pudding," I said sadly.

"It's because no one came from Amoy. Otherwise, they would have sent it," said my wife.

"I remember once I bought exactly the same kind of pudding in a Cantonese shop on Wuchang Road. I think I can still find it."

"No, you can't," challenged my wife.

"Of course I can," I took up the challenge.

By three o'clock in the afternoon I was already in a bus on my way home from North Szechuen Road with a big basket of *nienkao* weighing two pounds and a half.

At five, we ate the fried *nienkao,* and with the room filled with the subtle fragrance of narcissus, I felt terribly like a sinner. "I'm not going to celebrate New Year's Eve," I said resolutely; "I'm going to see the movies tonight."

"How can you?" asked my wife. "We have invited Mr. Ts—— to dinner this evening." It all looked pretty bad.

At half past five, my youngest child, Meimei, appeared in her new red dress.

"Who put on the new dress for her?" I rebuked, visibly shaken, but still gallant.

"Huangma did," was the reply.

By six o'clock, I found red candles burning brightly on the mantelpiece, their lapping flames casting a satirical glow of triumph at my Scientific Consciousness. My Scientific Consciousness was, by the way, already very vague and low and unreal.

"Who lighted the candles?" again I challenged.

"Chouma did," was the reply.

"Who bought the candles?" I demanded.

"Why, you bought them yourself this morning."

"Oh, did I?" It cannot have been my Scientific Consciousness that did it. It must have been the Other Consciousness.

I thought I must have looked a little ridiculous, the ridiculousness coming less from the recollection of what I did in the morning than from the conflict of my head and my heart at that moment. I was soon startled out of this mental conflict by the *boom-bah!* of firecrackers in my neighborhood. One by one, those sounds sunk into my deep consciousness. They have a way of shaking the Chinese heart that no European knows. That challenge of my neighbor on the east was soon taken up by my neighbor on the west, until it grew into a regular fusillade.

I was not going to be beaten by them. Pulling out a dollar bill, I said to my boy:

"Ah Ching, take this and buy me some heaven-and-earth firecrackers and some whip firecrackers, as loud as possible and as big as possible. Remember, the bigger and the louder the better."

So amidst the *boom-bah* of firecrackers, I sat down to the New Year's Eve dinner. And I felt very happy in spite of myself.

山水

NATURE

29 回 An Invitation from a Mountain Resident

LETTER TO PEI TI, B.A.

Wang Wei
A.D. 699 - 759

« A famous poet-painter, who started the school of "scholar's
painting," consisting of ink splashes and rapid lines, later made
famous by Su Tungpo.

Dear Pei:

In this month of December, the weather has been very mild,
and the old mountain is worth a visit. I knew you were immersed
in your studies, and did not want to bother you. I may tell you
what you missed: I often went into the mountains and stopped at
Kanpei Temple where after a meal with the monk, I started off.
I crossed the Pa [river] and saw the outer city wall sleep under the
moonlight. At night, I went up the Huatsekang [hill]. The golden
ripples of the Wang chased and floated with the moon, and on
the distant mountainsides, some lights flickered beyond the forests.
The sounds of dogs barking from some alley and of farmers
pounding rice were punctuated with notes from the temple bells.
By that time, the servants accompanying me had fallen asleep
and I sat alone, thinking of the days when we wandered together
on the mountain paths or sat on the bank of a clear stream and
wrote verse. Now I will wait till spring is here, when the green
things will have returned and blue hills lie in the distance, minnows
chase in the shallow waters and herons flap their wings. You will

find pheasants flying in the morning among the wheat fields and dew on the green banks. This will be not so far away. Are you coming? I would not write of these things and invite you to come unless I knew you would appreciate them. But there is a deep, resuscitating joy in it. Don't forget. I am sending this note by a woodcutter.

From a resident in the mountains,
Wang Wei

30 ▣ The Stone Bell Mountain

From

COMPLETE WORKS OF SU TUNGPO

Su Tungpo
1036 - 1101

« *Su Tungpo is probably the most loved character in Chinese literature. (See notes on Su Tungpo, selections 37, 59, and 64.)*

THE 'CLASSIC OF WATERS' SAYS, "At the mouth of Kuli stands the Stone Bell Mountain." Its commentator Li Taoyuan (died A.D. 527) states that "there is a deep water at its foot, where the winds and waves striking the rocks make a sound like that of great bells." People often discredit this statement, for bells and musical stones submerged in waves do not make such a sound, not to speak of rocks. Not until the Tang Period did Li Po [not the poet] visit the place, where he found two rocks from the water. When struck with a wooden handle, they made a clanging sound, dying away gradually like bells, one in a clearer and the other in a muffled tone. He thought he had thus verified the origin of the name. But I had my doubts, for there are certainly rocks which make a ringing sound when struck, but these were said to make sounds like bells. In June, 1084, I was making a voyage from Tsi-an to Linju, and my eldest son, Mai, was going to Tehshing in Kiangse. I sent him off to Hukou,* and thus we had an opportunity to visit it and see the stone bells. A monk

* Where the Poyang Lake empties into the Yangtse River. At this place, there are now two hills by this name.

sent a boy to show us. The boy took an ax and struck at some of the rocks near by at random, but there was nothing unusual about the dull thuds. I gave it up for hearsay and laughed.

That night, however, there was a bright moon, and I took a boat with Mai to the foot of the mountain. The river here was flanked by a high cliff almost a thousand feet high.* As seen in the moonlight, the rocks looked very much like some weird monsters or dark spirits in frightening postures. The hawks nesting above flew up with raucous cries upon hearing our approach. There was another noise like an old man coughing and chortling somewhere in the air. We were told that this came from a species of cranes [daws?]. I was quite moved and was thinking of turning back when a great noise came over the waters, booming and whining like drums and bells, which quite frightened the boatman. Upon close examination, I found that at the foot of the cliff were a number of stone caves of unknown depth. When the waves hit the caves, it made that roaring, surging noise. On turning back past Hanshan, at the point where the lake waters joined the big river, there was a huge rock in the middle of the stream, big enough to hold a hundred people. This huge boulder was full of holes and hollows, and the winds and waters sucking through them swish-swashed and made a booming noise, which joined with the clanging from the water caves to make a symphony.

I said to my son, "Mai, you see. That clanging from the caves will help you to understand the mention in history books of the sound of the bells of the Emperor Ching of Chou Dynasty, and the boom will help you to appreciate the description of the orchestra bells of Wei Shientse.† Evidently, what the ancient books tell us is true. One is often inclined to doubt ancient records until one personally sees these things. Li Taoyuan must have seen what we have seen, but he was not very explicit. The

* Actually about 500–600 feet.
† Su Tungpo could repeat phrases and whole passages from history books.

scholars usually would not take the trouble to take a boat to the foot of the cliff, so they could not have known. The boatmen know about it, of course, but they do not record it in books. Li Po verified it only superficially by knocking at a couple of rocks on land, and he never really found out where the sounds came from."

I write this down, to show that Li Taoyuan did not say enough and Li Po did not know enough.

« *The knowledge that these sounds were made by water striking stalactites will of course detract from the mystery and excitement of the piece. That the caves were full of stalactites is plain from the following comment from Lo Nien-an of the Ming Dynasty. And this, to my knowledge, is the only description of stalactites and stalagmites in Chinese literature.*

Comment by Lo Nien-an: In the spring of 1606, I passed Hukou. At the caves, both the formations from above and those from below were exposed, and they all looked like bells. The bells from above were especially curious. At this time, the water had receded and the whole base of the cliff was exposed. I went up and when I looked at the inside, it was like a battle array of spears and spearlike formations. Farther in, I saw what looked like hundreds of hanging curtains and screens. The interior was like a Buddhist tale of an undersea palace with its treasure of pearls, corals, and shells, shimmering in golden colors. Some hung down like drapery, some came up from the sides like bamboo shoots, and others had been smashed, looking like broken lotus roots, or like round lotus pods. In all my travels, I have never seen anything quite like it. . . . Tungpo came to the border on a boat, and did not see the whole caves exposed. That is why his description was not complete.

31 ▣ The Peach Colony

Tao Yuanming
A.D. 372 - 427

» *This famous piece by one of the greatest poets (see selection 18)
describes a colony of people separated from the outside world
for centuries, and embodies an ideal of people living in classical
simplicity in contrast to the chaos of his days. Today in Chinese, the phrase "peach colony" has come to mean "utopia."*

DURING THE REIGN OF TAIYUAN* OF CHIN, there was a
fisherman of Wuling. One day he was walking along a bank. After
having gone a certain distance, he suddenly came upon a peach
grove which extended along the bank for about a hundred yards.
He noticed with surprise that the grove had a magic effect, so
singularly free from the usual mingling of brushwood, while the
ground was covered with its rose petals. He went further to explore, and when he came to the end of the grove, he saw a spring
which came from a cave in the hill. Having noticed that there
seemed to be a weak light in the cave, he tied up his boat and
decided to go in and explore.

At first the opening was very narrow, barely wide enough for
one person to go in. After a dozen steps, it opened into a flood of
light. He saw before his eyes a wide, level valley, with houses and
fields and farms. There were bamboos and mulberries; farmers
were working and dogs and chickens were running about. The
dresses of the men and women were like those of the outside world,
and the old men and children appeared very happy and contented.

* A.D. 376–396, in the author's own lifetime.

174

They were greatly astonished to see the fisherman and asked him where he had come from. The fisherman told them and was invited to their homes, where wine was served and chicken was killed for dinner to entertain him. The villagers hearing of his coming all came to see him and to talk. They said that their ancestors had come here as refugees to escape from the tyranny of Tsin Shih-huang [builder of Great Wall] some six hundred years ago, and they had never left it. They were thus completely cut off from the world, and asked what was the ruling dynasty now. They had not even heard of the Han Dynasty (two centuries before to two centuries after Christ), not to speak of the Wei (third century A.D.) and the Chin (third and fourth centuries). The fisherman told them, which they heard with great amazement. Many of the other villagers then began to invite him to their homes by turn and feed him with dinner and wine.

After a few days, he took leave of them and left. The villagers begged him not to tell the people outside about their colony. The man found his boat and came back, making a mental note of the direction of the route he had followed. He went to the magistrate's office and told the magistrate about it. The latter sent someone to go with him and find the place, but they got lost and could never find it again. Liu Tsechi of Nanyang was a great idealist. He heard of this story, and planned to go and find it, but was taken ill and died before he could fulfill his wish. Since then, no one has gone in search of this place.

Comment by Yuan Chunglang (c. 1600): There has been a great deal of speculation about this piece which was written quite late [in the fourth century]. Many think there is such a wonderful colony. But how many really know for sure that it existed, and how many appreciate its meaning? Some hold the opinion that it was a temporary hallucination created by a fairy spirit, and some believe that there is no reason to doubt that such a colony which fled from the terrible times of the Emperor of Tsin is entirely possible. I regard such contentions as futile, for whether or not it was a hallucination or it really existed, the point is that the writer never saw the place and the events which he described, but thought it would be beautiful to have such a colony. It just flowed out of his mind as he began to write. We can see that he took the fisherman as a symbol of a man of simple tastes, and how he described his easy and carefree attitude as he went on his way. After his entrance to the valley, it was the author's intention to describe it as a scene of pastoral peace and beauty, such as may well be in our own world. That is why he says, "just like those of the outside world." Furthermore, he spoke of the escape from the turmoil of the Tsin regime, to emphasize his ideal of the ancient pre-Tsin times, the "Three Dynasties" of Confucius [stretching back to 2,200 B.C.]. Indeed the author speaks of himself elsewhere as "a man of the period before Fushi," before human civilization began. . . . The mention of Liu Tsechi shows his conception of such a man of high ideals to be alone worthy of revisiting it, and that is why he says that "since then, no one has gone in search of the place." For if there was really such a colony, the fisherman could not have missed it on the second journey, or other fishermen could not have failed to find it. It is clear therefore that the author merely intends to make the fisherman stand for a protest against the world's turmoil and for an ideal of peace and simple living. We feel that here speaks a great human spirit, laying bare his heart to us. One can look at it either way, as a protest against the increasing chaos and complications of the modern world, or as embodying a great ideal taking shape in the fisherman he had borrowed for the purpose. Interesting as the account may be in itself, the real meaning lies elsewhere.

32 ▣ The River of Folly

Preface to

FOLLY RIVER POEMS

Liu Tsungyuan
A.D. 773 - 819

« *Liu Tsungyuan, like most great writers of China, including such persons as Su Tungpo and Han Yu, lived a period of demotion in exile. It was the regular thing in past history for officials who had crossed the will of those in power or criticized the emperor's policy to be punished by being sent to some low post in remote districts. Liu Tsungyuan was sent to Kweilin and Han Yu to modern Swatow, as the cities are now called. Liu wrote this when in exile.*

THERE IS A RIVER which runs north of the Kuan and flows into the Siao. This is locally called the "Ran River," because, according to some, a Ran clan used to live here and, according to others, because there is a dyeing industry [*ran*] along the river. I was remanded to this district in the Kuan River district because of my folly, and have come to love this place. It is especially beautiful a few miles up, and I have chosen my home here. Since the written name of the river is yet undecided and the local people are in favor of changing it, I have changed its name to "River of Folly," following the precedent of the Folly Hill in ancient times, which took its name from the "Man of Folly." I bought a small hill above it and named it the "Folly Mount." Sixty paces northeast of the Folly Mount are springs, which I bought and christened "Folly Springs." The Folly Springs consist of six, all coming from the high grounds in different rivulets, which are called the "Folly Rivulets." I then had these springs dammed and surrounded with rocks and made into a pond, which is named the "Folly Pond." East of the Folly Pond stands the Folly Hall, and on the south stands the Folly Pavilion. In the center of the pond, I had a little isle made, called the "Folly Isle." The place is studded with choice, rare plants and special, selected rocks, and all have received the humiliating name of "Folly" because of me.

Water has been proverbially associated with wisdom. Why then is it humiliated here with the name of "Folly"? First, the river current is very low and is useless for irrigation purposes, and secondly, it is too fast and full of rocks in mid-current for navigation by big boats. Thirdly, it is narrow and shallow, unworthy to be a hiding place for dragons who control the rains and the clouds. It is therefore of no benefit to the world, just like myself. I find therefore some excuse for calling it the "River of Folly." Now the *Analects* tells us that Ningwutse "acted like a stupid person in times of chaos" [to save his life]. There we see a man who was clever and chose to appear stupid. Yen Huei [Confucius' favorite disciple] is said to "appear stupid, sitting and thinking all day." There is the case of a man who was a deep thinker and appeared stupid. They were not really stupid. In my case, however,* I live under a wise government, but have been stubborn and self-opinionated. Therefore there is no one more stupid than myself. If so, then, I have the indisputable right to father the name of this river.

Despite its defects, this river has many good points. It is beautiful, and it sounds like music as it rushes down the hills, so that it makes a stupid person like myself find it enchanting, unwilling to tear myself away from it. And like the river, I cannot fit in with the times, but I can console myself with writing which mirrors and reflects all creation and its myriad changes and washes away all

---

* Liu was careful here to say the right thing. For if he "grumbled" or did not admit his fault, the writing might be brought up against him as evidence of his insurbordination.

impurities, even as the river does. Thus fitting words of folly to celebrate the River of Folly, I lose myself in the universe, becoming a part of the vast creation, go back to the age of the nebulae, and mingle with the Inaudible and the Impalpable, hidden in a primeval stillness, unknown to the world. I have written eight poems on the River of Folly and have them inscribed on the rocks.

33 ▣ The North Peak of Lushan

THE GRASS HUT

Po Chuyi
A.D. 772 - 846

« Of China's major poets, Tao Yuanming, Po Chuyi, and Su
Tungpo stand in a direct line of tradition. Those who like one
generally like the other two, for it cannot be helped. Po never
ran into any serious political troubles in his life. This piece describes his lodge at Kuling, Lushan, with which his name is associated, and also shows that by his time, around A.D. 800, the
three religions of Confucianism, Taoism, and Buddhism were
commonly accepted by one and the same person without the
least trouble. The priests could do nothing about it. (See also
selection 63 by the same author.)

THE BEAUTIES OF LUSHAN [the Lu Mountain] top all
mountains of the world. On its north stand the Shianglu Peak and
the Wei-ai Temple. The view between the peak and the temple
again tops that of all Lushan. In the fall of A.D. 816, Po Lotien
[Chuyi] of Taiyuan saw the place and fell in love with it. He felt
like a wayfarer seeing his own home and never wanted to leave it
again. He therefore had a mountain lodge built here next to
the temple, facing the North Peak.

In the following spring, the house was completed. There are
three rooms, separated by two pillars, and two separate rooms on
the sides with four windows. Its dimensions and plans are exactly
as he had wanted. The northern door is made wide so as to let in
the cool air in summer, and on the south the roof is receded to
receive the warm sun in winter. The woodwork is unpainted, and

the walls are not whitewashed. There are stone steps, paper windows,* bamboo screens, and coarse linen curtains. The central hall is provided with four wooden couches, two unpainted screens, one lacquered *chin* [string instrument], and a few volumes of Confucianist, Taoist, and Buddhist books.

Since Lotien came here and took charge as its owner, he spends mornings and evenings admiring the mountaintops and listening to the springs below, and enjoying the view of bamboos, trees and rocks, and clouds. Very soon, he began to feel himself again, whole and fine and relaxed and at peace. The first night, he felt remarkably well; on the second night, he felt his heart was at peace, and on the third night, he felt as if he had lost his own identity like a disincarnated spirit, without knowing why.† He asked himself what had happened and found the following explanation.

There is a level ground about a hundred feet wide in front of the house, with a raised terrace in the center occupying about half the area. South of the terrace is a pond twice its size. The pond is planted around with wild flowers and bamboos, and in it are white lotus and white fish. Farther south again, there is a rocky stream, banked by old pines and cypresses, about ten spans in circumference and several hundred feet high. Its top branches reach toward the clouds, and its low overhanging boughs brush the pond. The trunks are crowded in with underbrush and creepers, while their thick foliage, spreading like giant parasols, shut out sunlight entirely. In summer, the air is like that of September. The paths leading to the house are paved with white pebbles, and only five paces from the back of the house, there is a rockery formed with odd hollowed rocks, covered with rare plants and grass, shining with mossy green and dotted with some red berries whose name I do

---

* Paper windows were common things in Peking, being translucent, cheap, and warm in winter. The exact literal name of this lodge is "Tsaotang," or "Grass Hut," a name popular at the time, also used by the great poet Tu Fu for his residence in Chengtu (Szechuen).
† Here, as in the end of the preceding piece by Liu Tsungyuan, the phrases used are those from Chuangste. This is also very often the case with Su Tungpo. This shows the great literary influence of Chuangtse, the Taoist.

not know. The colors remain that way all through the seasons. Then there is a flying cataract which comes down it and tea plants grow under it, which makes it an ideal place to make tea for those who would enjoy the leisurely life. East of the house, there is a small fall which splashes water over the rocky steps into a stone gully below. It makes a gurgling sound at night and shines in the morning sun like a chain of silver. On its west, a bamboo pipe leads from the north, receiving its water from on top, and the water breaks into several columns of fine spray like beautiful beads coming down from the eaves and disappears into vapor in the wind. In the environs, there are the flowers of the Embroidered Valley in spring, the mountain brooks of Stone Gate in summer, the gushing Tiger Stream in autumn, and the snows of the peak in winter. The views change from sunshine to cloudy and rainy weather and from morning to night in a manner impossible to describe or enumerate. That is why I say that the view here tops all in Lushan. Alas! a man is often proud of a house or a sleeping place he owns. And I am here as owner of all this bounty which unites all that is best and brings one so close to nature. Is it any wonder then that I should feel whole and fine and relaxed and at peace here?

In ancient times, the monks Hueiyung, Hueiyuan, Tsungping, and Lei Tsetsung* and others, eighteen of them, came and made their homes here and never left it again in their life. I can understand why they did so, although separated from them by a thousand years.†

I have often thought how all my life, from my youth to this day, I have always made it a habit to beautify my house with rocks and ponds wherever I stayed, even though it was for only a short

---

* These were great scholar monks, of the White Lotus Society, with its headquarters at Lushan, led by the great Buddhist scholar Hueiyuan (A.D. 334–416), known as "Master Yuan."
† Clearly rhetorical here, since the writer knew well that the White Lotus Society was formed here only four centuries before him. See also the next paragraph where he speaks of what he carries in his right and left hands.

time. It is my weakness. I was sent down here as assistant to the magistrate. The magistrate has pampered me with his kindnesses, and the Lushan, with its offering of nature's bounty. Heaven has granted me the time and the earth has bestowed upon me this place for rest. What more can I ask? For the present, there are still official duties which prevent me from spending my entire time up here. Perhaps later, when my younger brothers and sisters shall all have been married and my period of service shall have been completed, I shall then have the freedom to stay where I like. I shall then lead my wife and children by the left hand and carry my books and a *chin* in my right and retire here, to fulfill my heart's desire. The clear spring and the white rocks shall be witnesses to these words.

I came to live in the new house on March 27. On the ninth of April, twenty-two friends, including Yuan Chishu of Honan, Chang Yunchung of Fanyang, Chang Shenchih of Nanyang, and the elder priests of Tunglin and Shilin Temples, gathered to celebrate the housewarming with tea and fruit offerings. This is the record of the origin of the Tsaotang, the rustic summerhouse.

» Let me add something to what I have said in the introductory note about the three major poets in a direct line of tradition. They have something in common, which is an attitude of life. They were all three emancipated spirits, but not rebellious, took adversity with a sense of humor, and enjoyed life intensely. They were flexible, accepted what came in their way, and had a great zest of living. They loved humanity as much as they loved nature and were sensitive to its beauties, and always lived close to the common people. Their romanticism was restrained by reason, without trying to escape from life's responsibilities. They were mature. They did not serve religion, but made religion serve them. In this sense, they were true emancipated spirits, and being such emancipated spirits, they had humility in their hearts. That is a state of mind which comes through in their poetry, and their easy style was the natural outflowing of this spirit. Such is the stature of a great spirit. It is curious that Tao

Yuanming wrote a comparatively small volume of poetry, yet no one later poet could quite equal him because no one else could catch that peculiar elevation of the soul. Li Po is usually regarded as unique, of the type we call a fairy descended from heaven, and therefore I have not mentioned him in this connection.

HUMAN ADJUSTMENTS

34 🔲 The Half-and-Half Song

Li Mi-an
16th century?

« *This is the soundest and most mature philosophy of living comprised in a single poem that I know, although I know, too, that it is one of the most exasperating to the hundred-percenters.*

BY FAR THE GREATER HALF have I seen through
This floating life — ah, there's the magic word —
This "half" — so rich in implications.
It bids us taste the joy of more than we
Can ever own. Halfway in life is man's
Best state, when slackened pace allows him ease.

A wide world lies halfway 'twixt heaven and earth;
To live halfway between the town and land,
Have farms halfway between the streams and hills;
Be half-a-scholar, and half-a-squire, and half
In business; half as gentry live,
And half related to the common folk;
And have a house that's half genteel, half plain,
Half elegantly furnished and half bare;
Dresses and gowns that are half old, half new,
And food half epicure's, half simple fare;
Have servants not too clever, nor too dull;
A wife who is not too ugly, nor too fair.

— So then, at heart, I feel I'm half a Buddha,
And almost half a Taoist fairy blest.

One half myself to Father Heaven I
Return; the other half to children leave —
Half thinking how for my posterity
To plan and provide, and yet minding how
To answer God when the body's laid at rest.

He is most wisely drunk who is half drunk;
And flowers in half-bloom look their prettiest;
As boats at half-sail sail the steadiest,
And horses held at half-slack reins trot best.

Who half too much has, adds anxiety,
But half too little, adds possession's zest.
Since life's of sweet and bitter compounded,
Who tastes but half is wise and cleverest.

35 ⎒ On Going Around

"THE CURVED CITY"

Anonymous

« The central idea of this essay is "going around" as against a "frontal attack," embodying the principle of nonresistance. The modern phrase expresses it well: "If you can't lick 'em, join 'em." It defends the curve against the straight line, being bent against being straight, the indirect method against the direct method, the hidden against the open, the recess against the exposed area, the secluded against the ostentatious, etc. All these ideas are expressed in the Chinese language by one and the same word, chu, which occurs in the essay sixty-three times, but has to be rendered differently as "going around," "round," "curve," "bent," "indirect," "hidden," etc. Some of the play on the word is lost in the translation, but the main idea is quite clear.

SOMEONE ASKED ME why I call it a "Curved City."

"Because it follows the bends of the ground, as you see," I answered.

"So you like the crooked instead of the straight. Why don't you make it straight?"

"That I cannot do," I said. "You know that straight means straight, but you do not know that being curved does not mean being crooked. Look at the universe and all its things and study its principles. The firmaments go around us, and the earth turns round. The four seasons follow one another in a cycle, and the seven constellations rotate in the skies. The important thing in a mountain is its undulating sweep, in water its meandering curves, in a dragon its spinning around, in a tiger its crouching gesture before the pounce, in a bird its circling the sky, in an old cypress its twists and bends. Therefore the Wuyi Mountain is famous for its 'nine bends,' and a balcony for its 'hexagonal corners.' The 'four recesses' of a pond control the outflow of water, and the 'one graceful curve' of the crescent moon adorns the skies. The spring becomes more beautiful in the Serpentine Park [Chukiang, famous park south of Tang capital, Chang-an], flowers seem all the more surprising on a curved path, and friends lined up to drink on the bends of a curving stream enjoy it the more. Objects have their hidden parts, the heart has its secret corners, affairs have their complicated turns, and men's words have their intricate meanings and motives. That is why we say of a good artist that he has mastered the 'secrets' of the trade, and speak of good moral teachings as reaching the 'inner depths' of man, and we speak of a wise settling of affairs as a good 'round' compromise, and of helping to overcome difficulties as a 'roundabout' achievement. And, of course, there are the 3,300 rules of the so-called 'chu etiquette.' So you see the meaning of being round and curved is comprehensive and all-embracing."

"Then you hate what is straight?"

"I did not say that. In all arts and industry, all human affairs and relations, the combination of the straight and the curved makes for the best results. In archery, the bow is bent, but the arrow is straight. In a boat, the mast must be straight, while the sails must bend. In fishing, the line is straight while the hook is curved, and in carpentry and masonry, you have to have both the straight guiding line and the T square, and the compasses. Sometimes it is better to give a sly hint than straight advice to a friend, and kings and rulers can be made to see your point by a covered, indirect analogy better than by straightforward counsel. There are times when an official must carry out the law rigidly even to the point of killing his own close relatives, and other times when the father covers up for [refuses to inform on] the son and vice versa.* Con-

* These are classical statements referring to historial cases.

fucius said, 'In times of peace, speak and act by stern principles, but in times of bad government, act by stern principles but speak very carefully.' Sometimes one must act straight, and sometimes one must not. By going around, one accomplishes what is a straight purpose, and by being firm but polite, one gets at the heart of the matter."

"If so, then why do you choose the curve?"

"Ah, indeed! I would like to lead the ruler by straightforward advice but the ruler would not follow, try to influence friends by frank criticism but the friends would not listen. I tried to discipline the family by rigid rules but the family would not take it, and I tried to live by stern principles and society thought me lacking in tact. So in such a world, a man does not hold his head high against the sky, nor does he tread firmly upon the earth. He bows and kowtows and sits gingerly on a seat corner. He circles round the bank until he finds a place where he can ford the stream. He doubles up in his sleep for rest, bends his body or his arms when carrying things, and crooks his legs when sitting on the ground. Looking up at the sun, he tilts his head. So then we do everything indirectly; we try to circumscribe an obstacle, go around a difficulty, and answer by evasion. If a post does not pay enough, we 'stoop' to accept it, and when we find we cannot satisfy everybody, we have a compromise, or 'roundabout,' solution. We 'yield' to violence, 'suffer' sickness and sorrow, 'go around' and avoid those who would hurt us, and 'endure' and 'give ground' in time of turmoil and chaos. If someone calls me a 'cow,' I will 'roundly' admit it, and if someone calls me a 'horse,' I will 'roundly' admit that, too. There are so many applications of the principle of going around. Things which are curved are so useful, like the plowshare, the hollowed chisel, and the wicker baskets made of bent vines. Well, then, I would like to be the plowshare, the hollowed chisel, and the wicker basket."

"You seem to have made out a good case for the curved," my friend said. "Great historians sometimes bent their heads and great generals sometimes bent their knees. The great poet Tao

Yuanming sometimes bent his waist to make a bow. Confucius himself enjoyed sleeping head on a crooked arm. Well, well, you have made a good point there."

« There are two ways of carving a roast, one by cutting it through with a chopper, and the better way by prying around the interstices of a joint.

All nature moves in curves. I do not think it is possible to find a single straight line in plants, animals, and minerals. The heavenly bodies are proverbially round, and certainly clouds are never square. Canals are straight, but not rivers. A bird's leg is constructed like a spring suspension. In this is contained the esthetic principle of calligraphy. A good calligraphist never makes a straight line, but tries to suggest a sinuous paw or a curving vine. "A horizontal line should contain three bends," said Wang Shichih, the "Prince of Calligraphists." That is why I abhor the cubist paintings: they are products of an engineer's draftboard, not of an artist. A cubist does not even begin to understand the esthetics of natural forms. Functional architecture is all right for factory buildings. Definitely, art has sold out to commerce.

In morals, the combination of strength and grace is even more important in the development of human character. I think a wife can get very tired of a husband who says gracefully "yes, my dear" all the time. All beauty and all character come from the combination of strength and grace. Someday I would like to write an essay on this as a general esthetic principle.

36 ▣ How To Relax

Chang Nai
c. 1600

« *The Chinese title for this essay ("Shichishuo") means "The Mechanism of Rest." As in English, the word "to rest" is closely associated with "to refresh," "to restore," and "to recuperate," and further, even with the idea of growth. The Chinese word shi has all these meanings and, in addition, designates the "breath." This rest is regarded as a silent, continuous process, making for growth and restoration.*

Since coming to the capital, I have occupied a room, where there are two couches. Yu Shuho and I often sit and talk together, or light an incense and read, and when we are tired, we lie down, and after a while get up and read again. We rather enjoy this kind of life. Sometimes, returning to our room, I used to feel the place was too uncomfortably small, hardly conducive to rest and relaxation. Then I realized with a smile that the physical location should have nothing to do with it. Mencius spoke of the continuous process of "growth and recuperation" [shi] in trees and in men "day and night," and we speak of the expelling of breath in respiration as shi. We also speak of the growth and prosperity of plants and the multiplication of their kind in animals as shengshi and tseshi. It is clear then that this "rest" is associated with life, and not with death or cessation of activities. A good analogy is that of banking a furnace, or covering up a brazier with hot ashes; the fire goes on, ready to burst into flame when we add fuel to it. On the other hand, to mistake "rest" as a cessation of activities would be more like putting out the light in an oil lamp. This is the vulgar idea of sleep. When Mencius spoke of the "rest by day and night," he meant that the process of growth and restoring of balance was going on all the time. The breath is continually being inhaled and exhaled like the alternation of the sun and the moon, or like the ebb and flow of tides. It is a continuous process of repair and restoration of balance during activity, and not confined to the period of "rest" only. In this sense, a man who has trained himself goes through his daily business and contacts with people with possession of mind; he is never hustled when busy and deals with the problems simply and clearly. Mr. Yangming* kept on discussing philosophy even during his military campaigns, which is a good example to prove that one can be relaxed in time of busy activity. In plants, the flowers and fruit grow above while the roots are hidden below, but there is not a moment when waste is not being repaired and the plant is not being nourished. A system of vital energy is circulating all the time from its flowers and fruits to its roots, and when this flow of vital energy is lacking or failing, there is neither growth nor restoration.

Human life depends entirely upon this vital force. That is why it is said that one must keep poise to maintain it. All thinking and all deliberations come from this calm and poise, a state of complete rest from vexations when one can call oneself master of a situation. That is why it is also said, "Let the environment be disturbing, but let the mind be calm." For when the mind can master that equilibrium, one feels that the environmental circumstances cannot upset it. It is therefore not true that rest and relaxation depend upon one's physical location or circumstances.

The method is therefore not to seek relaxation in material conditions, but in the mind. One may well examine oneself: Am I calm or confused when there is a busy schedule morning and night? Do I sleep well? Do I talk too much, or give way too much to pride and anger? Am I dogmatic and self-opinionated, or am I

* Wang Yangming (1472–1528), a great philosopher of the Ming Dynasty who taught the identity of knowledge and action ("acting is believing"). Note the Chinese usage of addressing Mr. Wang as "Mr. Yangming," which is normal. "Mr. Yangming" is polite; "Mr. Wang" is entirely impersonal.

detached, looking at life from the outside? If I can answer these questions in the affirmative, then I am continually being refreshed, and all activities go to nourish my vitality even as the fire in a banked brazier. If not, this vital force is dissipated and almost used up through hustling and bustling. In that case, even when sitting idly with one's eyes closed, one's mind is occupied with a booming confusion of thoughts, which is not a real rest. Man depends upon food to nourish his blood and keep up the balance between waste and repair. Some who are troubled spirits dream troubled dreams at night, or sit idly like a wooden corpse in the daytime. There are people today who try to do this, shutting themselves up in a quiet meditation hall and acting like a disemboweled spirit. Where is the trace of vitality and growth? A popular saying goes: "Tsang-men [the busy street of Soochow] is a good place for study," meaning that one can do it if one is master of oneself.

Shuho thinks that one should have a couch by the side of one's desk, where one can lie down when tired from meeting people, or reading or writing, or after various amusements or a long conversation. That will be achieving what may be called a "small [temporary] peace." Mr. Lungchi says, "A perfect man rests, but does not sleep." The breath of life restores, but in sleep a man's soul wanders away from his body. To seek this relaxation during the time of action and work would be achieving what may be called the "great [deep-down] peace." I write this for Shuho.

« An ancient saying says, "Flowing water does not stink, and a door hinge which is constantly used does not rot." Chuangtse says, "A perfect man does not dream," the notion of a perfect man being one with great spiritual powers. The quotation from Mencius referred to also makes the idea plain. Mencius says, "How can nature remain beautiful when it is hacked at every day as the woodsman chops down trees in a forest? To be sure, the nights and days do the healing and there is the nourishing air of the early dawn, but this is soon dissipated by what he does during the day. With this continuous hacking of the human spirit, the rest and recuperation obtained during the night are not sufficient to maintain its level, and when the night's recuperation and rest are not sufficient to maintain its level, the man degrades himself to a state not far from that of a beast. People see that he acts like a beast and imagine that there was never any true character in him. But is this the true nature of man?"

37 ▣ Moments with Su Tungpo

From

COMPLETE WORKS OF SU TUNGPO

Su Tungpo
1036 - 1101

« Su Tungpo ("Recluse of the Eastern Slope," as he called himself) was really one of the greatest geniuses of all China's history, commonly acknowledged one of the greatest poets and
prose writers. He was also a great painter, and like all geniuses a
great many other things besides. Twice he was under detention,
once at Huangchow and once on the island of Hainan. His Journal and his letters to his friends during these periods show his
genial character and his wonderful sense of humor. Everything
he touched became beautiful.

1. Under Detention at Huangchow (1080–1083)
A. THE LINKAO HOUSE (1080)

My HOUSE IS ONLY ABOUT A DOZEN STEPS from the bank
of the river. The beautiful mountains on the south bank lie spread
before my window, and with the high winds and changing clouds
and misty weather, the view changes a hundred times a day. I have
never had such luck before.

— *Letter to a friend.*

After a drink and a good meal, the Recluse of the Eastern Slope
leans over his desk, with white clouds on his left and the clear
river on his right. Both the outer and the inner doors are wide
open, giving a direct view of the hills and the peaks. At such a time

197

I sit there as if I were thinking of something and again as if I were not thinking at all. In such a state of mind I receive so freely the bounty of nature spread before me, that I feel almost ashamed.
— *Journal.*

The great river lies only a few dozen steps below me and half of its water comes from the Omei Mountain, so that it is almost as good as seeing our home town. The hills and the river, the wind and the moon, have no owner; they belong to anybody who has the leisure to enjoy them. How would your new garden compare with mine? I suppose you have the advantage of paying the summer and autumn taxes on it, and the draft exemption tax besides, while I don't.
— *Letter to Mr. Fan.*

B. AT THE EASTERN SLOPE (1081–1083)

On my arrival at Huangchow, my salary was cut off, and I have such a big family to support. I am now compelled to practice the greatest economy. I allow myself to spend only 150 cash [roughly fifteen cents] a day. On the first of every month I take 4,500 cash and apportion them into even lots, and suspend these individual strings of cash on the ceiling. Every morning I take one string down by means of the hook used for hanging up paintings, and put away the hook for the day. Then I provide a large bamboo section, in which I save up what is left over for the day, with which I can entertain my friends. This is the method of Yunlao [Chia Shou]. In this way, I figure my money will last for a year. I shall think of some way to provide for the family when it's all used up. . . . I don't have to worry ahead. For this reason I haven't a single care in my breast.
— *Letter to Chin Kuan, 1081.*

A *night promenade at Chengtien* (1083).
On the twelfth night of the tenth moon of the sixth year of Yuanfeng, I had undressed and was going to bed, when the moon-

light entered my door, and I got up, happy of heart. There was no one to share this happiness with me, so I walked over to the Cheng-tien Temple to look for Huaimin. He, too, had not yet gone to bed, and we paced about in the garden. It looked like a transparent pool with the shadows of water plants in it, but they were really the shadows of bamboos and pine trees cast by the moonlight. Isn't there a moon every night? And aren't there bamboos and pine trees everywhere? But there are few carefree people like the two of us.

Script on the Snow Hall (1083).
To go about by carriage is a good way to acquire infirm legs.
To live in great halls and deep chambers is an ideal method to catch cold.
To indulge oneself with women is a sure way to destroy one's health.
To eat food with rich gravy is the proper way to develop stomach ulcers.

A *recipe for a long life, written for a friend* (1083).
1. Having leisure equals having power.
2. Going to bed early equals having wealth.
3. A leisurely stroll is as good as a drive.*
4. Eating late is as good as eating meat.*

2. Exile on Hainan Island
(South China Sea, 1097–1100)

WHEN I FIRST ARRIVED at the South Sea and saw a complete circle of water on the horizon, I felt disheartened and sighed, "When shall I be able to get out of this island?" But then I thought: the universe itself is surrounded by water. The Nine Continents are situated in the Great Ing Ocean, and China is situated in the Lesser Ocean. There is not a time in our life when

* Su Tungpo is here quoting Yen Cho of the third century B.C.

we are not living upon an island. Imagine that you pour some water on the ground. A little blade of grass floats on top of it, and upon this blade an ant is clinging for his life. The ant does not know what to do. In a little while the water dries up and the ant crawls away safely. Meeting other ants, it says with tears in its eyes, "Alas! I thought I would never see you again!" How could the ant know that in the twinkling of an eye, it would be able to go wherever it wants? It amuses me to think of this idea. I am writing this after a little sip with some friends.

— *Journal, September 12, 1098.*

I have been in this place over half a year and can somehow get along. I need not go into the details. Think of me as a monk who has been driven out of the Lingying Temple and is now living in a small cottage, eating simple peasant meals! I can live my life this way to the end of my days. As to malaria and other diseases, are there not diseases also in the north? One can die of all kinds of diseases and not of malaria only. It is true, there are no doctors around this place, but think how many people are annually killed by doctors at the capital! I know you will laugh when you read this, and cease to worry about me. When friends ask about me, just tell them what I have said.

— *Letter to Monk Tsanliao.*

This is January 15, 1099, the Festival of Shangyuan. I am living at Tanchow. Several old scholars have come to visit me. Kuo said, "Father, can you come out for a stroll? The moon is beautiful and the night is so calm." Happily I accepted the suggestion and we went out to the western part of the town and entered a temple. We passed through small alleys filled with the Chinese and the tribesmen. There was quite a crowd at the wineshops. By the time we returned, it was already midnight, and the servants were snoring in their sleep. Thinking that fortune and adversity were all the same, I laid my cane behind the door and laughed.

"What are you laughing at, Father?" Kuo asked. "I was laughing at myself and at Han Yu," I replied. "Han Yu was once fishing. He could not catch any fish, and thought he could catch them by going to another place. He did not know that by going to the sea, one does not necessarily catch big fish!"

— *Journal, January 15, 1099.*

3. A Note on Brewing and Drinking Capacity

I CAN CONSUME ONLY one pint a day. There is no one in the world with less capacity for wine than myself. But I like to see people drink. When I see my friends lift the cup and slowly sip the liquor, I feel uplifted in my spirit, and my joy is greater than even that of my friends. I never pass a day without visitors, and never have visitors without wine. Consequently there is also no greater lover of drink in the world than myself.

It has seemed to me that there is no greater human happiness than two things, freedom from sickness in the body, and freedom from worries in the mind. I have neither, but there are others who suffer from them. How can I make them happy when I see them? That is the reason why everywhere I go, I keep some good medicines and give them to those in need. And I especially love to brew wine for my friends. . . .

[In ancient times] Tungkaotse served at the palace and received three quarts of wine per day. His brother once asked him, "Are you happy serving the court?" "What happiness is there in serving the court?" replied Tungkaotse. "But there is considerable attraction in the daily gifts of three quarts of liquor from the imperial cellar!" There is no government ban on wine here, and I can brew it at home, obtaining thirteen gallons from ten bushels of rice. The five magistrates of Kukong, Canton, Huichow, Shunchow, and Meichow give me presents of wine from time to time, so that I'm having more than Tungkaotse. Tungkaotse called himself "Mr. Ten Gallons," but received only three quarts a day. He did not have enough for himself, and certainly could not spare it for his friends. As for me, if I were in his place and received that amount, two quarts and a half would go into the stomachs of my rustic friends. Tungkaotse was a friend of Chungchang Kuang. He practiced the art of prolonging life and foretold the day of his death and wrote his own epitaph. I am his friend, living a thousand years after him.

— *Journal, January 13, 1095.*

4. A Note on Medicine

« *Su Tungpo was quite an expert on medicinal herbs, as seen from his sundry writings. There still exists a book of famous medical recipes ascribed to him and Shen Kua, his contemporary. This is just one of his humorous notes.*

The late Ouyang Shiu once told me this story. Someone was sick and consulted a doctor. The doctor asked him how he got this illness, and he told him that he had been at sea and his ship ran into a storm. The doctor then obtained an old rudder bar which was deeply stained with boatmen's hand perspiration, had it scraped, and the scrapings were ground into a powder, mixed with cinnabar and Indian bread [tuckahoe]. The man drank this concoction and was said to get well. A statement in the Pharmacopoeia also says that powder made from old bamboo fan handles ground and mixed with *Ephedra sinica* [source of ephedrine] is used for stopping perspiration. Mr. Ouyang said then that very often medicines are prescribed on such reasoning, that it sounded like a joke, but sometimes did cure people. I told him that, in that case, a potion made from ground pens and ink should cure one of ignorance and idiocy. Following the same reasoning, to drink from the fountain of the ancient saint Poyi would cure one of greed, and to eat the leftovers of Prince Pikan would cure one of the disease of office seekers. It might also cure one of cowardice to lick the shield of General Fankuei, or one might kiss the earring of the beauty Shishih and be cured of ugly sores. On the seventeenth of leap eighth moon, 1088, my boat passed through Yingchuan district. I recall that twenty years ago, I met Mr. Ouyang at this place and had this conversation.

« Ouyang Shiu (1007–1072), one generation above Su Tungpo, was the greatest writer of his times. When he read Su Tungpo's composition, he said to his friends, "I see that this young man will come right up and win his place." Immediately, Su's position was established and they became fast friends.

5. Save the Child

« Su Tungpo built dams, worked on famine relief, instituted prison physicians, himself collected famine orphans and fed them. He was also the first to protest against the custom of drowning girl babies at birth. The following is, I think, one of his greatest letters, urging a plan to stop such homicide. And he was rewarded in a way no man could be rewarded; when he left Huangchow, the grateful parents lined up the village streets with tears in their eyes and babies in their arms whose very lives had been saved by his efforts.

TO CHU KANGSHOU, CHIEF MAGISTRATE OF OCHOW (1083)

Su Shih addresses you:

Yesterday I was at Wuchang stopping over at Wang Tienlin's place. He told me a very touching story, and after hearing it I could not eat. I think I can bring this to your attention, if not to others, and am therefore dispatching this letter to you through Mr. Wang. Other people might be too busy with their own affairs to take the time and trouble to attend to something which is outside their official routine.

Tienlin said to me that in the district of Yochow and Ochow [Wuchang], the poor farmers as a rule raise only two sons and one daughter, and kill babies at birth beyond this number. They especially dislike to raise daughters, with the result that there are more men than women and many bachelors in the country. A baby is often killed at birth by drowning in cold water, but

I have made bold to bring this matter to your attention because I know I am speaking to a true friend, and I crave your pardon for the intrusion.

> « For his own part, he established a Save-the-Child Association, and made his neighbor Ku, a very honest and philanthropic scholar, its president. The association collected money from the rich people, asking them to contribute ten dollars a year or more, with which they bought rice and cloth and cotton for quilts. Ku handled the money, and a monk at the Ankuo Temple was made treasurer in charge of records and accounts. These people went about the countryside to investigate cases of needy expectant mothers, and gave them presents of money and food and clothing if they promised to raise their children. Su Tungpo said that it would be a great pleasure if they could thus save a hundred children a year, and he himself contributed ten dollars per year. He was acting in the best tradition of Buddhism.
>
> It has always seemed to me that wherever the spirit of man lives, religion comes to life again. Whenever the spirit of man dies, religion also decays.

38 ▣ On Wealth and Commerce

Szema Chien
145 - after 85 B.C.

« *After the romantic poets, who seem to have no use for money, it may be refreshing to hear the views of an objective scholar trained in observing facts. Szema Chien, author of Shiki (or Shihchi), the great history covering the earliest times to his day, was the greatest historian of China, not only because of the important material he preserved, but also because of his great style, his scholarly judgments, and his intense personal feelings. In philosophy he was not a narrow, slavish follower of Confucius. Son of an astronomer-historian, with access to all the historical documents of the Han Imperial House, he supplemented them by extensive travels. Several centuries before him, there had already arisen a class of merchant princes, with great accumulation of wealth. The chapter on "Wealth and Commerce" contains many valuable economic facts of those days, but the following short excerpts reflect only his views and opinions on wealth.*

I DO NOT KNOW about prehistoric times before Shennung, but since the Yu and Shia dynasties (after twenty-second century B.C.) during the period discussed by the historical records, human nature has always struggled for good food, dress, amusements, and physical comfort, and has always tended to be proud of wealth and ostentation. No matter how the philosophers may teach otherwise, the people cannot be changed. Therefore, the best of men leave it alone, and next in order come those who try to guide it, then those who moralize about it, then those who try to make adjustments to it, and lastly come those who get into the scramble themselves. Briefly, Shansi produces timber, grains, linen, ox hair, and jades.

Shantung produces fish, salt, lacquer, silks, and musical instruments. Kiangnan [south of the Yangtse] produces cedar, *tzu* [a hard wood for making wood blocks], ginger, cinnamon, gold and tin ores, cinnabar, rhinoceros horn, tortoise shell, pearls, and hides. Lungmen produces stone for tablets. The north produces horses, cattle, sheep, furs, and horns. As for copper and iron, they are often found in mountains everywhere, spread out like pawns on a chessboard. These are what the people of China like and what provide the necessities for their living and for ceremonies for the dead. The farmers produce them, the wholesalers bring them from the country, the artisans work on them, and the merchants trade on them. All this takes place without the intervention of government or of the philosophers. Everybody exerts his best and uses his labor to get what he wants. Therefore prices seek their level, cheap goods going to where they are expensive and higher prices are brought down. People follow their respective professions and do it on their own initiative. It is like flowing water which seeks the lower level day and night without stop. All things are produced by the people themselves without being asked and transported to where they are wanted. Is it not true that these operations happen naturally in accord with their own principles? The *Book of Chou* says, "Without the farmers, food will not be produced; without the artisans, industry will not develop; without the merchants, the valuable goods will disappear; and without the wholesalers, there will be no capital and the natural resources of lakes and mountains will not be opened up." Our food and our dress come from these four classes, and wealth and poverty vary with the size of these sources. On a larger scale, it benefits a country, and on a smaller scale, it enriches a family. These are the inescapable laws of wealth and poverty. The clever ones have enough and to spare, while the stupid ones have not enough. . . .

Therefore, first the granaries must be full before the people can talk of culture. The people must have sufficient food and good dress before they can talk of honor. The good customs and social amenities come from wealth and disappear when the country is poor. Even as fish thrive in a deep lake and the beasts gravitate toward a deep jungle, so the morals of mankind come as effects of wealth. The rich acquire power and influence, while the poor are unhappy and have no place to turn to. This is even truer of the barbarians. Therefore it is said: "A wealthy man's son does not die in the market place," and it is not an empty saying. It is said:

> The world hustles
> Where money beckons.
> The world jostles
> Where profit thickens.

Even kings and dukes and the wealthy gentry worry about poverty. Why wonder that the common people and the slaves do the same? . . . [Here follows a long section on the economic products and conditions and the people's character and way of living of the different regions.]

Therefore you see the distinguished scholars who argue at courts and temples about policies and talk about honesty and self-sacrifice, and the mountain recluses who achieve a great reputation. Where do they go? They seek after the rich. The honest officials acquire wealth as time goes on, and the honest merchants become wealthier and wealthier. For wealth is something which man seeks instinctively without being taught. You see soldiers rush in front of battle and perform great exploits in a hail of arrows and rocks and against great dangers, because there is a great reward. You see young men steal and rob and commit violence and dig up tombs for treasures, and even risk the punishments by law, throwing all considerations of their own safety to the winds — all because of money. The courtesans of Chao and Cheng dress up and play music and wear long sleeves and pointed dancing shoes. They flirt and wink, and do not mind being called to a great distance, irrespective of the age of the men — all are attracted by the rich. The sons of the rich dress up in caps and carry swords and go about with a fleet of carriages just to show off their wealth. The hunters and the fishermen go out at night, in snow and frost, roam in the wooded valleys haunted by wild beasts, because they want to catch game. Others gamble, have cock fights, and match dogs in order to win. Physicians and magicians practice their arts in expectation of compensation for their services. Bureaucrats play hide-and-seek with the law and even commit forgery and falsify seals at the risk of penal sentences because they have received bribes. And so all farmers, artisans, and merchants and cattle raisers try to reach the same goal. Everybody knows this, and one hardly ever hears of one who works and declines pay for it. . . . Hence the poor work with their hands, those who have a little savings try ways and means to increase it, and the successful ones follow the fashions of the day. This is a general principle. If a man can make a living without incurring personal dangers, all clever men want to do it. Therefore those who produce wealth are the highest, those who trade on it the next, and those who get rich by crooked means are the lowest. If a man does not have the character of a religious hermit, but always remains poor and shiftless while harping on moral platitudes, he should be ashamed.

« The chapter closes with a description of the means and manner by which many merchant princes rose to great wealth from humble origins, some by clever speculation and hoarding in times of war, some by utilizing labor of slaves, and some by usury. Quite a few founded family fortunes by mining iron. The discovery of iron about the fourth or third century, or even as far back as the time of Confucius, brought wealth to many people. Some of the wealthy were said to live like kings.

39 ▣ Is There Retribution?

"LIFE OF POYI"

Szema Chien
145 - after 85 B.C.

« Szema Chien had an objective down-to-earth view of life, as seen
in the preceding selection. In the present selection, he expresses
what is at least an honest opinion on one of the most vexing
problems of religion—is there retribution?—and seems to doubt
that there is. The style is tense with personal emotions, though
they are those of a widely read scholar. He had a personal catas-
trophe. As Master Astronomer-Historian, he had the highest
post close to the emperor. He had recommended one General
Liling to fight the Huns in Turkestan. Liling was trapped, and
under the circumstances, surrendered rather than commit
suicide. The emperor was furious and had the general's immediate family exterminated. Szema Chien probably had tried to
intervene for his friend. The net result was that he himself was
castrated and thrown in prison. It was in the years under detention that he wrote the voluminous masterpiece called Shiki, preserving an enormous amount of historical material that otherwise would have been lost. Its scope and plan and comparative
chronological tables are staggering.

The name of "Poyi" (twelfth century B.C.) is synonymous
with that of a saintly hermit or recluse. He and his brother, Shuchi, were princes of a small kingdom. They both declined the
throne and finally it was given to another brother. When a con-
quering dynasty was founded, they refused to serve under the
conqueror and escaped to the mountains where they subsisted
on beans and eventually died of starvation. They were made immortal by Confucius's calling them "true men." Szema Chien
therefore posed the problem whether there is justice in the
world. I have omitted here the beginning, which expresses the

211

40   How To Be Happy Though Rich

From

THE ARTS OF LIVING (SHIENCHING OUCHI)

Li Liweng
1611 - 1679

« *Li Liweng was an original and versatile writer. He was not so
much a scholar as an artist of living. He wrote the popular guide
to painting Chiehtseyuan Huapu (translated by Miss Mai-mai
Sze, Bollingen Series 49) and a number of popular books, including one on making poetic couplets which I learned as a
child. He wrote twelve short stories and ten plays, with a tend-
ency to comic themes. The book The Arts of Living gives his
always original thoughts on musical plays, hints on acting, house
and interior, food and drinks, and horticulture. For further excerpts from his book, see selections 41, 45, and 52.*

MONEY IS THE MEANS for providing pleasures, yet too much
money also entails its disadvantages, and that is why it is difficult
to be happy though rich. When the people of Huafeng wished
lots of money and children and years [long life] for Emperor Yao
(traditional reign, 2357–2257 B.C.), it is recorded that he replied,
"Too much money means too many things to attend to." And the
people of Huafeng said, "You can give some away." Tao Chukung
[alias Fan Li, c. 473 B.C.] several times made a thousand dollars and
several times gave them away. That was because, like Emperor
Yao, he was afraid of the disadvantages of having too much money.
To teach rich men to enjoy life would mean to ask them to
give money away, which is difficult, to say the least. Having

money, one thinks of managing it to let it grow and have more. Once one starts to manage money, there are endless worries and all peace of mind is gone. Also one begins to worry about theft or robbery, or even about being stabbed in the bargain. The worries arising from such fears of theft and robbery are equally demeaning. Furthermore, wealth makes one a target for envy, and one feels no one really cares for him. What chance is there for enjoying life? Such indeed are the penalties of great wealth. Should one therefore conclude that it is impossible to be happy though wealthy? I think not. One cannot be expected to give a great deal of money away, but one can at least refrain from being grasping. This is especially appreciated in times of general poverty. Taking less interest for a loan or cutting one's shares from farmer tenants will immediately be appreciated by the poor, who will be very grateful. One gains a good reputation when one burns up an I.O.U. even though the debtor has been able only to pay the interest, or when one contributes money to the government or a public cause. This would be quite a contrast to what the rich people of today are doing. It would not hurt one's soul to do so, and would put an end to all envy and enmity. When one hears the tributes of the poor people, it is as good as having two orchestras, and when one receives honors or awards from the government, one's name goes down to posterity. Thus one obtains both honor and happiness. As to amusements, music, women, nice villas, pleasure parties, these things are easily available to the wealthy people as they are not to the poor. So what seemed to be difficult to attain can now be readily achieved.

41 ▣ How To Be Happy Though Poor

From

THE ARTS OF LIVING (SHIENCHING OUCHI)

Li Liweng
1611 - 1679

THE ART OF BEING HAPPY though poor consists in one phrase, to think "it could be worse." I am poor and humble, but there are people poorer and more humble than myself. I have a big family to support, but there are people living alone and without children, and widows and orphans. I have to work hard on a farm, but there are people without a farm, or who would rather work hard on their farm like me but cannot because they are sitting in jail. It is a way of thinking, or of looking at it. The same situation may look like hell to one and like paradise to another. On the other hand, always to want to compare oneself with one's betters will breed a state of mind conducive only to one's own misery.

I remember the story of a high official who was traveling abroad. It was summer and his bed was full of mosquitoes inside the net. He thought of his own spacious hall at home, where the summer mat was cooling to the body and many maids would attend to his comforts. The more he thought, the more miserable he felt. He was not able to sleep a wink. Then he saw a man walking about in the court of the inn, seemingly quite happy with himself. He was puzzled and inquired how he seemed to be so happy with the mosquitoes around and was not bothered at all. The man replied, "I once had an enemy and was put in jail. It was summer and the jail was full of vermin. But my hands and feet were tied to prevent me from escape. It was terrible to be bitten by insects and mosquitoes and not be able to do anything about it. There are mosquitoes now. But I move about and they can't touch me. In fact, it makes me happy to feel just the freedom of the limbs alone." The man saw one side of it and the other man saw the other side. The rich man felt quite lost when he heard the story.

WOMEN

42 ▣ The Origin of Foot-binding

"A NOTE ON WOMEN'S SHOES AND SOCKS"

Yu Huai
1617 - after 1697

« Yu Huai is a connoisseur of inkstones and of women, being best known for his volume on the singsong artists of Yangchow. He places the origin of foot-binding at the middle of the tenth century, while a commentator, Fei Shihuang, wrote a postscript to dispute it, believing its origin to be very much earlier. The case is not proven. What is clear is that foot-binding became popular in the latter part of the eleventh century. To make it easier to follow, it should be noted that the distinctive characteristics of bound feet with "bow shoes" are: (1) that in place of simple socks, long bands of silk, perhaps seven or eight feet long, were used to wind around the feet, and over these, a short embroidered ankle cover was worn, (2) that such feet were reputed to be very small, "three inches" being the goal, (3) that the curved, pointed form of the feet was called the "crescent" and the shoes were called "bow shoes." High heels alone, or pointed and up-turned fronts need not necessarily indicate foot-binding. "Lotus steps" and "bamboo shoots" (round and short and pointed at one end) are common expressions, and I think these do not always indicate the existence of foot-binding. The style probably originated in the licentious courts of certain rulers, the notorious "East Idiot Ruler" of South Tsi (c. A.D. 500) and the good-poet-but-bad-ruler Nantang Houtsu (reigned, A.D. 937–978), and became general custom later. In view of the exuberance of Tang poetry about women's beauty, its lack of specific reference to this curious custom should lead one to think that foot-binding was not yet the general custom in the Tang Period (seventh to ninth centuries). Yu Huai is probably correct.

There was no difference between the feet of women and of men in ancient times. The *Chouli* [classic on Chou governmental system] mentions the office of the "shoe man," whose duty was to look after the shoes of kings and queens. It mentions red clogs, black clogs, red and yellow silk braids, black curves, white shoes, linen shoes for formal, informal, and home use by the titled men and ladies. This shows that shoes of men and women were of the same form. In later generations, the small and slender bow shoes of women were prized for their smallness.

According to my research, foot-binding began with Li Houtsu of Nantang (reigned, A.D. 937–978). He had a royal woman attendant called Yaoniang [Miss Yao], who was noted for her slender beauty and her dance. He had a golden lotus made, six feet high and decorated with precious stones and festoons and tassels of silk. This golden lotus in many colors stood in the center. He made Miss Yao tie her feet with silk and crouch on top of it to suggest the form of a crescent moon. She danced on top of the lotus in her white socks and made pirouettes suggesting the clouds [with her long sleeves]. Many people then began to copy her style. This was the first beginning of foot-binding.

This custom was not started before the Tang Dynasty (beginning A.D. 617). Therefore, among the poems written by so many poets singing the beauty of women, endlessly describing with great interest their looks and gestures, the richness of their hair ornaments and facial make-ups and their dresses and skirts, and the delicacy of their hair, eyes, lips, teeth, waists, and hands and wrists, not a word was said about their "small feet." In the *Kuyofu* [*Ancient Songs*] it says, "New silk embroidery covers her white ankle and the arch of her feet was like a beautiful spring" [Han Period]. Tsao Tsechien (A.D. 192–232) has a line which reads, "She wears embroidered shoes for long walks." Li Po (A.D. 701–762) says in one poem, "A pair of gold-toothed clogs; two feet white as frost." Han Chihkuang writes, "Six inches of fine round skin dazzle in the light." Tu Muchih (A.D. 803–852) [a great philanderer and poet] writes, "It measures one foot minus four-tenths of an inch." The document "Miscellanies, Secret H"* of the second century A.D. says [describing a girl selected to be queen], "Her feet measured eight inches, and her ankle and arch were beautiful and full." Such mention of "six inches" and "eight inches" of white, soft, and full feet shows that the ladies' feet before Tang were not bent to resemble the crescent moon.

The case of the East Idiot Ruler of Tsi (c. A.D. 500) may come to mind. He made his favorite royal concubine Miss Pan tread on gold models of lotus flowers arranged on the floor, and said, "A gold lotus flower arises from her every step." This, however, refers to the models of lotus flowers which she trod upon, but is not meant to say that her feet themselves were lotuses. Tsui Pa mentions in his book on the origin of things, the *Kuchinchu*, that there were phoenix-head shoes with double *tai* [soles?], but there was no indication that only women's shoes were meant.

In the Sung Dynasty, few women bound their feet before the reign of Yuanfeng (A.D. 1078–1085). But in the almost four hundred years that followed, beginning from the Mongol Dynasty (A.D. 1277–1367) to the present, the unnatural fashions and exaggerations have steadily grown and run into excesses.

Ancient women all wore socks. On the day that Queen Yang Kueifei† died (c. A.D. 756) at Mahuai, a village woman picked up half of a pair of her embroidered socks. She exhibited this to the public, charging 100 cash for touching it. Li Po says in one of his poems, "Her feet are white as frost; she does not wear black-capped socks." One name for socks was *chiku* [ankle sheath].

* See selection 43.
† Probably the most famous, pampered, and extravagant queen of China's history who almost brought an end to the Tang Dynasty. A revolt by her lover, An Lushan, a Mongol or a Turk, caused the emperor to flee the capital. The general public opinion had been so enraged by the extravagances of her family that the army escorting the fleeing emperor refused to go farther unless their demand to have the queen killed be complied with. She was given a band of silk to hang herself with. Her corpse was shown to the commanders and the army marched.

When Emperor Kaotsung (reigned, A.D. 1127–1162) heard of the death of his prime minister, Tsin Kuei, he said, "Now I don't need to conceal a dagger in my *chiku*." Thus "socks" or *chiku* were worn by both men and women. The difference is that socks in ancient times had soles to them, as is not the case today. In ancient times, one could walk about in socks without shoes. Now we cannot. . . . Tsao Tsechien says, "She moves her light steps. Her silken socks become dusty." Li Houtsu writes, "She descends the perfumed steps in her socks, holding the gold-thread shoes in her hand." Such indeed is the difference in shoes and socks between the ancient and the modern times.

As to high heels, I do not find it mentioned in ancient books. This seems to be a modern invention. Some ladies of Wu make heels of sandalwood, covered with fine stiff silk. Some have carved heels, with a concealed perfume bag inside, so that they leave a trail of perfume as they walk about. This is a monstrous extravagance. I mention this because poems of the Sung and Mongol Dynasties made no reference to it, so that poets who want to write about ancient beauties should be careful on this point.

43 ▣ A Woman's Body

"MISCELLANIES, SECRET H"
("TSASHIH MI SHIN") A FRAGMENT

Anonymous
2nd century A.D.

« *The following is one of the most curious fragments that have
survived the ages. The name of the document, "Miscellanies,
Secret H," seems to indicate that it came from the secret ar-
chives of Han palace, the word* shin *in this context having no
meaning unless it was used as a word in the Chinese cycle for
labeling a series, like the letter H in the alphabet standing for
"Number 8." This is a record of the queen of Emperor Huan
(reigned, A.D. 147–167) of Han Dynasty, beginning with a report
of the physical examination of the queen when she was a girl of
sixteen, given by a woman servant of the palace. The rest deals
with the formal six ceremonies of engagement (first presents;
asking for name of the girl, her age, and her ancestors; divina-
tion; second formal gifts which was the formal engagement;
asking for date of marriage; and finally the wedding), and ends
with her "coronation" as empress. The woman's report is interesting because of its realistic details. The phrases she used are
not found in the usual literary language but belonged to her
spoken language. I give here only the woman's report.*

IN THE FIRST YEAR of Chienho (A.D. 147), the fourth
moon, day of Tinghai, Maid Wu of the Court of Serving Women
went with the edict of Pingshu [the day before] to the house of
Chamberlain Chao. The edict says, "We hear that the first poem
of the *Book of Songs* celebrated a royal marriage, and that the
choice of a good royal spouse has ever been the concern of good

rulers of the past. The chaste reputation of the bereaved young daughter of the late General Cheng Shang, has reached our ears. Let the Chamberlain go with Maid [Wu] to the late general's house, and examine her deportment and all intimate details and report faithfully. We intend to select her for the palace."

Bringing the letter of authorization, I [Maid Wu] and Chao went to the house of the late General Shang and found the family just having dinner. Our arrival created a great excitement in the house. The girl, named Nuying, left the hall and went to her inside quarters. Chao and I followed the instructions of the edict and studied her deportment carefully and were satisfied. Chao then went out and I went with Ying [the girl] to her private room, where I sent away all attendants and closed the door. At that time, the sunlight came through the shell windows and shone upon Ying's face, which radiated a brightness like the morning cloud or snow, so that I instinctively avoided looking at her directly. Ripples of light came from her eyes and her eyebrows were curved. She had red lips and white teeth, a long pair of ears and a pointed nose. Her cheeks were full and her chin well-formed, all in proper proportion. I then took off her long, bending hair ornament* and let down her hair, which was jet-black. I felt it in the palm of my hand, and it reached the ground, with more to spare.

This done, I asked her to loosen her underclothes. Ying blushed all over and refused, and I said to Ying, "It is a palace rule which must be complied with. Please let a poor old woman see it. Loosen the belt knot and I shall be very careful." Ying's tears came to her eyes and she turned her face away and closed her eyes. I then loosened her belt knot, and turned her toward the light. I smelled an exquisite smell. Her skin was white and fine and so smooth that my hand slipped as it touched it. Her belly was round and her hips square. It was like constructed cheese† and carved jade.

---

* This was a pin several inches long, made of light, soft metal so that it shook up and down as the girl walked. Hence the name used here, *puyao*, which means "shaking at every step."
† Literally "constructed fat." Such phrases are evidently from the woman's *patois*.

Her breasts bulged out, and her navel had enough depth to permit a half-inch pearl to go in. Her *mons veneris* rose gently. I opened her thighs and saw that the vulva was bright red, while the labia minora slightly protruded. I was satisfied that she was a chaste virgin. In general about Ying's body, her blood well nourished her skin, her skin well covered her muscles, and her muscles well concealed her bones. Her dimensions were right. She stood seven feet one inch,* her shoulders were one foot six wide, her hips three inches less [*sic*] than her shoulders. She measured two feet seven inches from her shoulders to the tips of her fingers, and her fingers were four inches from the tips to the palm, looking like ten pointed bamboo sticks. The length of her legs from the thighs to the feet was three feet two inches, and her feet measured eight inches. Her ankles and arches were round and full, her soles smooth, and her toes small.† The tight silk and closefitting socks were gathered in as with ladies in the palace. For a long time she stood speechless. I urged her quickly to thank His Imperial Majesty, and she bowed and said, "Long Live‡ the Emperor!" Her voice was like a wind moving among a bamboo grove, very pleasant to the ear. She had no piles, no bad marks, no moles and no sores, or defects in the mouth, the nose, the armpit, the private parts, or the feet.

I am a stupid humble woman and cannot express properly what I saw or felt. I make this secret report, properly sealed, knowing that my life depends upon Your Imperial pleasure.

« I think the end of this fragment about the empress's coronation is interesting. The emperor was seated in his throne, while the empress-to-be was seated in the center of the hall, facing him. The Grand Councillor stood outside under an awning to the east, with the empress's seal held by an officer by his side. When the formal letter of appointment was read, the empress-to-be-

* The foot in Han days was probably about seven tenths of a modern English foot, so that the girl was just under five feet tall.
† This line, rather than one describing her socks, is most important in my opinion as proof that her feet were not bound. Bound feet cannot have smooth soles, for the soles were bent and folded over.
‡ Literally *banzai*, which is Chinese for "ten thousand years."

said, "Long live the Emperor!" and was seated again. Grand Councillor Chiao took the seal in his hand and passed it to Chamberlain Chao, who received it kneeling. The chamberlain brought it up to the hall where it was passed to a lady in charge of the palace. This lady official passed it to a chiehshu (lady of a certain rank), who received it kneeling. The chiehshu passed it on to a chaoyi (lady of a higher rank), who also received it kneeling. The chaoyi then brought it to the empress. The latter bowed to the emperor and said again, "Long live the Emperor!" When this was done, the eunuchs blew the trumpets three times and a drum was beaten. The officials filed out. The empress was seated on her throne and a general amnesty was declared.

44 ▣ Professional Matchmakers

From

DREAM MEMORIES OF WEST LAKE

Chang Tai
1597 - 1689

« *The original title is "Lean Horses," local name for matchmakers.
The author describes the practice of Yangchow, nationally
famed as the center of luxury and the place where regular houses
trained girls to be singsong artists or concubines. The time was
the early seventeenth century.*

   *This piece describes what may be called the "concubine mar-
ket" and its efficiency. It is the most unromantic way of securing
a mistress; only coarse businessmen would buy a concubine this
way.*

AT YANGCHOW, there were hundreds of people making
a living from activities connected with the "lean horses." One
should never let it be known that one was looking for a concubine.
Once this leaked out, the professional agents and go-betweens,
both men and women, would swarm about his house or hotel like
flies, and there was no way of keeping them off. The next morning,
he would find many of them waiting for him, and the matchmaker
who arrived first would hustle him off, while the rest followed behind and waited for their chance.

Arriving at the house of the "lean horse," the person would be
served tea as soon as he was seated. At once the woman agent
would come out with a girl and announce, "*Kuniang* [mademoi-
selle], curtsy!" The girl curtsied. Next was said, "*Kuniang*, walk

45 ▣ On Charm in Women

From

THE ARTS OF LIVING (SHIENCHING OUCHI)

Li Liweng
1611 - 1679

« *See note on author, selection 40.*

THERE IS AN ANCIENT SAYING that "the power of exotic beauty fascinates." Exotic beauty means charm, although it has been commonly misunderstood as referring to "good looks" merely. Good looks, it should be understood, can never move us unless it has charm, and only then does the beauty become fascinating and exotic. People who think that all beauties can fascinate people need only stop to think why all the silk dolls and pictures of women can never move one, although probably their faces are ten times more beautiful than living women. Charm in a person is like the flame in a fire, the light in a lamp, and the luster in jewels. It is something invisible and yet seemingly palpable, something which can be seen and yet has no definite shape or body. That is why charm is always mysterious — why a woman with charm is regarded as being exotic, for to be exotic is to be exciting and mystifying, to be that which people cannot quite understand. There are women who make people fall in love with them at first sight, who once seen are never forgotten, and who make men risk all they have, glory, wealth, and even their own lives, in order to possess them. Such is the strange power of women's fascination, something which is elusive and defies all explanation.

232

Of all the things that I admire the creator of the universe for, and of all the mysteries of the universe, the charm of personality ranks the greatest. If I were God, I could give my creatures bodily shape and wisdom and knowledge, but I could not give them this something which is invisible and yet seemingly palpable, which exists and yet has no bodily shape, is seen for a moment and disappears again — namely, charm. For charm not only enhances beauty and attraction in women; it can make the old appear young, the ugly beautiful, and the dull become exciting. For silently and secretly it fascinates a man without his being aware of it. A girl who has only a third-grade facial beauty is as fascinating as another one who has better looks, if she has only charm. Take two girls, one who has only ordinary third-grade "looks" but has charm, and the other who has no charm but has better "looks," and put them side by side. People will like the third-grade and not the second-grade beauty. Or again, take a moderately good-looking woman without charm and another who has charm but is totally deficient in good looks and put them together and let people exchange a few words with each of them. People will fall in love with the one who has charm and not with the one who has merely good looks, which goes to prove that charm can substitute for a total absence of good looks. There are today girls who are otherwise common-looking, yet who can fascinate men even to the point of making them risk their lives for them. The secret lies solely in this one word "charm."

Charm is something which comes naturally to a person and directly grows out of her personality. It is not something which can be copied from others, for charm imitated is beauty spoiled. To knit her eyebrows was beautiful in Shishih, because it was natural to her, but would be actually disgusting if Tungshih were to assume the same pose, because she was born differently. It is possible to lay down rules for judging a person's face and skin and eyebrows and eyes by certain standards, but as for this thing called "charm," it is something that is immediately felt, but cannot be analyzed or put into words; for in its elusiveness lies its exciting power and fascination. . . .

I shall give a few examples of what I saw to show my meaning. I was once in Yangchow, trying to pick a concubine for a certain official. There were rows of women in beautiful dresses and of different types. At first they stood all with their heads bent, but when they were ordered to hold their heads up, one of them just raised her head and stared blandly at me, and another was terribly shy and would not hold her head up until she had been bidden to do so several times. There was one, however, who would not look up at first but did so after some persuasion, and then she first cast a quick glance as if she was looking and yet not looking at me before she held her head up, and again she cast another glance before she bent her head again. This is what I call charm.

I also remember that on a certain spring day, a number of people including myself were taking shelter in a pavilion to avoid a spring shower. Many girls and women, both ugly and beautiful ones, made a dash for the place. There was one woman in a white dress, however, about thirty years old, who stood by under the eaves outside the pavilion, seeing that there was no more room inside. The other women were all shaking their dresses, but there she stood, calm and poised under the eaves, without bothering to do so, because she knew that, exposed as she was, to shake her dress would only make her look ridiculous. Then the shower stopped and people rushed out only to rush back again when the shower came again. They found her quietly standing inside the pavilion, for she had anticipated it. She did not show an air of self-satisfaction; on the other hand, when she saw the other women standing outside with their dresses all wet, she did her best to wipe the water off their shoulders and sleeves, revealing then her infinite charm of movement as if God had ordained this crowd of ugly women to come there with their fussiness in order to show off her beauty to greater advantage. As an observer, I saw it was perfect; in the beginning she showed her charm by her poise when she was standing outside, and then she showed her charm in movement when she was helping the others. But the whole thing came naturally, for she could not have planned it. Her former poise and charm were just as natural as her subsequent activity. She had revealed this inner charm already when she was standing outside the pavilion, quiet and reserved and just her natural self, a charm which was just as effective and suitable to the circumstances of the time as her later movements and activity. . . .

Some readers may ask, Is it true that charm can never be taught, for we say that one can even learn to be a saint or a sage? I can only say in reply that charm can be learned, but cannot be taught. If it again be asked, Why can't it be taught if it can be learned? my reply is that people without charm can learn it by living together with people who have it. They will acquire it by daily example and contagion, like reeds learning to grow straight in a field of hemp. It comes gradually and naturally by a kind of invisible influence. To lay down so many rules for acquiring charm would be futile and indeed only make confusion worse confounded.

THE HOME AND DAILY LIVING

46 ▣ A Family Letter

From

TSENG'S FAMILY LETTERS

Tseng Kuofan
1811 - 1872

« Tseng Kuofan's family and official correspondence is probably better preserved than any other man's in the last century. His diaries and letters run probably to a million words. Tseng Kuofan was the general who saved the Manchu Empire during the Taiping Rebellion (1850–1864), and who in consequence was the most honored man in his days. This letter to his family is all the more remarkable for this reason. I have been curious to see how such family instructions turn out, and am happy to observe that his grandchildren and great-grandchildren today are active in the educational world, many of them having studied in England. His son Chitseh (1839–1890) was ambassador to the Court of St. James.

WHEN THE BRIDE [daughter-in-law] comes to our family, she must be taught to go to the kitchen and learn cooking and also put her hand to the spinning wheel. She should not be allowed to become idle because she comes from a wealthy home.

Can the eldest, second, and third daughters already make their own shoes? I should like to have the three daughters and one daughter-in-law each make me a pair of shoes every year,* as a

---

* Chinese shoes were usually made with cloth soles, reinforced by cardboard or felt, and were often homemade. The tip of the ladies' shoes usually had embroidery. The embroidered top was the important thing where a lady could exercise her ingenuity in design and colors. If a leather sole was wanted, she could have the shoes completed by a cobbler.

form of respect, but also so that I can see their needlework. They should also make dresses and socks with cloth made at home. In this way I can keep track of the industry or idleness of our womenfolk.

The families of officials nowadays tend to become idle rich, living in luxury. They set bad examples. When my three daughters are grown up, I want them married to simple middle-class scholar families which need not be rich.

Never neglect the planting of vegetables in the home garden. Breeding fish in the pond outside our front door helps to give a sense of growth and life all around. Raising pigs is also an important part of domestic economy. Do some of the bamboos at the back terrace dry up after autumn? We can see from these four things whether a family is active and industrious, or whether it is eating away its fortune. None of these four things — raising fish, pigs, bamboo, and vegetables — may be neglected. First we want to keep up the tradition of thrift and industry of our ancestors, and, secondly, these four things give a sense of life and growth. The moment one enters a door, one can see an air of busy prosperity. Even spending some money and labor on them would be thoroughly worth while.

47 ▣ The Home Garden

From

SHIAOCHUANG YUCHI

Chen Chiju
1558 - 1639

« *The writer was a great scholar and collector of rare books. He
was wealthy and refused office and lived in the beautiful rich district of Sungkiang. He devoted his time to publishing at his
own expense a famous collection of rare booklets, the Paoyentang Rare Books Library. (See also selections 90, 105, and 106
by the same author.)*

INSIDE THE GATE there is a footpath and the footpath
must be winding. At the turn of the footpath there is an outdoor
screen and the screen must be small. Behind the screen there is
a terrace and the terrace must be level. On the banks of the
terrace there are flowers and the flowers must be bright-colored.
Beyond the flowers there is a wall and the wall must be low. By the
side of the wall there is a pine tree and the pine must be old. At
the foot of the pine tree there are rocks and the rocks must be
quaint. Over the rocks there is a pavilion and the pavilion must
be simple. Behind the pavilion are bamboos and the bamboos must
be sparse. At the end of the bamboos there is a house and the
house must be secluded. By the side of the house there is a road
and the road must branch off. At the point where several roads
come together, there is a bridge and the bridge must be tantalizing
to cross. At the end of the bridge there are trees and the trees must
be tall. In the shade of the trees there is grass and the grass must

be green. Above the grass plot there is a ditch and the ditch must be slender. At the top of the ditch there is a spring and the spring must gurgle. Above the spring there is a hill and the hill must be undulating. Below the hill there is a hall and the hall must be square. At the corner of the hall there is a vegetable garden and the garden must be big. In the garden there is a stork and the stork must dance. The stork announces there is a guest and the guest must not be vulgar. When the guest arrives he is offered wine and the wine must not be declined. At the drink the guest must get drunk and the drunken guest must not want to go home.

48 🖻 Cut Flowers and Vases

Chang Tehchien
c. 1600

« Many authorities have written on this subject, including Tu
Chihshui and Yuan Chunglang. The following is probably the
best connected summary. On the more fascinating subject of arranging miniature landscapes, the best is still that by Shen Fu,
the author of Six Chapters of a Floating Life (see The Importance of Living, pp. 308–310). Su Tungpo has a piece about a
miniature landscape arrangement in his home, inherited from
his father. No dates of Chang Tehchien can be found, but this
piece bears a preface dated A.D. 1595.

1. VASES

THE SELECTION OF A PROPER VASE for flowers is the first
step. There are elements of season, copper vases for winter and
spring, and porcelain for summer and fall, and elements of size
and space, big ones for big halls and small ones for a studio or
library. Copper is preferred to gold and silver to avoid suggestion
of opulence, and vases with earrings should be avoided, as also a
symmetrical arrangement in pairs, to avoid their looking as if on
a temple altar. The vases should be more slender at the top than
the bottom for steadiness.

In general, slender and small vases are preferred to the wide and
big. The best is four or five inches* or six or seven inches, one foot
being the maximum. If the vase is too small, the flowers will not
keep for long.

* The Chinese foot contains ten inches, or 14.1 English inches. "Five
inches" means half a Chinese foot, or seven inches by English measurements.

Copper [or bronze] vessels that can be used for holding flowers are jars, bottles, goblets, and pots formerly used for holding wine but quite suitable for this use.

Antique copper [and bronze] vases and bowls or alms bowls which have been found underground are especially suitable, for from their long burial underground there has been a change from contact with the soil. They keep flowers as fresh as on the bough, so that they last longer and wither more slowly. Some flowers even start to form seeds in the pot, especially when the bases are very old and the water used is excellent. Earthenware which has lain buried for a thousand years acts in the same way.

There were no porcelain [tzu] vessels in ancient times till the Tang Period (beginning in the seventh century), and only copper [or bronze] was used. The use of kiln ceramics began with Tang.* Later came [the products known by their yao or kilns of] Chai, Ju, Ko, Ting, Lungchuan, Chunchow, Changsheng, Wuni, Shuanteh, and Chenghua. Thus a great variety of chinaware has developed. In point of antiquity, the bronze or copper vessels would be best. Among the porcelain, Chai and Ju [Chaiyao and Juyao] are priceless because they do not exist any more. Therefore the Kuanyao, Koyao, Shuanteh, and Tingyao rank among the best and most valuable today. The Lungchuan [Celadon], Changsheng, Wuni, and Chenghua rank next.†

There are ancient bronze jars, and Lungchuan and Chunchow vases of a very big size, two or three feet high, which have no other use. In winter, they can be used for big sprays of the plum

---

* Practically no one has seen a Tang porcelain, by which is meant high-fired enamel-coated vessels. The Chinese earthenware dated back to prehistoric times. But already in A.D. 950, we have the famous Chai ware, extremely thin and delicate, which presupposes an earlier development. The chinaware mentioned here begins with Chai and ends with Chenghua (1465–1487).

† Koyao and Kuanyao are Sung. In general, Sung ware (twelfth century) is monochrome, sometimes bluish green, like Kuanyao or Lungchuan, but especially valued is its white, such as Tingyao, with faint markings of different kinds. Bright-colored porcelain was introduced in the Ming wares, such as Shuanteh and Chenghua (fifteenth century).

flower, but sulfur must be thrown into the water [to prevent cracking from ice formations].

2. DIFFERENT FLOWERS, GRADED FOR BEAUTY
[omitted]

3. CUTTING

Flowers should be cut from near-by gardens in early morning with the dew on them, chosen from the half-blooms. Thus their fragrance and color will keep for several days. If cut after the sun is high up and the dew is gone, they will last only one or two days, besides having less brilliance and fragrance.

In cutting flowers, choose the twig for its bend and posture, perhaps fuller on top than below, weighted on the right or on the left, or curling together, or straggling and curving in one direction. Or a branch may perhaps stand out boldly alone, full and round both on top and below. In putting them in the vase, see that they bend or turn up, or incline or stand straight, in a harmonious grouping and height, so that each seems to say something, such as the postures chosen by artists for painting. Thus their natural beauty may be preserved. A straight, full, and shaggy twig of flowers cannot be considered in this art of *chingkung* [vase arrangements].

All flowers whether grown on trees or grass can be used for vases. But in picking them, soft branches must be picked with the hand, while stiff boughs must be cut with shears. A lover of flowers will bear this in mind.

Stiff branches (suggesting rugged strength or character) are easy to choose. The most difficult to choose are flowers from grass bushes. Unless one has seen a great many famous paintings, the arrangement easily becomes common.

4. VASE ARRANGEMENTS

As soon as a branch is cut, it should be quickly put in a vase with a small neck, which must be stuffed up to keep the vital force [*chi*] contained in it. Thus it will last several days.

Generally, the flowers should match with the vase in size, being slightly higher than it. For example, if the vase is one foot, the flowers should stand one foot and three or four inches from its mouth. If the vase is six or seven inches, the flowers should show eight or nine inches, to give an agreeable effect. If too high, the jar easily topples over, and if too low, the arrangement will lack elegance.

With flowers for small vases, the idea is that they should look slender and well formed, and should never be stuffy or over-crowded. If only one branch is placed, choose one which has an enticing posture with a twisting movement. If two branches are placed, one must be lower than the other, with the effect that they seem to come out from the same branch, or so arrange them that each branch faces a certain direction and they seem to fit in as one living branch. A binding twine must be used to fix their relative positions.

Although one always tries to avoid a stuffy effect, it is equally true that there must not be too few or too small flowers for the vase. Where such is the case, surround it with small slender twigs around the base of the arrangement. That will save the situation.

Only one or two kinds of flowers should be used for one vase. A little mixture of more kinds will make the arrangement confusing and disagreeable. Exceptions here are the autumn flowers.

5. FEEDING AND CARE

Flowers in nature get their nourishment from the dew. Therefore one should best use rain water, which is similar in nature to the dew. In some cases, honey or boiled water may be used. The artist must suit the nourishment to the particular needs.

The first important thing is to have a jar of collected rain water. In default of this, clear water from a lake or river may be used. Well water should be avoided because it contains salt and is bad for the flowers.

The water in the vase mostly contains poison. Therefore the water should be changed every morning to make the flowers last. They wither easily in two or three days if the water is not changed.

At night, the vase may stand in the open where it is sheltered from wind. Thus it will keep for several days. This is like *ginseng* [root for long life] provided by nature.

6. SPECIAL NEEDS OF DIFFERENT FLOWERS

The dark plum flower* — cauterize the point where it is cut, and wrap it up with clay.

The tree peony [*mutan*] — heat the broken joint with lamplight until it is soft.

The gardenia — lightly hammer its roots until they are frayed, and rub in a little salt.

The lotus — tie up the bottom with tangled hair and wrap it up in a ball of clay.

The cherry apple — wrap the bottom up with mint leaves and soak it in water.

Outside these few kinds, flowers can be cut and placed in vases without more ado. The tree peony takes honey well, and the honey will not be affected by it. By using boiled water with bamboo twigs, the hollyhock, the touch-me-not, and the Indian lotus, the leaves will not wither [easily?].

7. THINGS TO AVOID

Generally there are six things to avoid: (a) use of well water, (b) neglect in changing water, (c) handling with greasy hands, (d) injury by cats and mice, (e) contact with tobacco smoke or lamp smoke, and (f) a completely closed room with no movement of air. Any one of these things is bad for the flowers.

* I have never seen this flower abroad. The fruit is of the dark plum variety. There are two Chinese kinds, the *li*, which is light-colored, and the *mei*, which is dark. This flower of the *Prunus* genus is highly prized not only because it blooms in snow with pale pink flowers, but also because it has a singular beauty in having stiff and slightly twisted branches, and flowers standing on the branch without leaves, suggesting cool independence of spirit, pointing out straight into the cool air. It has also a very subtle fragrance. Chinese poetry and paintings associate it with moonlight shadows and snow. Its elegance of posture is similar to a twig of quince, or to forsythia which has light yellow blossoms like *lamei*, which is winter sweet.

8. PROTECTION OF THE VASE

In winter [when the water in a vase may freeze] there are no good flowers except the narcissus, the winter sweet [*lamei*], and the dark plum [*mei*]. Here wide-mouthed vessels, like ancient wine goblets or wine jars, should be used, and an inner tube made of tin placed inside it containing water for the flowers so as to avoid cracking. When a small vase is used, put some sulfur in the water and keep it near a southern window near the sun in the daytime and put it near the bed at night to prevent freezing. Another way is to use unsalted meat juice, having taken care to remove the fat first. Thus the flowers will blossom without injury to the container.

When boiled water is used for certain flowers, first keep a certain amount in an ordinary jar, keeping its mouth closed tightly. Wait until it is cool, then put it into the vase with rain water so that the vase will not crack. Be sure to remember this, or a valuable vase may be so spoiled.

49 ▩ How To Enjoy Birds

Letter to

BROTHER MO, FROM "FAMILY LETTERS"

Cheng Panchiao
1693 - 1765

« Cheng Panchiao was famous for his paintings of bamboo, of which I am the fortunate owner of one. He was even more loved and admired for his great simplicity of living, his contempt for officialdom, and his love and compassion, of which this letter is a good example. I have translated all sixteen of his family letters in The Wisdom of China and India. This man had a true sense of values. (See also selection 96 by this wonderful man.)

My only son was born to me in my fifty-second year. Of course, I love him, but there is a correct way of loving one's children. Even in games, he should be taught to show the heart of mercy and generosity, and avoid cruelty. What I hate most is to have caged birds; we enjoy them while they are shut up in prison. What justification is there that we are entitled to thwart the instincts of animals to please our own nature? As for tying up a dragonfly by the hair or tying a crab with a piece of string, it affords the children some fun only for a little while, and soon the little thing is dead. Now nature creates all things and nourishes them all. Even an ant or an insect comes from the combination of forces of the *yin* and *yang* and the five elements. God also loves them dearly in his heart, and we who are supposed to be the crown of all creation cannot even sympathize with God's heart. How then is the animal world going to have a place of refuge?

Snakes and centipedes, tigers, leopards, and wolves are most dangerous animals. But since Heaven has given birth to them, what right
have we to take their lives? If they were all meant to be killed, then
why in the first place did Heaven give them life? All we can do is
to drive them far away so that they shall not harm us. What wrong
has the spider committed by spinning its web? Some kill them without mercy on the fairy tale that they curse the moon or that they
may make the walls crumble down. On what authority is such a
statement based, by which we kill animals' lives? Will this do?
Will this do? As I am away from home, you should watch over my
son. Develop his heart of kindness and stop his cruelties. Don't
spare him because he is your nephew, and not your son. The children of our servants are also a part of humankind. We should be
equally kind to them and should not permit our children to bully
them. When there are fish or eatables, we must also share them
with their children and see them happy and jump about. If our
own children are eating and let the servants' children stand far
away looking on, their parents will see it and, while pitying them
and being unable to help them, will shout to them to go away. Is
this not heart-rending for the parents? Now to be a scholar and be
a college graduate or a doctor is a small thing; the important thing
is to be reasonable and be a good man. Read this to sister-in-law
Kuo and sister-in-law Jao, and let them know that there is a proper
and an improper way of loving their children.

Postscript: Regarding what I have just said about not keeping birds
in cages, I must say that I always love birds, but that there is a
proper way of doing it. One who loves birds should plant trees, so
that the house shall be surrounded with hundreds of shady
branches and be a country and a home for birds. Thus, at dawn,
when we wake up from sleep and are still tossing about in bed, we
hear a chorus of chirping voices like a celestial harmony. And when
we get up and are putting on our gowns or washing our faces or
gargling our mouths or sipping the morning tea, we see their
gorgeous plumes flitting about. Before we have time to look at

one, we are attracted by another. This is a pleasure that far exceeds that of keeping one bird in a cage. Generally the enjoyment of life should come from a view regarding the universe as a park, and the rivers and streams as a pond, so that all beings can live in accordance with their nature. Great indeed is such happiness! How shall the keeping of a bird in a cage or a fish in a jar be compared with it in generosity of spirit and in kindness?

50 🀒 The Origin and Preparation of Tea

From

THE BOOK OF TEA (CHACHING)

Lu Yu

C. A.D. 740 - 804

« *The following consists of excerpts from the Book of Tea as abridged in the Commentary with Additions edition by Chen Chien of the Ming Dynasty, written in 1475. Lu Yu's book, which is well preserved, became the classic on tea and gave many details on the growth and preparation of tea, utensils used, regions where particular brands were grown, etc. Chen Chien made many additions. However, only extracts are given here which are thought to be of interest to the general public. One interesting difference between the earlier and the later author is that at the time of the eighth-century author there existed tea bricks, consisting of tea ground into powder and pressed into bricks, whereas in the Ming Dynasty this method of preparing tea for general use was eliminated. Such tea bricks were convenient for transportation, and in the eleventh and twelfth centuries there existed regular "Horse-and-Tea Bureaus" on China's northwest borders. The tribes in Chinese Turkestan had come to like tea and used to barter horses for tea. There was then a regular trade in tea under government license known as chayin. Another peculiarity in the early use of tea, as mentioned in Lu Yu's book and elsewhere, was that among some people tea was taken with salt. Su Tungpo confirmed this custom in his native province of Szechuen. Sometimes tea was mixed with ginger, and cinnamon, and among the Mongols with mare's milk and in Tibet with fried rice flour, which is the staple food of Tibetans up to this day. The Ming authors highly disapproved of adding anything to tea, not even jasmin or other flowers.*

The TEA PLANT [Thea, of the same genus as the camellia] is like *kualu* [variety of camellia]. Its flowers are white like the white rambling rose. The best kind grows on rocks, the middle quality on rocky soil. Those that grow wild are the best; those cultivated are second in quality. They grow best on cliffs facing south near dark forests. The purple variety is best, the green next to it. The bud-shaped are the best, the tiny sprouts next to them. Curled leaves are the best; flat leaves are next to them.

Among the utensils used are different kinds of baskets for picking, caldrons and double boilers [for frying and steaming], mortars and pestles [for pounding and grinding into powder], molds and fixtures and rollers [for making bricks, discarded in Ming times], and various bamboo sieves — three feet long, two and a half feet wide, with a handle of five inches — with holes of different fineness for sorting the leaves. A double-decker drying stack for drying them is made of wood. When the leaves are half dry, they are placed on the lower deck, and when completely dry, on the upper deck. [Speaking of tea bricks] a big "string" [put through with a hole in it] weighs one catty, a middle one half a catty [or eight Chinese ounces], and a small one four ounces. A drying apparatus consists of a box with wooden frame and bamboo matting, with a cover on top and a bottom with a door on the side for placing inside it a vessel containing slow-burning charcoal. In the moldy season of Kiangnan, tea is dried by charcoal fire.

Tea is picked in March, April, and May [Western calendar]. The bud type grows on the surface of rocks and is four or five inches tall, picked when the tiny buds are beginning to unfold in the early morning. The sprout type grows in bushes, with three, four, or five branches. One should pick the central stalk, going especially for the tiny sprouts. It is not picked on a rainy day or when the air is saturated with cloud vapor (as is often the case on hilltops). After picking, it is steamed, then roasted, then pierced through and packaged.

Spring water is best [for making tea], next rain water, and next well water. Among spring waters, those that come in swift, clear currents over rocks can be used. River water must be taken from places far removed from close human habitation. In well water, wells that are constantly being drawn from are preferred.

In boiling water to make tea, the stage when tiny bubbles begin to form with a little singing noise is called the "first boil." The second stage is when a series of bigger bubbles begin to form around the edge [of the container], and the third stage is when the water forms billows. It must be taken off the fire at once, or the water becomes too "old" and the tea is spoiled.*

« A Note on Tea. The treatise goes on to enumerate the earliest historical references to tea, books on it, and paintings of tea preparation and tea culture.

What seems to me should be the conclusion regarding the discovery of the use of tea is as follows: There was mention of the tea plant in the first and second centuries A.D., but no clear indication that it was used as a drink in Yang Shiung (53 B.C.–A.D. 18), Shuowen by Shu Shen (c. A.D. 100) and in Erhya (Han Period).

In the third century A.D. there was the first clear indication of drinking tea in Chang Hua's Powuchih — "When true tea is drunk, it keeps one awake." This was the period of the Three Kingdoms and early Chin. Tea was regarded as a delicacy. Wei Yao of Wu District was "secretly given tea to take the place of wine." Liu Kun also wrote to his brother to send him tea, which was not at the time obtainable everywhere.

The indication is that tea was first in use in Wu (modern Shanghai region), although the tea plant of another variety was known in Szechuen.

Beginning from the year A.D. 300, tea came into clear evidence as a drink. Emperor Hui (reigned, A.D. 290–306) was given tea to drink on returning to his capital. The year 307 is crucial in that it marks the invasion of the northern hordes and the migration of many Chinese south of the Yangtse, chiefly around the Wu region. One man, on crossing the river, was laughed at for

* It is possible that here the absolute boiling point is to be avoided before water is poured into the pot, in order to preserve the aroma.

not knowing tea. Also in the Wu region, we find the first mention of a man making a lot of money from selling tea as a drink in the streets in the time of Emperor Yuan of Chin Dynasty (reigned, A.D. 317–322). By this and the following century, it became common to use the phrase "tea and fruit." And this went on during the Southern Dynasties with the capital at Nanking (A.D. 420–588).

It is interesting to note that the words for tea in English and French come from the southern pronunciation of the Chinese word, as seen in the Amoy dialect pronunciation of tay (like the French thé) which was also the earlier English pronunciation of the word "tea." In Russia, whose tea came from northwest China, from Hankow north, the northern mandarin pronunciation of the same word, cha is used. In Cantonese, again, the word is pronounced cha, which accounts for the Portuguese form, chá.

51 回 The Nine-blessings Couch

Ting Shiungfei
17th century

SINCE MY RETIREMENT LAST YEAR, I have stopped all social activities and am doing a great deal of sitting quietly by myself. I have thought that what I really need is a good couch on which to take up my sitting with crossed legs like a Buddhist monk, all else being unnecessary luxury. One day I saw a good, firm couch in the place of one of my friends and loved it. My friend forthwith gave it to me as a present. I was delighted with it and had it put in the center of Peaceful Mind Hall. With a coil of burning incense, and letting the curtains down, I feel it is so spacious and comfortable that I seem to have left the world far behind me. I thought of Mr. Lai Chutang, generations ago, who after long years of study of Taoism had been able to dismiss all worries from his mind. With such a peaceful mind he always had a perfect sleep, and he counted his blessings, which were nine in number, and called his bed by that name. Today I have counted my blessings, too, while resting in bed. They are as follows: I am happy that (1) I have a good collection of books; (2) that I have a wife who loves reading and writing; (3) that I cannot drink; (4) that I do not understand chess; (5) that nobody wants me; (6) that I have found a famous master; (7) that I am able to live with my family in such beautiful surroundings; (8) that I am free from sickness; and (9) that though I am still under fifty, I am able to delegate all matters to my sons and live like a free bird. Thus I am able to take after the example of Mr. Lai, who lived less than a hundred years ago, and both of us have found our happiness in a couch. This couch shall go down to posterity as "the Nine-blessings Couch."

256

I note also here that what Mr. Lai called his nine blessings were the following: (1) that he was born in China; (2) that he lived in time of peace; (3) that as a Confucianist he came to hear the teachings of Tao; (4) that both his parents and his elder brother lived a long life; (5) that his children's marriages were early arranged and completed; (6) that he had no concubine; (7) that he had already reached beyond the age of sixty; (8) that he was born of a mild, easygoing disposition; and (9) that he suffered from no ugly disease.

» *The Taoist Chang Shingkung wrote a comment, counting his own nine blessings, seemingly all opposite the above writer's, which shows that all is a matter of point of view.*

Comment by Master Chang Shingkung: I have also nine things which I am happy about: (1) that I have so few books in my possession; (2) that I have no wife who loves to bother with reading and writing; (3) that I can drink when I like, and indulge in talk while drinking; (4) that I love to play chess, or watch others playing in silence; (5) that I have gradually come to overcome my dislike of common people; (6) that I have found a master, and also that I can also go without a master; (7) that I travel without the family; (8) that I love to be sick which gives me time for some deep thinking; and (9) that my children are married and deeply in love.

» *A true Taoist would give the palm to the writer of the comment. For he is already a master of himself in whatever circumstances.*

52 📖 The Arts of Sleeping, Walking, Sitting, and Standing

From

THE ARTS OF LIVING (SHIENCHING OUCHI)

Li Liweng
1611 - 1679

« *I have selected here three sections from Li Liweng's interesting chapter in* The Arts of Living *on the enjoyment of daily living. (See introductory note, selection 40.)*

THERE ARE MANY WAYS of enjoying life that are hard to hold down to any one theory. There are the joys of sleeping, of sitting, of walking, and of standing up. There is the pleasure in eating, washing up, hairdressing, and even in such lowly activities as going about naked and barefooted, or going to the toilet. In its proper place, each can be enjoyable. If one can enter into the spirit of fun and take things in his stride anywhere any time, one can enjoy some things over which others may weep. On the other hand, if one is a crude person and awkward in meeting life or taking care of one's health, he can be the saddest person amidst song and dance. I speak here only of the joys of daily living and of the ways in which advantage may be taken of the commonest occupations.

1. THE ART OF SLEEPING

There was a yogi who traveled about, teaching the secrets of conservation of life force and of prolonging life, and he wanted to teach me. I asked him what he could do to attain longevity and where such blessings were to be found. I thought it would be fine if his methods agreed with my way of thinking, and if not, I could at least befriend him.

This man told me that the secret of longevity lay in controlled breathing, and peace of mind was to be sought through séance. I said to him, "Your ways are hard and forced, and only people like you can practice it. I am lazy and like motion. I seek joy in everything. I am afraid it is not for me."

"What is your way then?" he asked. "I should like to hear it and we can compare notes."

And this is what I said to him:

In the natural scheme of things, it is meant for man to spend half his time in activity and half at rest. In the day, he sits, moves, or stands, and at night he rests. If a man labors by day and does not rest by night and continues this day after day, you can get ready and wait for his funeral to pass by. I try to keep my health by dividing half my time in rest and half my time in activity. If something troubles me and prevents me from sleep, there's the danger signal! I should count my remaining years on my fingers!

In other words, the secret of good health lies in a good and restful sleep. One who sleeps well restores his energy, revitalizes his inner system, and tones up his muscles. Compare a sick man with a healthy person. A man who is not permitted to rest will get sick; his eyes become sunken, and all kinds of symptoms appear. A sick man becomes worse without sleep. But after a good sleep, he wakes up full of eagerness for life again. Is not sleep the infallible miracle drug, not just a cure for one illness but for a hundred, a cure that saves a thousand lives? To seek health by controlled breathing and the hard exercises of yoga would only involve great concentration and effort to keep awake instead! Would I throw away the best medicine in the world for an untested formula?

The man left in anger and I did not argue with him.

An ancient poem goes, "After a long, sound sleep in bamboo-shaded quiet, I feel so far removed from the day's turmoil. If the hermit of Huashan comes to visit me, I shall not ask for the secret of becoming an immortal, but of sleeping well." A modern saying goes, "First rest your mind, then rest your eyes."

There is a proper time and a proper place for sleep, and there are certain sleeping habits which should be avoided. To be specific, one should rest between 9 P.M. and 8 A.M. To go to bed before nine is too early; it is a bad sign to be craving for sleep like a sick person. To sleep after eight in the morning is bad for health, like all oversleeping. Where would be the time left for other pleasures? I know a friend who never gets up before noon, and anyone visiting him before noon is kept waiting. One day I sat miserably in his parlor waiting, and with ink and brush ready, I playfully parodied an ancient poem and wrote as follows:

> I am busy sleeping,
> Throughout the whole morn.
> If I live to seventy,
> Five and thirty are gone.

Although it was done in fun, it is close to the truth. One should only sleep at night as a rule. The pleasure of an afternoon nap is understandable, but it should be reserved only for summer when the day is long and the night is short. It is natural that one tires easily in the heat, and it is as good for a man to sleep when tired as to drink when thirsty. This is common sense. The best time is after lunch. One should wait a while until the food is partly digested and then leisurely stroll toward the couch. Do not tell yourself that you are determined to get a nap. In that way, the mind is tense and the sleep will not be sound. Occupy yourself wtih something first and before it is finished, you are overcome with a sense of fatigue and the sandman calls. The never-never land cannot be chased down. I love that line in a poem which says, "Dozing off, the book slips out of my hand." Thus sleep comes without his artifice or knowledge. This is the secret of the art of sleeping.

Next, one must consider the place, which should be cool and quiet. If it is not quiet, the eyes rest but not the ears. If it is too hot, the soul rests but not the body, and body and soul are at loggerheads. This goes against the principle of good health.

Lastly, we will consider the sleeper himself. Some people are busy, and others have plenty of time. Logically, the man of leisure needs little sleep; it is the busy man who needs it most of all. But often the busy man cannot sleep well. He rests his eyes in sleep but not his mind. In fact, he gets no rest from sleep at all. The worst of it is to think of something during the half-awake hours of the morning and suddenly remember something he hasn't done or someone he hasn't seen. It is very, very important! He must not sleep another wink or something will be spoiled! That very thought drives away all sleep. He becomes tense and gets up more keyed up than before. The man of leisure rests his mind before his eyes are shut, and his mind wakes up refreshed before his eyes are open, happy to slumber and happier to wake up. Such is the sleep of the man of leisure.

Yet in this world how many such men are there? All men cannot lead a life with nothing to do. Therefore a method must be found. It is best to dispose of the urgent business of the day in the morning, and delegate to others those things that are not finished. Then one knows that everything is in order and under control. He can afford to seek the pillow and go for that slumber which is described as the "dark, sweet village." He will then sleep as well as the man of leisure.

Another thing: to enjoy a perfect sleep requires a peaceful conscience. Such a man will not be "frightened when there is a knock on the door at midnight," as the saying goes. He will not mistake the peckings of chickens in the barnyard for policemen's footsteps!

2. THE ART OF WALKING

The rich man will go out only in a horse and carriage. It may be called a comfort and a luxury, but it can hardly be said that it fulfills the intention of God in giving man a pair of legs. He who does not use his legs is *ipso facto* deprived of the use of his legs. On the other hand, a man who uses his legs is giving exercise to his entire body. That is why an ancient poor scholar* boasted that "a leisurely stroll is as good as a drive." Now to drive or to go on foot are both methods of transportation or locomotion. A man who is used to driving or riding on horseback can learn to enjoy the pleasures of a walk. Perhaps he comes upon a beautiful view or beautiful flowers on the way, or stops to talk with a peasant in his palm hat or meets a recluse philosopher turned woodcutter in the deep mountains. Sometimes one might enjoy a drive, and sometimes a walk. Surely this is better than the obstinacy of that proud scholar of ancient days!

What the poor man can be truly proud of is not the fact that he uses his legs, but that he does not depend on others for going anywhere. If he is not in a hurry, he can go slowly, and if he is, he breaks into a run. He does not have to wait for someone else, and he is not dependent on the carriage, unlike the rich man who is helpless when the driver is not there. The poor man has fulfilled the intentions of God in giving him legs to walk with. It makes me happy just to think of this.

3. THE ART OF SITTING

No one knows the art of living better than Confucius. I know this from the statement that he "did not sleep like a corpse [with straight legs] and did not sit like a statue." If the Master had been completely absorbed in keeping decorum, intent on appearing like a gentleman at all hours and being seen as a sage at all times, then he would have had to lie down like a corpse and sit like a statue. His four limbs and his internal system would never have been able to relax. How could such a stiff wooden statue expect to live a long life? Because Confucius did not do this, the statement describes the ease of the Master in his private life, which makes him worthy of worship as the father of all cultured gentlemen. We should follow Confucius's example when at home. Do not sit erect and look severe as if you were chained or

* Yen Cho, of the third century B.C. He was a Diogenes who refused gifts of money and power from a king.

glued to the chair. Hug your knee and sing, or sit chin in hand, without honoring it with the phrase of "losing oneself in thought" [as Chuangtse said]. On the other hand, if a person sits stiffly for a long time, head high and chest out, this is a premonition that he is heading for the grave. He is sitting for his memorial portrait!

4. THE ART OF STANDING

Stand straight, but do not do it for long. Otherwise, all leg muscles will become stiff and circulation will be blocked up. Lean on something! — on an old pine or a quaint rock, or on a balcony or on a bamboo cane. It makes one look like one is in a painting. But do *not* lean on a lady! The foundation is not solid and the roof may come down!

53 ▣ Hints to Hosts and Guests

Shen Chungying
c. 1600?

« *A great many treatises bearing this name (Shangcheng) and relating to wine dinners have been written, among which I select the following as the best.*

ONE SHOULD DRINK WITHIN ONE'S LIMITS when on an excursion to dangerous high places, when on a voyage, when the ground is full of thistles, when something important has to be attended to on the morrow, when traveling alone without servants, and when recently recovered from an illness.

Sometimes a host spends a great deal of money on food and fails to provide good wine. Would it not be more sensible to save some money from the food and provide good wine?

The object of a friendly dinner is to enjoy oneself. Sometimes while a wine game is going on, a guest does not pay attention, and when it comes to his turn, he is at a complete loss as to what it is all about, which spoils the fun.

Sometimes a host counts on some guests not turning up and arranges the places accordingly. An awkward situation arises when there are more guests than places for them, causing last-minute confusion, which is damnable.

Guests should leave when it is just right. Some guests overstay their welcome, causing great inconvenience to the host and his servants. This is especially hard in extreme cold or hot weather.

Wine served at a dinner should be uniform. Sometimes strong

wine is followed by light, or the two come together mixed or improperly warmed up. This is considered bad service.

To descend upon a dinner uninvited or without being expected is permissible only among the best of friends. Sometimes such intrusion is disgusting, particularly when associated with taking too much liberty. The guests can only wink at each other to show their disgust. Why does anyone want to lose his self-respect?

There are people whom you have never met at dinners but who grow suddenly very hospitable because they want to ask you a favor. After their object is accomplished, they forget all about you again. Such people should be avoided.

One cannot feel too happy about a party where the guests break up in a hurry, perhaps on account of rain or snow, or because of a long distance to travel, or to get into the city before the closing time.

It is not nice to see some guests nibble at the fruit or cold dishes before the others have come. But it may be the host's fault when a dinner is held up because the guest of honor is late and the host fails to give something to quell the hunger for his first guests.

I do not know when the finger-guessing game started. But it is just a pastime, enjoyable only when people do not cheat in timing or use tricks. Otherwise, it is not worth while.

Good servants help to attend to the service and can follow intelligently a wine game. Servants who steal food or drinks, or are uncouth and rude, or have disgusting manners, only spoil the dinner.

It is a pity when there is a good wine game and no worthy participants, or when a good drinker does not find one with equal capacity to keep him company.

Sometimes a guest is fined to drink, but cannot take it. He begs to be allowed to drink the next time, which is a good idea for both host and guest. Sometimes the officer of the game insists on his drinking until the man throws up. This is very silly.

I do not approve of a host who does not urge his guests to drink or fails to provide dice, nor do I approve of stuffy guests who are strict on principles and refuse to take part in wine games.

There are some people who give a dinner in expectation of being invited in return and who like to compare the lavishness of dinners, as if their lives depended upon such trifles. That is a form of vulgarity.

Guests and host should be neither too formal nor too informal. Some guests decline to take even a low seat and hold up the dinner with their false modesty, or a host provides a too meager dinner while he gorges himself without regard to his guests. This is damnable.

Sometimes guests meet those who are from different professions. They make themselves ridiculous by dropping names or talking about their official affairs. The same thing is true of successful candidates of the government examinations who like to harp about their taking degrees.

If a host cannot drink himself, he should ask some of the guests who can to take his place at dinner to prevent the dinner from getting too dull. There is not much fun in sitting to a sumptuous dinner in a freezing atmosphere.

Some rich or influential people make a show of cordiality at dinner and make all sorts of promises which they promptly forget. Some other people try to ingratiate themselves at table. Both kinds are despicable.

It is a point of bad manners when the guests leave each other after dinner without a friendly feeling, or do not offer to take those without transportation in their carriages or boats. But of course drunken guests or objectionable persons should be avoided.

One should not treat monks when they are at table any differently from the others or make fun of their religion. It is neither good form nor sensible behavior.

There may be less well-read persons among the guests. One should not be too critical of them. For men are born differently, some more intelligent than others. A cultured man will be nice to all.

One should guard against using unrefined language, or use of abusive language, or misbehaving under the pretense of drunkenness, or making a scene.

Some people are too free and easy and keep on demanding more and more of the food which they like. This is bad manners.

One should have regard for one's neighbors at table. Some guests spread their arms about and drink like oxen without regard for those sitting next to them. Such conduct is hateful.

A cultured gentleman tries to avoid the following: incoherent and silly talk when drunk, putting things back on the plate, pouring wine back into the bottle, bringing too many attendants with him without consideration for the host.

Excuse and allowance must be made for a host on busy occasions like a wedding or a funeral when he cannot be expected to attend to all details of the guests' comfort.

A birthday is, according to the ancients, a painful day of labor for the mother. On such a day, or when celebrating a baby's first full month, one should try not to be extravagant, and should avoid slaughter of animals, as a religious consideration.

When a party is held in a garden, it is bad manners to allow the servants to pick flowers and fruit and break branches.

Rich men seldom invite their poor relatives to dinner. But when they meet another wealthy person, or a V.I.P. or a notorious racketeer or a popular courtesan, they entertain most lavishly. It is their folly.

Snobs show themselves at once at dinner parties. It is seen in the way they listen to and show respect to some important guest, or even to a vulgar, illiterate millionaire. Or some young people show no respect for elders or behave as if they were not present. These are all signs of lack of culture.

There are dinners given when one does not pause to reflect how sad it is, such as a dinner given to yamen runners and employees during a lawsuit, when the host perhaps has to sell his child to provide such entertainment. Equally sad is the dinner given by a squanderer of a family fortune, without the host realizing how sad it really is.

Sometimes the guests become very uncomfortable when the wine games are too strictly carried out by the umpire, or badly carried out, with the result that good drinkers have no chance to drink and others are made to drink beyond their capacity. Or sometimes the umpire is not at his job and lets everything go to pieces.

It can happen that a guest of honor cannot drink. He must exercise restraint upon himself and allow others to enjoy themselves.

At wedding dinners, one should be especially careful to see that one does not bring along servants who may make drunken scenes. The same is true of dinners given by families involved in a lawsuit.

It is necessary to have an umpire or presiding officer to see that wine games proceed in order, especially when there are many guests. But it is not proper to have another deputy umpire, or even a supervisor to supervise the presiding officer.

It is a most exasperating thing to have to send servants to urge invited guests to come who will not come until they are sent for again and again. From noon till sundown, the servants run till their legs are tired, those looking for their appearance wait until their eyes are tired, the other guests wait in hunger, and the host is embarrassed about whether to ask the guests to be seated at table or not.

Guests are sometimes invited to meet a guest of honor, and the host depends upon their co-operation. Sometimes guests who have been notified in time arrive late after the guest of honor, or others join in making cruel demands upon the host. Such drunks are beneath contempt.

It is also annoying to see a host unprepared or short of things when the guests have arrived.

Dinner should be given according to one's means and station.

One can foretell that a well-to-do family which is unduly stingy with its food cannot amount to much in the future, and also that a common scholar who is too extravagant is not going to keep up for long.

At a dinner with new relatives or children, one should not talk of poetry and history, which will embarrass those who cannot follow.

One gives dinners and entertainments according to what is suitable to one's means. One should not waste, nor just blindly follow custom. To be stingy when one should spend and to spend when it is not necessary are both out of place.

A man sometimes promises gifts or dinners when he is drunk and forgets all about it. And he may make this into a habit. He is not conscious of it, but to others he can be very tiring.

It does not speak of good manners when one is a vegetarian and does not make it known until he is seated at table and refuses to touch this or that. Then the host or the other guests find out, and it puts the host in a most awkward position of having to produce something suitable on the spot.

A dinner may become very dull when there is no challenge to drink among the guests. On the other hand, when two guests get too engrossed in their mutual challenges, the other guests may be neglected. Both the host and his guests should use some tact to bring about a change.

54 ▣ Fashions in Cuisine

From

THREE CUSTOMS AND TEN SINS
(SAN FENG SHIH CHIEN CHI);
A FRAGMENT

Anonymous
probably 17th century

« *The above is one of the two surviving fragments of a book found presumably in Soochow. It is not found in any other collection except Shuoku, edited by Wang Tao (1828–1897). Wang Tao was the scholar whom James Legge depended upon for the translation of the Chinese Classics in the Sacred Books of the East. Wang Tao was involved in the Taiping Rebellion in the mid-century, and after its defeat lived as a political refugee in Hong Kong. He traveled to England and was well received in church circles. He was really a great scholar. It is a pity that he did not indicate how the manuscript was discovered, or whether he had found only these two fragments which he published. The book is a record of changing social customs, mostly wicked, of the Soochow-Changshu region. The other fragment, which is not translated here, deals with a woman of notorious morals who ruined almost all the families in the village and who even in her sixties bewitched young men with her charms. Wang Tao merely indicates that the author lived in the Manchu Dynasty (after 1644). From internal evidence, it seems he lived around 1675.*

IN THE *Yangku Manlu* by Hung Shun of Sung Dynasty, (c. twelfth century), there is a story about a female cook. It says that in the capital, the middle and lower classes preferred to have daughters rather than sons. Every time a girl was born, she was carefully brought up and protected like a jewel. When she began to grow up, she was given training in some special line according to her talent, so that her service would be wanted by the rich families. These young women for household service were classified into several kinds, such as "personal maids," "skilled women," "sewing women," "housekeepers," "actresses," "washing women," "musicians," "cooks" etc. These were all sharply divided professions, and among these the lowest was that of a female cook. But, even so, only the most wealthy families could afford to keep them.

The story is told of the experience of one official who employed such a female cook. There was a certain magistrate who came from a poor family and who had filled posts in several districts. His habits were frugal, and when he was back home on account of his parent's mourning period,* he was short of servants and his food was badly prepared. He remembered that once at the capital he had tasted an extraordinary supper at the home of a friend, prepared by a *chuniang* [female cook]. There happened to be someone going to the capital and he sent a letter to a friend asking that he look for one for him. Most of them would not leave the capital, but some time later his friend wrote him that he had secured one *chuniang*. She was just over twenty and had recently left a high official's home, had great skill and was quite pretty, and understood writing and arithmetic. He was sending the girl down south immediately. In less than a month's time she arrived. At the suburb station, she sent her husband† ahead with a note in her own handwriting. Her calligraphy was very good and well formed. It began

* Every official, including a prime minister, had to resign for three years during the period of mourning for a parent's death. Concealment of such a funeral and continuing in office, when exposed, would be a very serious crime in the eyes of the law. Nothing of importance to the state could excuse breaking the Confucian custom of loyalty to one's parents. It was practically considered obscene.
† In the other fragment the author notes that when the Mongol Dynasty collapsed, the Mongol soldiers were segregated. Their women soon earned more money than their husbands, who waited outside rich men's homes to take them home.

with the usual polite phrases about how happy she was to come
to serve him and to begin service that very day, etc., and at the
end begged him to send a soft sedan chair to receive her so as to
keep up proper form. It was couched in a very refined language,
not what a common woman would be able to write. The magistrate
was greatly delighted. When she entered the house, her deportment and manners were perfect. She was in a red jacket and green
skirts and bowed to the others and retired. This was more than
the magistrate had expected, and all his friends proposed that they
should have a dinner to celebrate. On her part, the woman was
anxious to show her skill. The magistrate told her that he would
give a formal dinner later, but for the present he would like to
have a small household dinner with five courses of "five-inch"
[small] dishes. The woman asked for his orders in the way of meat
and vegetables, and the magistrate wrote them down and gave the
list to her, asking among other things for lamb's head and *pâté d'ail*
[garlic paste]. The cook took the order, then opened her writing
case and wrote down the things to be bought [by other servants].
In this list she put down ten lambs' heads and five catties of garlic,
the other things in proportion. The owner thought that that was
a great deal but did not want to make her think that he was stingy.
When the foodstuff was all bought, the cook opened her baggage
and took out her kitchenware, consisting of various pans, spoons,
big and small, soup plates, etc., and asked a maid to show them to
the master. They were beautiful and shining, consisting all of
"white copper,"* each vessel worth about twenty taels of silver.
The other kitchen utensils, like knives and chopping boards, were
also of a very fine quality. Everybody was impressed. Then she put
on her apron, with silver chains around her upper arms. With a
sweeping gesture, she entered the kitchen and sat on a large hard-
wood settee. Slowly she got up to prepare her food, handling her
knife most expertly. In preparing the lambs' heads, she had them
rinsed and put on a table, then began to pick the meat from the
jowls and threw all the rest away. On being asked, she said,

* Copper alloy with nickel in it, as mined in Yunnan.

"Gentlemen don't eat those things." The others picked up the thrown-away parts and put them away, and she laughed and said, "Are you people going to eat dog's food?" In preparing her garlic paste, she scalded the garlic with boiling water once, took off all the leafy parts, leaving the stem, which she cut up into lengths according to the diameter of the dish to be used. Again she peeled the outer layers and took only the yellowish, tender middle part. This she soaked in wine and salt, and threw all the rest away without stint. But her food was something of a dream, tasty and crisp and fragrant, and extremely neat in appearance. The friends cleaned up the plates and looked at each other in admiration. After dinner, the *chuniang* came in, made a double bow and said, "I am glad that my food meets with your approval. Please give the regular gratuity." The magistrate was embarrassed and did not know what to say. The *chuniang* suggested, "Why don't you follow the usual practice?" Then she took out several slips of paper from her coat pocket and presented them, saying, "This is what I used to get." The magistrate looked at it, and found that for a formal dinner she was given 10,000 cash and twenty pieces of silk, and half of that amount for a small dinner. The magistrate thought he was trapped and could only do what was demanded of him. In private he told his friends, "How can I afford to give such dinners and keep such a cook?" In about ten days, he dismissed her on some pretext.

This was the custom prevailing at the time of the Northern Sung when people were willing to spend money on food. Even thrifty people were sometimes forced to follow the custom. How much more so is it today? I have already recorded all the customs of keeping actresses and the songs and dance and entertainments under the head of "Customs of Professional Women." But even in worship of the dead, sacrifices of animals are made before the priests start to chant their prayers. In places of amusement, lavish and choice dinners are given before the songs and dances start. So a good dinner is the usual preliminary to song and dance. That is why I have included the matter of food under the category of "Customs of Professional Women."

[Concerning present-day customs] the attention to good food began in the city [Soochow or Changshu] with the pawnbroker Fang Shihmou. He gave extravagant dinners. In place of Sung porcelain dishes, which were considered too small, he used large bowls for keeping fish and in place of three-inch dishes he used big ones such as are used for holding Buddha's hands.* His "golden lacquer leg of pork" consisted of an entire leg which had been prepared with brown sugar and sweet sauce, served whole on the table. His "crystal leg of mutton," prepared with white sugar and white wine, was also served entire on the table. Roast chicken and duck were always served in pairs, also entire. Most of his other dishes were like that, and the rich families began to copy him. In the Ming Dynasty the regular custom was to serve only six courses, or even five, using small dishes, and sometimes there was a wooden dish, shaped like a fish with scales and all, containing some beans.† Now the custom has greatly changed.

Assistant Commissioner Chien was a rich man before he became an official and grew richer still. He loved to give dinners when he was at home. His wife was an expert cook, her dishes being distinguished by three qualities: novelty, delicacy [nongreasiness], and choiceness. Some of her famous dishes are the following:

LAMB KIDNEY

First take the raw kidney and cook it lightly with the skin on. Then take it out, skin it, and cut it into thin slices. Sauté it with crushed walnut until the walnut oil has penetrated the kidney. Add spices, old wine, and A-1 soy sauce. Fry in deep oil. Its taste is better even than bear's paw.‡ When lamb kidney cannot be obtained, pig kidney can be prepared in the same way.

* *Shiangyuan*, a large variety of citrus, with one end shaped like fingers.
† The custom still persisted in Honan, as I am informed by my friends. It is based upon a pun. The word for "fish" is *yu*, which also means "enough to spare." It was a lucky word to have enough to spare, and guests on coming to the end of the dinner would raise their chopsticks and say "we have enough to spare."
‡ Bear's paw is an old as Mencius (372–289 B.C.) but is still a delicacy in the Manchurian provinces. It is a cartilaginous substance, cooked until gluey like Provençal tripe, but is distinctly nongreasy.

TURTLE SKIRT

Take only turtle found in creeks, and not those from Kiangpei [north of the Yangtse, in Kiangsu]. Cook a little and cut the "skirt" [fleshy part with black skin] and peel off the black skin with a pair of pincers, leaving an absolutely clean white meat. Fry in crackling pork fat with ginger and cinnamon powder. It melts in the mouth and has a piquant aroma. The guests would not know that it was turtle meat. Therefore it was given a special name of *hun fenpi* [a gluey pâté, but made with meat].

STEAMED WILD DUCK

Domestic-fed duck which is fat and juicy is not uncommon. One must take wild duck caught with a net. Feather it clean. Take out the entrails and stuff it with sweet sauce,* soy sauce, and old wine. Sew up and wrap it on the outside with a freshly made *fuyi* [hardened sheet of bean curd].† Steam until thoroughly soft. Then skin it from neck to leg and open up the joints and bone it, leaving only the head and the legs. Cook this entire over a slow fire with spices, sweet sauce, soy sauce, and old wine along with its own juice until the sauce is almost dry. Then serve.

Other animals which are greasy, like the guinea hen, *tsihmao* [porcupine?], and eagle, should be steamed with a wrapping of *fuyi*, so that the meat will taste moist with the natural fat kept in.

DUCK'S TONGUE

A large quantity must be collected from cooks or restaurants. After cooking, take out the thin cartilage in the center. Slice in half lengthwise, and stir-fry [or sauté] with the tender part of bamboo shoot and champignon in sesame oil. Sprinkle in a little sweet white wine. The guests will think it is a kind of prepared champignon but the taste is different. This ranks first among the hors d'oeuvres.

* *Tienchiang*, sweet and sour, made with juice of shellfish.
† This is always done for wrapping roasts to prevent escape of juice while in the oven.

PICKLED COXCOMB

The pickled coxcomb comes next among the delicatessen. It is also collected from various restaurants or cooks. Wrap in *chuan* silk and marinate in *tsao**** overnight. Sesame oil and sweet white wine dregs can also be used. Sauté it with tips of bamboo shoot and champignon. The guests will like its flavor without knowing what it is.

CHICKEN AND DUCK GIZZARDS

Next among the delicatessen comes the gizzard. It is also collected from restaurants and cooks and soaked in sediment of wine. Cook it with good spring water to make a delicious soup, with fresh tips of bamboo shoot or fresh, tender *sunghua* mushroom.†

PIGEON EGG SOUP

Make reservations for eggs with breeders of pigeons, paying down an advance. One needs about twenty of these to make a bowl of soup. Boil them in water and take off the shell. There will remain white, translucent lovely balls to put in soup. At the same time, make flour balls with flour from lotus root, with stuffing of crushed pine seeds made into a paste with the finest foreign sugar. These white flour balls can go with the pigeon eggs in the same soup. Sometimes the guests will take home a few of these white flour balls, smelling their subtle fragrance all the way. This is a most distinguished, exotic soup.

CARP'S TONGUE SOUP

The tongue will also have to be collected. It is drenched with white wine and cooked with good spring water to make soup, with a pinch of fine onion. Served at the end of a wine dinner, it is most delicate.

* Grains from a distillery, the dregs or sediment of wine casks, regularly used in marinating foodstuff.
† This grows under pines and is prized for its flavor.

BLACKFISH TAIL SOUP

Choose a large blackfish and cut off its tail to use for soup. Boil it in plain water. Take out and cut into thin threads, after taking off the tail bone. Mix with bamboo shoot, mushroom, or seaweed in the soup. Or add a little lotus root flour [like corn starch] and a few drops of rice vinegar. Taken after a wine dinner, it cools one's spirit and has a flavor which keeps in the mouth. This is also a recherché recipe.

The above tend toward the exotic. The usual rich food seems to be ignored. Perhaps these things are prized for their special nutritive value, or perhaps the Assistant Commissioner did not like rich food. A competitive spirit developed among families to outdo him by more fancy dishes, but he seemed to stick to his principles of novelty, delicacy, and choiceness. Thus there was another change in cuisine fashions.

Then followed Mr. Chao of Taiyuan with his steamed eel, and Mr. Chen of Yingchuan tried to better Mr. Chao with his boneless mullet. The cook Shu made a name with his stewed shad in spring; then Mr. Shao Shengshih tried to better Mr. Shu with his shad in all seasons.

CHAO'S STEAMED EEL

Choose a big fat eel with a full belly. Throw away its head and tail and innards. Chop into one-inch sections, and rub them with natural salt. Arrange the pieces in a pewter heater* packed with sweet white *niang*† and place the heater inside a boiling pan of soup. After a while, add the best-quality soy sauce. When the spine shows through the flesh, pinch off the bone right inside the heater. Then cover the sections with a thick coating of chopped onion, pepper, and good white pork fat. Keep them in the heater surrounded with boiling water until the pork fat has melted at the

* *Shuan*, a pewter jar used to keep spirits warm by being held suspended in boiling water.
† Fermented rice, like *tsao* a regular substance for marinating food.

bottom and serve. This food is extremely rich in flavor. It makes a gourmet's mouth water just to mention it.

CHEN'S STEAMED BONELESS MULLET

Mr. Chen gave money to the wholesale fish dealers with an order to reserve big mullets exclusively for him. He wanted to outdo Mr. Chao, and chose the mullet instead of eel, and he also cooked it by means of a heater. The fish is slashed in two from the back, leaving the belly connected. The head is kept. Pack white fermented rice at the bottom of the heater and place the fish over it, and steam without direct contact with boiling water until it is done. Then take off the spine and nip off all the bones clean. Close the two halves again, with head and tail intact. Again cover it with chopped onion, pepper, salt, and pork fat, and steam again until it is thoroughly soft. It is served in the heater. It is boneless and tender and soft with a very delicate flavor. The guests can hardly wait for the host's invitation to eat by his raising chopsticks.

SHU'S STEAMED SHAD

Shad is a tasty fish, considered among the best seafood in the south. It used to be steamed or boiled. Mr. Shu in general copied the method of the above two in preparing eel and mullet, but added only white foreign sugar and did not chop the fish into sections. The scales are not removed.* The result is a very tasty and clean piece of fish, rich in flavor, different from shad prepared in other ways. His shad became very much sought after.

SHAO'S SHAD IN ALL SEASONS

Mr. Shu could provide shad only in spring, but Mr. Shao was able to provide it in all seasons. When asked how he did it, he explained that it was not easy. In late spring, he asked his servants who understood how to preserve fish to go to the river port provided with cash and the preservatives, like foreign sugar, pepper and salt, and the best kind of *tsao*, or fermented rice. They went to

* Much of the flavor comes from the fat contained in the skin of shad.

the fishermen's homes, and as soon as fish came in, the entrails were taken out but the scales were kept. Foreign sugar was rubbed into the inside and over the scales. They packed a jar at the bottom with a heavy layer of *tsao*, adding some pepper and natural salt. The fish was placed above the *tsao* and again covered with *tsao* and pepper and salt. This was continued until the jar was almost full, when the contents were pressed firm with the hand and the mouth sealed with fine clay. After reaching home, the jars were buried underground to keep them cool. This was what Mr. Shao told his friends.

SAUTÉED PORCUPINE

But this is nothing compared with the trouble in preparing porcupine. Yushan [in Kiangsu, north of Soochow] is close to the sea [the Yangtse River mouth] where river porcupines come in large quantities in the spring. Everybody knows that it is poisonous, and there were few who dared to eat it until Mr. Li Tsening came along. He was a wholesale dealer, grew rich, and took an interest in food. The first thing was the careful preparation of the "porcupine paste" made of yellow beans a year before. Only the best yellow beans were used. First the brown and black beans were removed, then the yellow ones with small black dots or purple grains on them, until the mass consisted entirely of pure yellow. Every piece had to be scrutinized. This was cooked until it was soft and made into a yellow paste with the addition of Huai wheat flour. In June this was mixed with a little white salt and exposed in the hot sun, with a veil to keep out dust. When this was done, it was put in a jar, which was covered with an earthen basin and sealed with lime. This was the "porcupine paste." It is said that in the making of the paste the slightest presence of black or brown beans, or those with black or purple markings, when eaten with porcupine would kill a person. Or when dust got mixed in during the preparation, it would also be harmful. That is why so much care had to be taken. Men were then sent to a clear river, where boats carried several jars of the river water. All washing and cooking of porcupine was done with this river water. Take several pairs of porcupine, gouge out their eyes and embryos in the stomachs. Slash out their spines and clean out all blood. Use a silver pin to pick out all remaining clots of blood on the fat. Cut out the meat and boil it in water with the skin on. Then take it out, place it on a wooden board, and pick out all bristles without exception with fine pincers. Then cut the flesh and skin into squares, with bone and skin and flesh and all, and sauté with pork fat. After this, fry the meat in hot oil, mixing in the yellow bean paste prepared a year ago. Whenever the pot is opened, the cover should be held over it to prevent dust from falling in. Take a paper roll, dip it in the sauce, and light it with a match. If the paper roll lights, the meat is done; if not, it is not done yet. Usually a large quantity is prepared (because of so much trouble), but when prepared it must be eaten and must not be kept over. It was found that thus prepared, it was absolutely harmless, and for this reason, Li's porcupine became famous and very popular. Every year, about March or April, friends would collect money to have a dinner at his place, and everybody was excited and busy, as if the porcupine feast was a great event of the year. And they ate and ate almost every day until the arrival of the beginning of summer.

BROILED CRABS

Crabs are best produced in lakes. The yellow kind with big claws are called "golden claws." Crabs used to be boiled. Later someone thought that, in boiling, some of the flavor was lost. By tying up the claws and putting them in baskets for steaming, the flavor was better preserved. Then there came Pockmark Chou who introduced a new method of broiling them when he came back from the capital. He opened a wineshop in West City and it was a roaring success. He first boiled the crabs, then, dipping them in sweet wine and sesame oil, put them on an iron grill to broil. In a short while, the shell rose as if it was ready to burst, and the shell of the two claws and eight feet was all cracked by the heat and the joints at the belly fell open. It was only necessary to prick the shell lightly with one's fingers and the shell fell off, leaving only the meat and the roe. Each man was given a portion on a small dish, which he ate after dipping it in vinegar prepared with sliced ginger. It was delicious and very simple without the usual trouble in getting at the meat. But he would not reveal the secret. Others tried to copy it, but the crab was scorched black and still the shell remained as before. Then someone circulated the story that this Pockmark Chou used to hire beggars to catch hundreds of snakes in spring. When the snakes were cooked, there floated on top a coat of oil. This snake oil was collected and secretly applied. When he told people that he used sesame oil, it was really snake oil. The story was believed, and the people stopped going to the shop, which after three or four years was closed. Then the custom of eating steamed crabs came back to the town. At first it started with the clerks and officers connected with water transportation. Each person was provided with a set of special tools for eating them — a small hammer, a small knife, and a pair of small crackers, for breaking, cutting, and picking the crabs. This became a popular custom, in which even the cultured gentlemen joined.

SHARK'S FIN AND SWALLOW'S NEST

At this time, sea trade was still forbidden. Seafood which came from Fukien and Kwangtung was as expensive as gold, and people were satisfied with their local products. Soon the ban on overseas trade was lifted, and overseas food began to arrive. It was then the custom never to give a formal dinner without a delicacy from overseas, and first among these was the "big" dish, by which was meant the edible swallow's nest. It costs five or six dollars a catty in Canton and double that amount in Soochow. Then there was shark's fin of various qualities. People liked these novelties and soon forgot the taste of fish and meat.*

---

* I am certain that the value of shark's fin and swallow's nest was not based on their intrinsic tastiness but on their rarity (i.e., "snob appeal"), exactly like caviar. No one could make much fuss over peanuts, which are much tastier than either shark's fin or caviar. In both cases, these foods were valued because they came from a distant

TABLE SERVICE

Modern extravagances extended to the table service. Certain kinds of food had to be served in Koyao [twelfth century] plates, and certain others, although quite ordinary, had to be served in Shuanyao [Shuanteh, fifteenth century] ware. Food had to come from a great distance and the utensils used had to be period pieces. Thus just attention to food itself was not enough, and once more the fashion in eating changed. Therefore Sun Fengkung wrote his *Tungshulu* and Lu Pipu wrote his *Shihching-chu* [treatises on food]. These were a literary man's pastimes, but still they showed the popular love of good food. I have no idea what future readers of this book will think of the whole subject.

« *The writer's tone is slightly moralistic, but he wrote as if he was engrossed with the subject of progressive immorality, so that I am sure he was quite charmed by it, as shown by his keen observations and interest in details. Has not every writer of realistic fiction claimed that he wanted to expose something for man's spiritual uplift?*

---

country and were considered "rare" and unusual. Caviar comes from Russia, and shark's fin and swallow's nest come from the China Sea and the Indonesian regions. In the days of sailing boats, transportation was difficult enough, apart from the dangers involved in obtaining both shark's fin and swallow's nests, the latter being built by a special species of swallows in caves under cliffs by the sea. Of course both delicacies are gelatinous substances, almost tasteless in themselves, but they are always prepared with the most expensive soup. Cotton cooked in chicken and turtle soup might also taste heavenly.

55 ▣ Eggplant Terrine

From

THE RED CHAMBER DREAM

Tsao Shuehchin
c. 1717 - 1763

« The Red Chamber Dream *has for its background a house garden and a large family living in fabulous luxury. Phoenix is the daughter-in-law running the big household. Grandauntie Liu is an old peasant woman about seventy living on a farm, now visiting the garden. Grandma Chia is the head of the family, about the same age as Grandauntie Liu. The latter cuts a comic figure here, but her solid reliance on her farm plays an important part toward the end of the story when the family fortune crashes.*

GRANDAUNTIE LIU WAS DRINKING the big cup of wine, holding it between her two hands and gulping it.

"Slowly, slowly," said both Grandma Chia and Auntie Shueh. "Or you will choke."

Auntie Shueh then asked Phoenix to bring up some more dishes, and Phoenix said, "Grandauntie, name it and I will produce it, whatever it is. I will feed you with my chopsticks."

"I don't know any names. Whatever you offer must be good," replied Grandauntie.

Phoenix then got hold of bits of the eggplant terrine and put them in Grandauntie's mouth. She said laughingly, "You eat eggplant every day. Taste some of ours and see if you like it."

"No joking. This is not eggplant. It never tastes like this," said

283

Grandauntie. "Why, if eggplant tastes like this, I will plant only eggplant in my farm and not anything else."

"But it is true. We are not joking with you," said everybody.

"Is it?" exclaimed Grandauntie in wonder. "There must be something wrong with my taste. Please young auntie, give me another bite and let me taste it slowly."

Phoenix gave her another bite from the terrine. Grandauntie chewed it very slowly and then said with a smile, "There is a suggestion of the eggplant flavor. But still it does not taste like eggplant. Tell me how you make it. I can prepare it at home."

"That's easy," replied Phoenix. "Just take some fresh eggplant, and take off its skin. Cut the pulp fine and fry it in deep chicken fat. Then take some dried shredded chicken and mix it with champignon, fresh bamboo shoot, mushroom, banksia rose petals, hardened bean curd, and different preserved fruits. Cut all this up into mince and boil it in chicken soup until the soup is almost dry. Sprinkle a little sesame oil, and moisten it with wine dreg oil. Keep it in a porcelain jar and seal it tight. When you want to eat it, just take it out and dress it with fried boned-chicken claw. That is all."

"Oh, my Buddha!" said Grandauntie, putting out her tongue. "That will take ten chickens to prepare it. No wonder it tastes so good." Then she continued to sip her wine slowly.

藝術

ART

56 ▣ From an Artist's Notebook

From

PURPLE PEACH HALL MISCELLANY (TSETAOSHIEN TSATUO)

Li Jih-hua
1565 - 1635

« *Li Jih-hua was a painter of the "literary man's" style and a connoisseur. Most artists have recorded their chats about art in some notebook or other, but such writing usually lacks the lightness and joy of Li's work. Incidentally, he met the great Italian missionary Matteo Ricci, as he recorded in a small paragraph, included here. All such notebooks are truly random notes in that the range of subjects noted is as wide as that of a literary man's conversation, from the strange and unfamiliar and exotic to the touching and delicate problems of everyday living. I have selected and translated here such passages as may interest a Western reader, particularly those showing insight into an artist's life and his problems. I begin with a note which touches on the theme of the following selection describing the communion with nature of the great painter Huang Kungwang (Tsechiu, 1269–1358) of the Mongol Dynasty, who called himself "Grand Idiot Taoist."*

MAGISTRATE CHEN ONCE TOLD ME THIS about Huang Tsechiu. He used to sit in a thick bamboo grove, among rocks and brushwood, in some deserted mountain. He seemed lost in thought and people could not make out what he was doing. Often he went to the place where the river joined the sea, and watched the tossing and surging waves. He stood there transfixed, unmindful of howling storms or moaning sea spirits. Alas! perhaps this is the reason why the Grand Idiot's work has such depth and power, almost equal to that of the Creator.

The ancient painter Ku Kaichih (A.D. 345–411) painted portraits and Chang Sengyu (c. A.D. 502–556) painted dragons, and both did not fill in the eyeball at once, the idea being that the whole expression depended upon it. The painters of landscapes regarded the moss like the eyes on a face and spent a great deal of thought on filling it in. I have heard that Paishi (c. 1155–c. 1235) had a trunkful of landscapes, all with the moss unmarked. He said to people, "I don't feel up to it today. Someday when my head is very clear, I will do it."

A painter must understand give-and-take. By "taking" is meant grasping and sketching in the rough contour of things. Though it is important that such strokes be firm, yet the great thing in such strokes is a lightness of spirit — continuing and breaking at places. If one draws a straight line, it becomes dead and wooden and laborious. By "giving" is meant the omissions, any discontinuity being carried on in space, like the faint outlines of distant hills or the lopped-off branches of trees, which seem to exist and yet not to exist.

Sometimes, walking in the country, one sees a strangely beautiful rock or tree. One should take out pen and paper and make a rough sketch of it. This is similar to Li Ho's method of writing [poetry] on slips of paper and throwing them into his bag.*

Let your painting develop like floating clouds, sailing into space and going around rocks, spreading out here and obstructing the sunlight there, with complete spontaneity. That is the way to achieve an effect of nature. Then it will hold. Practicing calligraphy is like washing pebbles. When the dirt on the surface is washed off, the colors and brilliance of the pebbles reveal themselves naturally. In both cases, the vitality comes from careful observation in spare time and high concentration and mastery at the time the brush touches the paper.

* See following selection.

The reason why the moderns cannot compare with the ancients is that they have not the vital force of the latter. This vital force does not come from strenuous effort, as if one could do a piece of creative work just by setting one's jaws tight. Then what is it? The answer lies in this: stand aloof from thoughts of fame and profit and take a cultured, detached view of life, so that one's spirit comes nearer and nearer to that of the ancients. Then one will have taken hold of oneself, and be ready for the discovery of that great world of freedom in beauty.

My disciple Huang Changfu asked me for a handwritten script, and I wrote the following grading of antiques in their order of value:*

1. Calligraphy of Chin and Tang. [See table of dynasties following.]

2. Paintings of Wutai and Earlier Sung.

3. Ancient rubbings [prints from inscriptions] of Sui, Tang, and Sung.

4. Calligraphy of Su Tungpo (1036–1101), Huang Tingchien (1045–1105), Mi Fei (1051–1107), and Tsai Shiang (1012–1067).

5. Paintings of Yuan Dynasty.

6. Calligraphy of Shienyu Chu (1257–1302), Chao Mengfu (1254–1302), and Yu Shihnan (A.D. 558–638).

7. Paintings of Ma Yuan (during Southern Sung) and Shia Kuei (between 1195–1224).

8. Paintings of Shen Shihtien (1427–1509) and Wen Chenming (1470–1559).

9. Cursive scripts of Chu Chihshan (1460–1526).

10. Correspondence of other famous writers.

11. Bronze vessels before Han and Tsin, with brilliant greens and reds.

12. Ancient jade.

* This order of preference is of course personal, with emphasis on calligraphy.

13. Tang inkstones.

14. Famous, well-authenticated swords and *chin*.

15. Good Wutai and Sung editions of books.

16. Quaint rocks with rugged lines and beautiful form.

17. Old dwarf pines, fine rush grass sharp like needles, in a good basin.

18. Charming dark plums and bamboos.

19. Imported high quality incense.

20. Rare, beautiful foreign novelties.

21. Choice tea and good wine.

22. Delicacies of food from land and sea.

23. White porcelain and earthenware of an unduplicable color.

A scholar should know the relative value of things, like the order of the Founding Knights of the Tang Empire in the mind of the great founder. One should not follow the commercial dealers who place the highest value on the brittle porcelain of Shuanteh and Chenghua.*

When Meng Chang (A.D. 919–965) obtained a copy of the drawing of Chung Kuei [subduer of evil spirits] done by Wu Taotse (eighth century), he asked Huang Chuan [a famous painter] to make a change in it. Chung Kuei was gouging out the eye of a devil with the forefinger of his left hand, and Meng Chang wanted Huang to change it so that the thumb was doing it. Huang made a new drawing and presented it to him, saying, "When Wu made this drawing, the whole force of Chung Kuei's body was concentrated in the forefinger. I cannot change it [without changing the whole posture]. Your humble servant cannot hope to equal Wu. But the whole force of this painting of mine is also concentrated, on the tip of the thumb." I often tell this story to people who come to me with a piece and composition and beg me to correct it, and make them understand why I decline.

* These were comparatively recent in the author's time.

CALLIGRAPHY*

We must learn calligraphy as young men learn boxing or wrestling. Everybody knows how to close a fist or to stand firm. What one must learn is the posture for springing into action. If the posture is right, the wrestler can spring and leap and have the opponent in his mortal grip. The onlookers see all the rhythmic movements, the writhing and tugging and well-timed punching.

In writing characters, one must keep the spirits calm and feel suffused with an air of well-being, which he directs to the tip of his writing brush. Thus the writing flows out like a gentle breeze, or dots like sweet rain, or lashes down like a cataract, or pauses and is poised like curling and twisting angry pines. It goes fast or slow, as the situation demands, sweeps out or cuts in, never a step transgressing the way of the ancient models. The mind becomes the master, doing what it likes. In this way, one can hope to gain a little place among the calligraphists.

MATTEO RICCI

[After discussing the people of Europe and their astronomy, the author continues.] In the last years of the previous reign, Matteo Ricci came out with ten associates, sailed 60,000 li [20,000 miles!], passing through more than a thousand countries, and reached Indo-China after six years. By the time he had reached the Kwangtung province [in which lies Canton], his fellow travelers had all died. Matteo had magic which protected him from all harm, and he understood controlled breathing and internal vision [yoga],

---

* The esthetics of calligraphy is based on the beauty of movement, not of static proportions. The nearest analogy is to call it dancing on paper, with its pauses, twirls, and well-timed stately steps. What makes it difficult is that it cannot be corrected. Each character written is evidence of a complicated involuting movement of the brush, and the pleasure consists in following that movement. The same beauty of mastery may be seen in the drives and cuts and chops on the tennis court as played by a champion. On the very sensitive, specially prepared paper, every slightest nuance or hesitation in the movement is recorded as on a photographic plate.

so he was free from sickness. He stopped at Kwangtung for over twenty years and understood the Chinese language and writing. He had a reddish beard and blue eyes and a rosy complexion. He was very polite, bowing when he met people, and people loved him, believing that he was a good man. I met him in the fall of 1597 at Kiukiang, and had a good talk with him. He showed me some strange things from his country, a painted glass screen, and a sand filter shaped like a goose egg. It is filled with sand which falls down to the lower end and can be reversed, and is used for keeping time. He had with him the sacred books of his country, which were ornamented with gold and precious stones. Its paper was smooth like a lady's flesh — I do not know what it is made of. He said that this was made from barks in his country and made thin like that. He was already over fifty and looked like one between twenty and thirty, being a distant tribesman who has learned the truth [in the Taoist sense]. He has roamed the world and come this far, and is not thinking of going home.

Money and women. There are two things in this life which most quickly dissipate a man's energy and shorten his life — money and women. Magicians say that they can transmute base metal into gold to help people and that by practicing the art of love one can prolong life. Thus one can both get a great deal of pleasure and receive benefits. It is a very tempting proposition. But I do not believe it. I think it is too good to be true.*

« *For convenience, it is useful to memorize the centuries of the dynasties frequently mentioned:*

* The art of "riding women" for health and long life, of "absorbing *yin* to strengthen *yang*," is at least as old as the time of Han Wuti second century B.C.). The *Hanwu Kushih* of Pan Ku tells of many Taoists who by practicing this art lived to a great old age, without their hair turning white. The Emperor Han Wuti encouraged such magicians in his search for the magic formula of prolonging life, and he himself never slept without women. The legend was that he was a kind of maniac, and after his official burial in a mausoleum, when the palace girls were sent off to a monastery his ghost came to visit them, but other people could not see it. The number of women was therefore increased to five hundred to please him, and then the ghost disappeared.

A BRIEF SYNOPSIS OF CHINESE DYNASTIES

XXII–XIX B.C.	Shia ⎫
XVIII–XII B.C.	Shang ⎬ "Three Dynasties"
XI–III B.C.	Chou ⎭
end of III B.C.	Tsin
II B.C.–A.D. II	Han
mid III	Wei (forming with Wu and Shu, the Three Kingdoms)
mid III–IV	Chin (Eastern Chin from 317)
V–VI	"Northern and Southern Dynasties" (including Sung,* Tsi, Liang, Chen)
C. A.D. 600	Sui
VII–IX	Tang
first half X	Wutai, or "Five Dynasties"
latter half X–XIII	Sung (Southern Sung from 1127)
end of XIII–mid XIV	Yuan (Mongol)
mid XIV–mid XVII	Ming
mid XVII–1912	Ching (Manchu)

* This Sung of Northern and Southern Dynasties is usually referred to as "Liu Sung" to distinguish it from "Southern Sung" (1127–1276). "Liu" is the name of that ruling house.

57 回 Communion with Nature

Postcript to

"LI HO'S LIFE"

Lu Kueimeng
? - C. A.D. 881

« That poets live close to nature is well known. Sometimes this
becomes an obsession with nature, in Thoreau fashion. This is
the case of the two poets mentioned in this piece, Li Ho (A.D.
791–817) and Meng Tungyeh (A.D. 751–814), of the Later Tang
Period. Li Ho was an extraordinary poet who died young, and
who was said to have a "devilish" talent, saying things that no
one else would have thought of. The same was true of Meng.
The lesson is that Li and Meng were physically immersed in nature where those lines were born and where Meng learned to observe the minutest details of plant and animal life. The writer
of this piece, Lu, was eminently fit to write it, for he himself
lived the same kind of life. He had two great loves, tea and fishing, and used to spend entire days fishing, carrying with him
some volumes of verse and a clay stove for brewing tea while on
the fishing boat. A similar habit he shared with Li Ho was that
he would write something and throw it into a cloth bag, but
then he would forget all about it. Creative work carries with it a
form of intense love which borders on mania before it can become a success.

YUCHISHENG'S* BIOGRAPHICAL SKETCH of Li Ho says that
the poet used to go out every day on a donkey, followed by a boy
servant. The donkey carried an old bag. Whenever he had a good

---

* "Yuchisheng" means "Jade River Student." See note on Chinese
names at the end of this selection.

couple of lines, he would write them down and throw the piece of paper into the bag. At night, upon his return, he would take these slips out and compose them into poems.*

When I was a boy living at Liyang, I was told by a white-haired old clerk of the government this story about the poet Meng Tungyeh. In the reign of Tsengyuan (A.D. 785–804), he was a poor scholar and was made an assistant magistrate of Liyang, formerly called the Pingling county. About two miles south, there is a rapids called Touchin [Throw Gold] Rapids, extending about two and a half miles in length. On the east of the road, there are the old ruins of the old Pingling city, with a wall enclosure of over one thousand paces. The tumble-down ruins of the walls stand three or four feet high, heavily covered with underbrush. Many old chestnut-leaved oaks, a dozen spans in circumference, cast their shadows over the place, and the ground is covered with wild under-brush and herbs, and is full of caves and depressions. As it lies on a low level, little ponds are formed where fish and turtles make their homes. In general, it is a dark, somber, and deserted place, suggesting the ages past. No one goes there except woodcutters and fishermen. Tungyeh fell in love with it. Every day or every other day, he would go out there on a donkey, accompanied by a young employee of the office, and head for the Touchin islets. Arriving there, he would sit in the shade of an old oak tree, by the side of some pool, and sing his lines until sundown. This habit continued, to the great detriment of his office duties. The magistrate was exasperated and requested permission from the prince to have someone else do Tungyeh's work and share his salary. Tungyeh's financial condition became difficult and he left.

I have heard it said that those who indulge in hunting and fishing slaughter life which is given by nature. If life may not be destroyed, how is it permissible for a poet to watch and observe and pry into and expose the secret of every little moment of such [plant and animal] life, so that from morning till eve these living

* His mother seeing him so occupied with those slips of paper, said to him, "You are going to kill yourself with those papers."

things have nowhere to hide? How is it possible that God should not punish such transgressors? Changchi [Li Ho] died young, Tungyeh was poor, and Yuchisheng died before he could secure an office at the capital. It must be so! It must be so, indeed!

    « A Note on Chinese Names.   *The above postscript shows the use of Chinese names and the confusion brought about by one person having several names. Li Ho's social name was Changchi, and Meng Tungyeh's regular name was Meng Chiao. Yuchisheng, at the beginning of the postscript, is the poetic name of the poet Li Shangyin (A.D. 813–858), who was equally known by his social name, Yishan. As seen in the piece, Li Ho is referred to by his regular name and his social name, while Meng Chiao is referred to by his social name, Tungyeh, and Li Shangyin is referred to by his fancy poetic name. It is impossible to be completely consistent by using either the regular or the social name, and Chinese writers do not. Some writers are more often referred to by their social name, such as the case of Su Tungpo, whose regular name was Su Shih.*

    In general, scholars always used to have two names, and many had three or more. The first, ming, is the regular name, the name by which the person signs himself in official papers; it corresponds to his legal name in the West. The second, tse, is his social name, by which his friends and others should address him. Thus, the signature in a letter is not the name by which one should address the writer in reply. This social name has, as a rule, some connection in meaning with the regular name. The more hidden the connection through some obscure classical passage, the more "refined" or "elegant" the person thinks he is: of some 15,000 current characters in a dictionary, a good 10 per cent are "current" only because they occur in personal names. This is pure pedantry and should be eliminated. Whereas the first kind of name is given by parents, the second is usually chosen by the person himself, and is usually more poetic. When a man becomes a poet or an artist or an owner of a villa, he adopts more fancy names, such as "Owner of Such-and-such Studio," etc. This third class of names can be called the poetic names. In some cases, a person had an honorary posthumous title conferred on him. All these names bring about an extreme state of things and demand some familiarity in reading literature.

I give here the extreme case of the painter Fu Chingchu (1606–1683). To begin with, he is always known as Fu Chingchu, which is not his regular name. Few people know his regular name, which is Fu Shan. At first his real name was Fu Tingchen. Then he became Fu Shan; his social name became Fu Chingchu, with other subsidiary social names like Fu Jenchung, Fu Sehlu, and Kungchihta, also just Kungta. This already takes us into the realm of his assumed fancy names. Since he was a painter and calligraphist, he began to assume any number of fancy names, with which he signed his scripts and paintings. He was "Red Gown Taoist," "Rock Taoist," "Leaving Alone Bad Spirits" (Shuili), "Six Rules" (Liuchih), "Old Man of Red Cliff," "Squire of Red Cliff," "Old Man of Dirt Hall," "Owner of Black Lamb Temple," "Old Man of Nightless Temple," "Guest of Mountains" (Fu Chiaoshan), "Guest Resident of Huang Mountain" (Chiao Huangshan), "Old Man Guest Resident of Huang," "Wine-drinking Taoist," "Wine and Meat Taoist," "Believer Not in Monastery" (Chushih), "Old Zen Buddhist of Bitter Wine" (which he loved), also "Saint of Mountain" (Chen Shan) or "Guest Resident Mountain Saint," "Taoist of Five Peaks," "Taoist of Dragon Pool," "Old Man Watching Transformations," "Great Laughing Disciple," and a long one, "Disciple Hearing the Truth at the Dragon Pool." Like those Tang princes who had several cuncubines and three dozen children, he could not have remembered them all himself. The total is, according to my count, thirty. I believe he holds the record. Social names are still used today by many, but not by all.

I have, in principle, stuck to one name for a person in this book so far as it is practicable.

« *The following is a collection of various important artists' opin-*
ions on the first law of rhythmic vitality, enunciated by Shieh
Ho, which has remained the keystone and inviolable principle
of Chinese painting throughout the ages. It is interesting to note
that Chinese literary criticism and art criticism began to flourish
in the third to fifth centuries in the southern dynasties around
Nanking, when North China was overrun by barbarians. There
was developed a self-conscious art and a rather effeminate soft-
ness of living.

WHAT ARE THE SIX LAWS of painting? They are: (1) rhythmic vitality, (2) skeletal pattern and basic strokes, (3) verisimilitude, or likeness to objects, (4) details belonging to particular
objects, (5) composition, and (6) copying models and spontan-
eous variations. — Shieh Ho (c. A.D. 479–501) *in Ku Huapin Lu.*

THOSE WHO JUDGE PAINTINGS by fidelity to objects speak on
the mental level of a child. — Su Tungpo (1036–1101) in a poem.

SOME ANCIENT PAINTERS might be lacking in accuracy of
form, but they had the bones and spirit. One has to judge such
paintings apart from accuracy of form. This is something difficult
to explain to the uncultivated. On the other hand, some modern
paintings have accuracy of form, but no rhythmic vitality. The
proper approach is through aiming at rhythmic vitality which
governs factual resemblance.
— Chang Yenyuan (c A.D. 860–890) in *Litai Shuhua Chi*

MANY MODERN PAINTERS draw a few simple lines, or else let
themselves go unashamedly and pile up things on the silk without

rhyme or reason by saying, "I am not concerned with the question of whether the painting resembles objects or not." These people do not understand that "not insisting on verisimilitude" implies that one should rather try to suggest resemblance to the things without formal resemblance. Those painters who merely cover up a painting with lines and blotches like furniture laid topsy-turvy in storage have no right to discuss it.

— Wang Fu (1362–1416) in *Shuhua Chuanshi Lu*.

THE STRANGE BEAUTY of "Cranky Old Man" [Huang Kung-wang, 1296–1358] lies not in his fidelity to form, but rather in his disregard for it. It is where he departs from it that he enters into the spirit of the creation, like a celestial steed lost in the clouds. Many modern painters try to aim at accuracy of form, and the more they try the farther away they get from the spirit of things.

— Yun Shouping (1633–1690) in *Pingoushiang Kuan Huapa*.

IN A PAINTING, aim first at the general concept of rhythmic vitality, and then the filling in of actual forms. Then weigh and consider. But if one has not a clear idea of the general developing movements and starts to think about the laborious details, one will have lost the rhythmic vitality already.

— Han Chuo of Sung (eleventh to twelfth centuries) in *Shanshui Chunchuan Chi*, quoted in *Huafa Yaolu* by Yu Shaosung, a contemporary.

IT IS HUMAN NATURE to prefer careful workmanship to slipshod work, the decorative to the simple and unadorned, the graceful to the rugged and the fine details to suggestions of all-round atmosphere, and the brilliant-colored to the subdued. The best in art can never go by such crude standards. On the other hand, there are many who mistake the ingenious and clever for true beauty, the boldly and crassly assertive for true strength, the immature and childish for true depth, and the awkward and superficial for true detachment of spirit. To neglect the first laws of rhythmic vitality and general conception in favor of such trite characteristics is to misunderstand the true meaning of a literary man's painting.

— Chen Yinchuo (contemporary) in
The Value of Literary Man's Painting.

« *It is not clear, but it is possible that in referring to those who make the four kinds of mistakes, the author had in mind Picasso, Rouault, African art, and the budding abstract artists, in that order.*

59 ▣ Painting the Inner Law of Things

From

COMPLETE WORKS OF SU TUNGPO

Su Tungpo
1036 - 1101

» *The following is probably the clearest statement by Su Tungpo of his concept of painting the inner spirit of objects. The word for this inner spirit is li, the philosophic idea of Universal Reason, or Reason in all things. The Sung Neo-Confucianist philosophy is usually known as the philosophy of li. This is the positive side of Chinese Impressionism, of which the protest against mere verisimilitude is merely the negative side. Dissatisfaction with mere photographic accuracy is one thing; to know where to go from there is another. Su Tungpo himself is one of the very greatest painters.*

It HAS BEEN MY OPINION concerning painting that men and animals and buildings and structures have a constant material form. On the other hand, mountains and rocks, bamboos and trees, ripples of water, smoke and clouds do not have a constant form [*shing*] but do have a constant inner spirit [*li*]. Anybody can detect inaccuracy in the constant forms, but even specialists often fail to note mistakes in painting the constant inner spirit of things. Some artists find it much easier to deceive the public and make a name for themselves by painting objects without constant forms. When one makes a mistake in the form or contour of an object, however, the mistake is confined to that particular part and does not spoil the whole, whereas if one misses the inner spirit, the whole painting falls flat. Because such objects do not have a constant form, one must pay special attention to their inner laws. There are plenty of craftsmen who can copy the minute details of objects, but the inner law of things can be comprehended only by the highest human spirits. Yuko's [Wen Tung, c. 1019–1079, a cousin of Su Tungpo] paintings of bamboos, rocks, and dried-up trees may be said to have truly seized the inner spirit of the objects. He understands how these things grow and decay, how they twist and turn and are sometimes blocked and compressed, and how they prosper and thrive in freedom. The roots, stalks, joints, and leaves go through infinite variations, following different rhythms independent of one another. And yet they are all true to nature and completely satisfying to the human spirit. These are records of the inspirations of a great soul. . . . Those who understand the inner spirit of things and examine these paintings carefully will see that I am right.

60 ▣ A Painting of Five Hundred Lohans

From

WENCHIH (A COLLECTION OF ESSAYS)

Tsin
c. 1079

» *"Lohan" is the Chinese word for Buddhist saint, or arhat (ara-*
hat). In many great Buddhist temples, there is often an annex
housing clay statues of five hundred lohans, with very realistic
facial expressions. This piece is contained in a Chinese
selection of "beautiful writings," Wenchih — with a preface
dated 1613 — where the author is given as "Anonymous"
with the surname "Tsin." Tsin's own note about this piece gives
the clear date of January 15, 1079. No one can say that the
world of Buddhist beliefs is uninteresting.

Author's Preface: Our family have been Buddhists for generations.
I once saw a sketch by Han Yu [eighth century] about a certain
painting and was greatly impressed by its succinctness and clarity
with attention to details, so that on reading it, one felt like seeing
the painting itself. This I am trying to do in writing this record
of the painting of lohans. I am not a good writer and dare not hope
that I have succeeded, but merely note this fact to show why I
have done what I did.

Buddhist disciple Tsin,
— January 15, second year of Yuanfeng (1079).

I. SCROLL OF FIVE HUNDRED LOHANS.

1 person having attained samadhi [final calm of all thoughts]
in a niche.

1 person sitting with crooked legs under a tree, lecturing.

8 persons standing on the sides, to the right and left, listening.

6 persons lecturing.

6 persons studying sacred texts.

1 person standing looking at a text, leaning on a cane.

1 person putting the text away after having finished his lesson.

6 persons each* sitting in a circle and discussing with hand gestures, playing with a fly swatter or cane, and talking with each other, chin in hand.

5 persons going toward the pagoda.

1 expounding Buddhist philosophy to lions.

3 persons behind him, seated.

1 person sitting on a cobra, with a cane planted near by.

6 persons with their backs toward trees looking up at distant magpies.

4 persons looking at climbing monkeys.

4 persons looking up at cricling phoenixes.

4 persons watching deer.

5 persons bending over and playing with lambs.

5 persons coddling storks.

1 person picking lotus pods.

5 persons behind him.

5 persons writing something on a banana leaf.

2 persons holding a banana leaf and wetting their brushes.

6 persons drinking tea with burning incense on the side.

3 persons washing their alms bowls in a stream.

* This word "each" may be a misprint, and accounts for a difference of 12 persons. As it stands, it seems to indicate 3x6 or 18 persons instead of 6. However, even if this is counted as 6 the total still exceeds 500.

1 person going home after having washed his bowl.

1 person washing his clothes.

1 person wringing out his clothes near a tree.

1 person going home with washed laundry.

1 person just coming to wash.

1 person watching from across the bank.

1 person washing his shoes [sandals].

1 person putting his shoes on after having washed them.

1 person going away in the act of putting his clothes on.

6 persons sitting together with their palms closed.

8 persons bowing before the light from the sacred relic.

4 persons feeding hungry ghosts.

5 persons feeding hawks and ravens.

5 persons feeding fish and turtles.

6 persons going up to the clouds.

1 each of the following: one showing a multicolored light from his fingers, one with a halo surrounding his alms bowl, one sprouting a spring of water from his forehead, one whose heels are stepping over a fire, one person with bare shoulders washing his gold earrings, standing with his hands . . . [misprint unclear here].

7 persons receiving requests to go to the believers' homes for vegetarian feasts.

6 persons receiving gifts of "dragon's daughter" pearls.

4 persons receiving gifts of flowers arranged like pairs of lions.

7 persons receiving gifts of flowers meaning "being born in Paradise."

5 persons receiving gowns from visitors accompanied with three cows.

7 persons receiving gifts of Turkish wheels.

4 persons receiving precious gifts from Hu [northwestern tribesmen] accompanied by two camels.

5 persons receiving gifts from kneeling sea spirits.

3 dragon-riders.

3 tiger-riders.

3 on horseback.

3 on saddled elephants.

3 lion-tamers.

1 person having a shave.

1 person shaving him.

1 person waiting to be shaved after a bath.

1 person taking off his clothing.

1 person folding away his clothing.

2 persons repairing broomsticks.

1 person holding a foot ruler.

3 persons sewing.

16 persons spread out looking at a spring coming from under rocks.

3 persons crossing a stone bridge.

4 persons coming to the bridge.

2 persons walking with canes.

3 guides.

3 helpers.

3 persons in sandals, carrying umbrellas.

1 person adjusting his dress for a walk.

[Besides the 244 persons enumerated above], there are an additional 123 persons in eighteen groups, spread out on the banks of a curving stream, or meeting each other on the mountain paths in various positions, as follows: sitting, walking, yawning while sitting on the ground with crooked legs, resting on canes, carrying bamboo hats, counting beads, carrying white ropes.

There are another twenty-eight groups totaling 139 persons, in varying positions, as follows: sitting or walking or standing, looking back toward the storied buildings, leaning on balconies, standing on high places over edges of cliffs, looking up or looking down, or turning their heads sideways, or looking out of the corners of their eyes, or peering into the distance, or watching the foreground.

This makes a total of 500 [actually 506, or 518] lohans.

In addition, there is Buddha sitting in the center. Beside him [not included among the lohans] are two bodhisattvas sitting on lotus seats, one on a lion, the other on an elephant, holding a *juyi* [ceremonial jade] or a lotus blossom, wearing jeweled hats and downhanging tassels of beads. Ten disciples stand at the back, bare-shouldered and barefooted, holding their palms together, and sixteen persons have come to pay their respects. There are also two good spirits in armor, holding a sword and a battle-ax, standing on the right and left. This increases the number by thirty-one.

There are, besides, sixteen boy servants carrying sacred texts, tea trays, attending to the house, and carrying pots and pans or removing dishes. There are fourteen devils, some riding on dragons or tigers, horses, and elephants, receiving gifts of food, or carrying messages, having black beaks and scales on their bodies and wearing jackets short at the back, or peering from behind trees. Furthermore, there are nineteen miscellaneous persons, among them some white-tunic tribesmen, offering fragrant flowers and rare animals, coming for a visit, some driving buffaloes, some carrying baskets of things on elephant backs, dressed in coats of armor and armed with bows and arrows, standing in admiration [of the Buddha]. In addition, there are forty-three kinds of birds and beasts, big and small, like phoenixes, storks, magpies, ravens, dragons, tigers, yaks, elephants, lions, horses, buffaloes, camels, cobras, lion cubs, and monkeys.

[This brings up the total to 580 persons] but the principal theme of the painting are the lohans, and therefore this is known as "A Painting of Five Hundred Lohans."

According to the story, this painting was done by a monk of the

Wu region by the name of Faneng. The lines and strokes are not without flaws, but the picture delineates with great charm the moods and expressions of the people with an unsurpassed sympathetic understanding. The ancient painter Taikuei used to hide behind a drapery after he had completed a picture of a buddha and listened to the criticisms of the onlookers and made his corrections accordingly. Thus it took him several years to complete a picture.

I imagine Faneng must have done the same before he could accomplish such a task. I do not think he could have dashed it off in a hurry.

« *Compare the above piece with selection 16, "The Mortal Thoughts of a Nun."*

61 ▣ Sound Mimicry

Preface to

AUTUMN SOUNDS
(A COLLECTION OF POEMS)

Lin Tsehuan
c. 1650

DURING THE AUTUMN DAYS, Che Aitzu [Lin Tsehuan] used to lock himself up indoors, and often he felt restless and did not know what to do. But whenever he heard of gossip and anecdotes, he dipped his pen in ink and wrote some poems. When these poems were collected together, he called them "autumn sounds." One day several of his friends dropped in to see him, and he asked them to stay and have a drink. He asked his guests to say what sounds they liked best respectively. "The sounds of the loom and the spinning wheel and of children reciting their lessons," said one of them. "What a good father!" said I. "The sounds of scolding footmen outside and of music and singing in the inner court," said another. "So you are given to luxuries," I commented. "The sounds of mother-in-law and daughter-in-law playing chess," said a third. "How romantic!" A friend who had remained hitherto silent, advanced with a large cup filled with wine and said:

"May I tell you something you never heard of before? There is a great imitator of sounds in the capital. On festive days, he sets up a screen eight feet high in the northeastern corner of the hall, and sits behind the screen with nothing except a table, a chair, a fan, and a sounding board. The guests sit around. By and by from behind the screen are heard two taps with the sounding board, which is the signal for silence. At first, they hear a dog barking far away in some alleyway. Then a woman wakes up and yawns; she tries to wake up her husband and says lewd things to him. The husband at first makes no reply but mumbles in his sleep. The woman keeps on jerking him, when the conversation between the two becomes clearer and clearer, and there is a creaking of the bed. Then the baby wakes up. The husband asks the woman to feed the baby, and while the baby is sucking and crying, the woman pats the baby and coos it to silence. Meanwhile, the husband has got up and is clearing himself, while the mother is also trying to make the baby urinate. This, however, wakes up the older child, who begins to cry vociferously. There is then started an immense confusion of sounds — of the woman patting the baby with her hand and cooing, the baby crying and sucking, the older child just waking up, the bed creaking, the husband scolding the older child, and the sounds of discharge in the night pot and the wooden pail. While the guests listen amazed with outstretched necks at this medley of realistic sounds, they hear the husband going to bed again. The wife then asks the older child to get up and clear himself also, and when this is done, they all get ready to go to sleep again. The baby is falling asleep. The husband begins to snore, and the rhythm of the wife patting her baby becomes slower and slower until it stops entirely. Then they hear a mouse going about the room and overturning things on the floor, while the woman coughs in her sleep. While the listeners begin to sit back and take it more easily, they suddenly hear a loud cry, 'Fire! Fire!' The husband gets up and shouts, the wife screams, and both children begin to cry. Very soon it seems there are hundreds of people shouting, hundreds of children crying, and hundreds of dogs barking, while through and above all this are heard the sounds of structures falling, fire cracking, wind blowing, water pouring, and men struggling and crying for help in a general pandemonium. The sounds are so real that the listeners' faces turn, their knees shake, and they almost take to their heels. But all of a sudden, a tap is heard and all sounds cease. When the screen is taken away, they see nothing but a table, a chair, a fan, and a sounding board."

Indeed here is a great painter of sounds. I set down my friend's words and let this serve as the preface to the *Autumn Sounds*.

62 ⌘ Beautiful Singing

From

LOATSAN YUCHI (A NOVEL)

Liu Ao
c. 1850 - 1910

« Liu Ao was a victim of obscurantism. He was a progressive and
wanted to introduce railways to China. He also opened a public
granary for famine relief. Accused of co-operating with mis-
sionaries, he was exiled to Chinese Turkestan, where he died.
His novel is an exposure of official corruption.

The Taming Lake is situated at Tsinan, capital of Shantung.
The time: around 1900. Little Jade, called "Fair Maid," and her
sister, called "Dark Maid," both enjoy a tremendous reputation. Dark Maid has just sung in her own exquisite manner and
someone has mistaken her for Fair Maid, when another in the
audience says:

"No, THIS ONE IS DARK MAID, Fair Maid's younger
sister. She learned all her singing from Fair Maid. . . . One can
admire Dark Maid's singing and say why, but Fair Maid's singing
just sweeps you along. Dark Maid's art can be imitated, but Fair
Maid's art cannot. For some years, people have been trying to learn
her style, including the singsong girls; one could reach the level of
Dark Maid at best, but no one could come anywhere near Fair
Maid." Meanwhile, Dark Maid had disappeared behind the stage.

At this time, the garden was full of people, talking and chatting
amid the cries of vendors of melon seeds, peanuts, wild plums, and
walnuts. While the garden was filled with all this din of human
noise, there appeared on the stage a maid of eighteen or nineteen,

312

dressed just like her sister. She had a small, oval face, fair in complexion, slightly better-looking than the average, and there was an air of pleasant refinement without cold dignity. With a slightly bent head, she came forward and stood behind the table, and gave a light shake to her sounding boards used for keeping rhythm. Strange to say, in her hands, these two stupid metal pieces seemed to be filled with a strange, rich rhythm. She then tapped the drum lightly, and looked up at her audience. The light of her eyes was like that of an autumn lake, and had the cold splendor of a midnight star. As she turned them about, everyone in the audience, including those sitting in the remote corners, thought she was looking at him. That look of hers alone laid a spell on those present. The hall became as quiet as if the emperor had appeared. You could hear a pin drop to the floor.

Little Jade opened her red lips, showing her white teeth, and began leisurely a few bars. At first, it was quiet and low, making the audience feel that there was something extremely satisfying about it. It was as if all their bowels had been ironed over with a warm iron and set at ease, or as if they had just eaten *ginseng*, so that every single one of the 36,000 pores on their body was glowing with joy. After a dozen lines, the pitch gradually rose higher and higher, until all of a sudden it shot high up like a steel wire reaching a height that made everyone aghast with amazement. Who would think that after lingering there for a second with a few turns and flourishes, it would go higher, and holding it suspended for a moment with a few turns, again higher she would soar, and this would go on three or four times until she was caroling in the clouds? It was like a man climbing the Taishan Mountains: when he started out, he thought that rocky Aolai Peak was in cloudy regions, and when he had reached Aolai Peak, he began to see the Fan Rocks, and when he had reached the latter, the vision of Nantienmen opened up before his eyes. The higher he went, the stranger and more awesome the view became. When Little Jade had reached the top, suddenly she let it go and took a swoop downward, and it was like a flying eagle winding its way from the heavens down the thirty-six peaks of Huangshan. Backward and forward she carried her song, until gradually it sank lower and lower, reaching the depth of inaudibility. In that spell of quiet, everyone held his breath. After a moment, a voice rose as if from underground, and this time, it clamored forth straight up and broke out into an orgy of sounds, like detonating fireworks that shot into the sky and spread out into lines of fire of different colors. And in its ascent, it was met by a symphony of other sounds, and the *pipa* players began to use all fingers in quick succession, the noise of the accompaniment waxing and waning in perfect harmony with the singer's voice. It was as if we were transported to a garden of spring flowers and caroling birds, filling the air with swift, changing, competing melodies. All of a sudden, the singing and the instrumental music stopped, followed by a thundering applause from the audience.

When the din of applause had died down, a young man of about thirty in the audience said with a Hunan accent: "I used to read an ancient book, saying that 'the melodies remain in the air for three days,' and found it difficult to understand. Now I begin to understand. After listening to Little Jade's singing, my ears hear nothing but her haunting melodies for days, whatever I do and wherever I go. When Confucius said that music made him 'forget the taste of meat for three months,' it must have been something like this. . . ."

63 ▣ The Sound of the *Pipa* on the Water

"THE PIPA HANG"

Po Chuyi
A.D. 772 - 846

« *This is one of the most touching and most popular of Po's writings. The hang (pronounced harng) is a recitative poem, rhymed and in meters, convenient for recital to the accompaniment of an instrument. The pipa, sometimes translated as "lute," consisting of four metal strings, has a wide range of sound effects, descriptive of quiet moonlight on river banks or of the din of battle. It is scraped or plucked with metal caps on the fingers. The piece is chiefly narrative and tells of the poet's encountering a woman player and her sad story. I believe it is better to translate it into prose, although some of the effect of such poetry is lost. The original form accounts for the short sentences.*

ONE NIGHT I WAS SENDING A FRIEND OFF to the riverbank at Kiukiang.* It was autumn and maple leaves and reed flowers swooped and flicked and snapped in the wind. I dismounted to find my friend already in the boat. We had a drink, but missed music. It was a dismal parting and I was going on my way. At this time, the river was flooded with a hazy moonlight. Suddenly there came over the water the sound of a *pipa*. I changed my mind and told my friend to delay starting a bit. We were curious to find out where the music came from and learned that it was from a player

---

* This is the same district where the poet built his mountain lodge in Lushan. See selection 33, "The North Peak of Lushan."

315

in another boat. The *pipa* had stopped and we hesitated a while as to how to approach and invite the player to come over. We then moved our boat over near to the other boat and introduced ourselves, begging to have the pleasure of seeing the player, for we were going to warm up some more wine, relight the lamps, and have dinner again. It was after repeated pleading that she came out, and when she did, she half covered her face with the instrument.

She adjusted the strings and plucked a few notes, but even before the melody began, we were struck with its langorous tone. And as she went along, with her head bent, the sounds were soft and muted, sad and plaintive and meditative, as if she were telling the story of her frustrated life. I felt that there was a long story behind it. Gently she scraped or plucked the strings, and I recognized the melody of "Nichang," followed by that of "Liuyao." The notes gathered up speed, those from the lower strings falling like fast raindrops and those from the higher trailing like whispers, and these were mingled together, giving the effect of marbles of different sizes falling into a jade plate. Then the melody was like orioles chirping and chattering in trees after a rain, while a covered spring gurgled below. And the water seemed to freeze suddenly as the sound of the strings came to a stop. It seemed that she could not go on and we held our breath in that moment of silence. When it started again, it broke out like water rushing forth from a broken silver vase, and again it was like the clash and clang of battle of men on horseback. When it was finished, she took out the stop in the center, and rattled her fingers across all four strings, making a sound like the tearing of silk. The people in both boats were struck speechless, and only a white haze hung over the middle of the river. Quietly she put back the finger caps in their place among the strings, and readjusted her dress and made a slight gesture of rising from her sitting position as a form of courtesy.

She then told us her story. She was born in the capital, but is now making her home at the Hamoling [Frog Hill]. She said that she had begun to learn playing the *pipa* from the age of thirteen at the Court of Musicians No. 1.* She often won high praise from her professors and was the envy of many girls. Oh, she was very popular. Every time she played, she received she did not know how many pieces of silk for presents. And she could afford to break silver brooches and hair ornaments, and her blood-red skirt was often splashed with wine. It was that kind of gay life she had in her youth year after year. Then her younger brother went into the army and her elder sister died. In time she lost her youthful glamour and now carriages rarely appeared in front of her establishment. When she was in her thirties, what could she do but marry a businessman?† The merchant was too busy attending to business and had left upriver a month ago to buy tea. So she was left alone on the boat, facing the cold water and the silent moon all by herself. Sometimes she cried herself to sleep, thinking of the days of her youth.

I was already saddened by her music, and now after I heard her story, I clicked my tongue in pity. And this I said to her: "We are both travelers in this wide world. We do not need to have met before to be friends. I was demoted from the emperor's court last year and sent down here to Kiukiang. The hardest thing here is to hear good music. Sometimes for a whole year I go without the sound of woodwind or of strings. The place is on low-lying ground and near the river, and houses are surrounded with rushes and wild bamboos. What can one hear except the song of cuckoos and the sad cries of monkeys? To be sure, there are folk songs and country pipes, but it rather grates on one's ears. So it is quite an agreeable

* A government institution for training musicians and actors and actresses.

† This line is considered by the Chinese readers as one of the saddest lines and is often quoted. One day, three centuries later, Su Tungpo was matching quotations from poetry with a famous courtesan. "What about the end [of a courtesan's life]?" asked Tungpo. The courtesan, Chintsao, quoted this line, and then was struck with its pathos and decided to become a nun. Marrying a businessman was considered an anticlimax for an educated lady.

surprise to hear your *pipa* tonight; it's like fairy music which my ears have missed for a long time. Come on, stay a while and play some more for me while I write this poem in your honor."

She felt greatly touched, standing there listening to what I said. Then she sat down again and played for me. And the notes fell fast, and they were sad and cut into one's heart. All who heard it shed tears, and the one who shed most was myself, for my black gown was wet.

« *Po Chuyi wrote in a simple style, not florid or over embellished. He was already well known, and poems like this were immediately picked up and sung by professional singers.*

文學

LITERATURE

64 ▣ Tungpo on the Art of Writing

From

COMPLETE WORKS OF SU TUNGPO

Su Tungpo
1036 - 1101

« *The best things said about writing in general are still those said by Su Tungpo in his letters to his friends. There are many good things in Wenshin Tiaolung, a very penetrating book on rhetoric and literary criticism by Lu Chi (A.D. 261–303) but its style was marred by the parallel constructions, which inevitably became pompous bad prose. Tungpo was like the polestar of his days, completely worshiped by a host of admirers, and among these there were four, and later six, scholars, whom he highly thought of and was willing to accept as his disciples. The impression of their correspondence is that he was like a genial great professor, charming, at ease, and sincere. One word from him and a scholar's name was made. Often people submitted their writings to him for his opinion, and he would be sincere and frank, but polite. I give here only excerpts from these letters.*

THE STYLE OF SAILING CLOUDS AND FLOWING WATER

I have looked over your poems and prose. In general, writing should be like sailing clouds and flowing water. It has no definite [required] form. It goes where it has to go and stops where it cannot but stop. One has thus a natural style, with all its wayward charms. Confucius said, "If a statement is not beautiful, it will not be read far and wide." Again he said, "In writing, all one asks is successful expression of an idea." One may think that if a statement merely aims at expressing one's thoughts, it will not be beautiful. That is not true. It is not easy to express exactly a fugitive idea or a passing thought. First of all, it is difficult to see and appreciate it in one's mind and heart — not one in a million can do it — and even harder to express it by writing or by word of mouth. When this is done, that thought or idea is given proper expression, and when one can do this, one can do anything with writing. Yang Shiung (53 B.C.–A.D. 18) loved to dress up his superficial ideas in archaic, abstruse language. For if he said clearly what he thought, it would be shown to be something everybody knew already. . . . These are examples of his superficiality. This is something about writing which can be spoken about only to those who really understand. I mention this merely in passing. Ouyang Shiu (1007–1072) said that writing is like gold or jade, with a definite market price for a certain quality. Literary reputation is not something which can be made or minimized by someone's expressed opinion. — *Letter to Shieh Minshih.*

THE COMPULSION TO WRITE

Writers in ancient times wrote, not because they decided they wanted to write, but because they could not help writing. It is like clouds and flowers of vegetation which take form naturally as a result of accumulation of certain forces. They have to seek expression of what is in them. I have heard my father say that the ancient sages said things because they had something which must be said. My brother Cheh and myself have written a great deal, but we have never presumed to think that we are so engaged in writing.—*Preface to Poems on the Southward Voyage.*

THE NEED OF INDIVIDUALITY

Never has the plight of literature been worse than today. The cause for this is to be sought in Mr. Wang (Anshih, 1021— 1086.* He is a good writer, but he wants everybody to agree with

* Wang Anshih was a great social reformer, but curiously also a good poet. The emperor had complete confidence in him and gave him power to enforce his socialistic schemes. This he did by driving away from the court every single man who did not agree with him, Su Tungpo among them.

himself. Even Confucius could not make two individuals alike; he could not change the character of his disciples, Yen Huei or Tselu. But Wang wants the entire world to accept his ideas. Two pieces of good land can both produce certain crops, but they do not produce the same kind of crops. Bad land, on the other hand, can produce one kind — a deadening uniformity of reeds and rushes which extend for miles and miles. This is the uniformity of thought which Wang wants.

— *Letter to Chang Wenchien* (a disciple).

THE UNIVERSAL VALUES OF WRITING

It is very hot these last few days, and I do not know how you feel. I have received your long letter and a scroll of prose and poems. I am sorry to have delayed answering until now. There are many people who write today, and many who write agreeably well. But there are few who show that ease and self-mastery and simple freshness as you do. I am glad to have read them, and shall not be selfish but will let the world know about it. There is one thing in life that there is no mistake about: no lasting reputation can be palmed off on the public. Literature is like gold or jade; there is a regular market value for certain qualities. It is true that the elder generation can help the younger writers by their comments. But in the end the quality of a writer will be determined by the reading public, and is not based on any one person's opinion. In the case of a few, like Huang Tingchien, Chang Wenchien [Su's accepted disciples], I was merely a discoverer of their talents. People heard what I said, and held their reservations, and only after a certain time elapsed was there a consensus of opinion, and they got their dues. I did not have the power to create reputations. And not only I, but also the generations preceding me. As to academic honors, these are in the lap of the gods. I have nothing to do with it. I am telling you all I think in this letter. Shall be going away from the capital soon. Can I see you? — *Letter to Mao Pang.*

ON THE SIMPLE, NATURAL STYLE

Mr. Chao (Wuchiu, later one of Su's disciples) sent me his long sentimental poem [*sao*]. On careful reading, I found it had a rich beauty of phraseology. His family seems indeed to have many talents. But I have a little idea to suggest, and I want you to put it to him gently. A man should aim first of all to write naturally and simply, and let that extra richness of thought and expression come naturally when it comes — overflows as it were as a natural, effortless consequence. I think Chao is a little too young. But break it to him gently, not because we want to spare him, but because it may affect that great young drive in him. Put it casually in the course of a friendly conversation. What do you think?

— *Letter to Huang Tingchien.*

ON CUTTING DOWN

I have received your poems in ancient *fu* and modern *shih* forms. I am pleased with the swing of rhythm and the many fresh ideas. But they are a little overwritten. Later you must try to cut down a little. Don't do it now. Your composition gives the impression of a swelling spring river. Let it rise to its highest limits. When the frost comes and the water level goes down, you will find the regular banks. But you should know it now.

You have kindly shown me the essays on Tang history by Sun Chih-han, whom I do not know. . . . He has many ideas there with which I agree. I have also read Ouyang Shiu's biography, with Szema Kuang's postscript, which are indeed very expressive. But why do you want me to write this piece by Ouyang in my handwriting for stone inscription so as to "immortalize" Chih-han? He can well enough stand on his own, even without Ouyyang's piece.

Why should he have the vulgar idea to want to achieve immortality by means of a good calligraphy? You have always been most kind to me, but don't do it by overcomplimenting me more than I deserve. The scholars of today are overambitious. They want people to compare them to Confucius or the duke of Chou;

any comparison from Mencius down would not satisfy them. This is a trend that should be stopped. I have come to realize that I ran into so many troubles because I was actually a lesser man than my reputation made me out to be. God will not stand for this. It is as bad as to receive a high post without having done anything for the country. I really wish people would stop rumors about me that add to my conceit. That will make matters worse for me. . . .
— *Letter to Li Chih* (almost a disciple).

« *All great men are humble. Su Tungpo was humble, in spite of his self-evident genius. One may find such among writers, but in politics, a truly humble great man is a rarity. What a difficult test for greatness!*

65 ▣ The Familiar Style

From

THE IMPORTANCE OF LIVING

Lin Yutang

« *It may be presumptuous for an editor to include his own comments on the art of writing. There is, however, some excuse for this, for the idea of the Kung-an School, or the School of Self-Expression (see selection 67) has not been fully represented. The following, first published here in* The Importance of Living, *was originally written in Chinese, the greater part being the statement with which I launched the fortnightly Jenchienshih, devoted to promotion of the familiar essay and reviving of the Kung-an School.*

A WRITER IN THE FAMILIAR STYLE speaks in an unbuttoned mood. He completely exposes his weakness, and is therefore disarming.

The relationship between writer and reader should not be one between an austere schoolmaster and his pupils, but one between friends. Only in this way can warmth be generated.

He who is afraid to use an "I" in his writing will never make a good writer.

I love a liar more than a speaker of truth, and an indiscreet liar more than a discreet one. His indiscretions are a sign of his love for his readers.

I trust an indiscreet fool and suspect a lawyer.

The indiscreet fool is a nation's best diplomat. He wins people's hearts.

326

My idea of a good magazine is a fortnightly, where we bring a group of good talkers together in a small room once in a fortnight and let them chat together. The readers listen to their chats, which last just about two hours. It is like having a good evening chat, and after that the reader goes to bed, and next morning when he gets up to attend to his duties as a bank clerk or an accountant or a school principal posting notices to the students, he feels that the flavor of last night's chat still lingers around his cheeks.

There are restaurants for giving grand dinners in a hall with gold-framed mirrors, and there are small restaurants designed for a little drink. All I want is to bring together two or three intimate friends and have a little drink, and not to go to the dinners of rich and important people. But the pleasure we have in a small restaurant eating and drinking and chatting and teasing each other and overturning cups and spilling wine on dresses is something which the people at the grand dinners do not understand and can never "miss."

There are rich men's gardens and mansions, but there are also little lodges in the mountains. Although sometimes these mountain lodges are furnished with taste and refinement, the atmosphere is quite different from that of the rich men's mansions with vermilion gates and green windows and a platoon of servants and maids standing around. When one enters the door, he does not hear the barking of faithful dogs and does not see the faces of snobbish butlers and gatekeepers, and when he leaves he does not see a pair of "unchaste stone lions" outside the gate. The situation is perfectly described by Yuan Chunglang, a writer of the seventeenth century: "It is as if Chou, Cheng, Chang, and Chu [Sung doctrinaires] are sitting together and bowing to each other in the Hall of Fushi, and suddenly there come Su Tungpo and Tungfang Shuo, who break into the room half naked and without shoes, and begin to clap their hands and joke with one another. The onlookers will probably stare in amazement, but these gentlemen look at each other in silent understanding."

66 ▣ Literature and Complexion

From

WEST-GREEN RANDOM NOTES

Shih Chenlin
c. 1693 - 1779

Wu is a studious young man who has read the entire Twenty-one Histories, punctuating them himself with red ink. . . . When he was young, he loved most the ancient philosophers, for he thought that they showed real insight into human life and expressed original thinking which is corroborated by our own experience. But among literature, he likes the random essays best. For in these idle chats casually expressed, there was no thought in the authors' minds of "making literature," but the sentiments often reveal our innermost secrets. "There are different kinds of composition," he said. "Some are school compositions, some are for the imperial examinations or for social occasions, and some follow the trends and fashions of the times, to please the public. The philosophers' works are written by thinkers, but random essays are written by poets. The writings of thinkers give one wisdom and have a practical bearing on life. The writings of poets please one's spirit, beautify one's complexion, and prolong one's life."

« I am burning six candles to translate this piece. The power in Manhattan has failed — a most rare and most curious thing. But it is a rare pleasure also. When shall a man again enjoy the pleasure of translating Shih Chenlin by the light of candles in Manhattan? I shall never forget it. As for why I do this when the temperature is in the 90's, the answer is that a man will do anything for complexion. The last line above tells the story. Besides, one keeps cool this way.

328

67 ▣ The Discovery of Self

Preface to

SELECTED POEMS OF LANGHUAN

Chang Tai
1597 - 1689

« *The literary schools mentioned here which the author tried in his younger days to imitate, are known generally as (1) the Kung-an School of the three Yuan brothers, led by Yuan Chunglang, flourishing around the year 1600, and (2) the Chingling School, a reaction against the first, led by Chung Poching (died 1625) and Tan Yuanchun (died 1631). The Kung-an School emphasized the expression of a writer's personality and a style of natural simplicity, sometimes carried to the point of bareness. The other school went in for a style packed with the intricate, the abstruse and difficult. Shu Wenchang, the idol of the author and of Yuan Chunglang, was an eccentric genius, poet, and playwright who lived from 1521 to 1593. The style here is deliberately quaint. (See note on Chang Tai in selection 27.)*

IN MY YOUNG DAYS, I loved [Shu] Wenchang, and began to learn writing verse in his style. Because [Yuan] Chunglang liked Wenchang also, I also began to learn to write like Chunglang who liked Wenchang. I never tried to write like others before these two. Later I liked the Chingling School and thought of writing like Tan and Chung, but never really had the time to master it. My friend Chang Yiju liked the latter school. He made an anthology of poetry from the Chung and Tan point of view, and from the same point of view selected my poems which tried to be like Chung and Tan but could never equal them. He said my

329

poems very much resembled Wenchang in spirit, and he left these alone and selected only those which more or less caught the Chung-Tan spirit. I decided to reform, and burnt all those poems which suggested resemblance to Wenchang, and tortured my brains to write nothing except that which was in the Chung-Tan tradition.

After ten years, I examined myself and found that I had failed to learn the style of Chung and Tan. For my nature was born like Wenchang. I might change a few words to give the verse a different complexion, but my bones could not be changed. I began to realize that the writing of a man is like the form and shape and petals and arrangement of flowers. These grow spontaneously in accordance with their inner nature, and take certain forms without mistake and without fail. One can graft another variety, and although certain changes may be produced, the main structural forms cannot be changed. I had already burnt those poems à la Wenchang. Now if I burned also those poems seemingly à la Chung and Tan, but essentially à la Wenchang, I would have to burn everything I ever wrote. I decided to spare these in time, and had copies made for my children, so that they would know that once their father was also a poet, that he both learned poems à la Wenchang and burned poems à la Wenchang, and but had now decided to preserve some which resemble Wenchang. These I preserve so that part of Tsungtse (myself) which resembles Wenchang may be preserved, and the Wenchang which is copied by Tsungtse may also be preserved through me. So if Tsungtse and Wenchang are both preserved, then the Wenchang spirit in Wenchang poems burned by Yiju will also be preserved. My old friend Wu Shi used to say that I am a reincarnation of Wenchang. He came especially to collect his poems and my discarded poems. But the poems of mine which he published are not equal to the poems of Wenchang which were published before. This means that already in his previous life Wenchang was not as good as Wenchang.

Now if one is going to take that Wenchang which was not as good as Wenchang and try to put into a pigeonhole the Tsungtse which resembles Wenchang without trying, Tsungtse will not submit to such treatment. The ancients said well, "I will try to get along with my own self." So I must learn to express myself.

The fifteenth of August, 1654.

68 ▣ The Moral Censor

From

HUAYANG ESSAYS

Shih Chenlin
1693 - c. 1779

THERE WAS AN OLD GENTLEMAN OF SHIN-AN with a long beard. He was very proud of it. He had started to grow it while still in his youth, and his vanity made him tend it every day. "No crab claws, and no swallow tails, please," he prayed to his beard every day. In three years, his beard grew to a very respectable shape and length, so that the townspeople called him "the Bearded Gentleman." When he grew old, the title was changed to "the Old Gentleman with the Long Beard." He had the habit of lecturing young people. Of all the things he could not stand the worst was loose morals or flirting with girls on the part of the youths. And the young men felt abashed and listened quietly when he talked to them. In time, the scholars began to look upon him as a moral censor and a stern schoolmaster, but treated him with great respect.

He was carrying on business in Soochow, and one day was returning home to Shin-an. There were about a dozen young men who were going home, too, and they all expressed the hope that the bearded gentleman would not be traveling on the same boat with them. When they went on board, however, there was the bearded moral censor, sitting erectly in the middle. Their hearts went down, for the voyage took about ten days, and it looked like it was spoiled for them already. The old gentleman saw them going away to take another boat and shouted at them. Under the circumstances, the young people turned back sheepishly and took their seats.

When the voyage began, they found that the boatman had a beautiful young daughter by the name of Laniang. There was a cabin on the stern which was occupied by one of the young men by the name of Huang Mingkao. The bearded gentleman warned him several times not to flirt with the young girl, until Huang gave it up and said, "If you don't trust me, why don't you take the cabin? I will move out."

"That will do also," said the old gentleman, giving his beard a soft brush with his fingers.

It was most unfortunate that soon afterward the old man caught cold, so much so that he had to cover his face in his quilt. He was afraid of light in the daytime, and in the night he preferred to sleep without candles. The young people were much put out and uncomfortable throughout the voyage, and dared not make any noise.

After ten days, the boat arrived at Shin-an. At nightfall, the old man was all wrapped up and sent ashore shivering and put in a sedan chair. He was so covered that no one could see his beard as he took the sedan chair. But they thought it was natural.

The young people turned around and said to the boatman, "You should have taken better care of the old gentleman and not allowed him to get so sick."

"Sick?" replied the boatman's daughter. "I have something to cure it." Thereupon she threw a package to the young man Huang.

Huang opened it and saw it contained the old man's beard, gray in color and over a foot long.

The party was greatly amazed.

"How did you get it?" they asked.

"What do you think?" replied the girl. "His beard was my price."

69 ▣ Little Half Catty

Huang Choushing
1611 - 1680

THERE WAS A CERTAIN MAN whose name we will not
mention. He was nicknamed "Little Half Catty." The name came
about because it was a rare thing when he allowed himself to
buy meat, and when he did he would buy only four ounces [which
was only one fourth of a catty of sixteen Chinese ounces]. He did
not think it sounded nice at all to say "four ounces," but preferred
to call it "half catty." When asked to clarify, he corrected it by
calling it "little half catty." I am enchanted by it and must therefore tell the story, as follows:

Heaven be praised! He is going to buy meat! What an extraordinary thing, for he never drank, and seldom tasted meat for a
whole year. Now he is going to buy meat. Heaven be praised!

He called together his servants and announced his intention. He
opened his trunk with his right hand and took a weighing rod in
his left. There were some cash in it. Very carefully he picked out
a tiny piece of copper and solemnly handed it over to the boy.
Quite overcome with emotion, tears stood on the brink of his
eyes. The servants looked at one another in surprise, and the boy
knelt down and asked, "Shall I buy a catty?"

The gentleman was struck speechless with this most unheard-of
idea, and was raising his hand to strike.

"Half a catty, then," corrected the boy.

The gentleman's sense of injury was still evident, and the boy
was confused and could not guess what the master wanted.

"Please tell me, how much shall I buy?"

The master put out four fingers, and said, "Buy a *little* half

337

catty." He really meant half of half a catty, but it sounded better.

The boy then left the house, but the master followed him quietly behind, taking care not to be observed. He leaned on the doorpost while the boy went into a butcher's shop. When the boy had delivered the money and the butcher was raising his knife to cut the meat, the master suddenly walked up and said, "Wait a minute. This is my meat. I am paying for it. Don't you give me under weight."

"No, sir," replied the butcher quickly. "Why, to you I would give you extra for a present, all right?"

"Some more," demanded the gentleman.

The butcher added a tiny bit.

"Some more!" repeated the gentleman.

The result was that he got six ounces instead of four. The gentleman returned with a triumphant face.

Now when they reached home, the boy was taking the meat to the kitchen.

"No," said the master. "You are not going to hurry away with that meat. Call the maid from the kitchen. This is food, God's given food, do you realize? I will not stand for any waste of God's bounty. We will do justice to it. Call the maid, and I shall personally give the instructions on what to do with it."

When the kitchenmaid came in, he said to her solemnly, "I do hereby hand over to you this meat. I want to get the best out of it, and do you be careful in cutting and preparing it. First, cut some and make it into cold roast cut into dice for sacrifice to my beloved ancestors. Secondly, reserve a portion for entertaining guests and my students. Allow a third portion to be well cooked for the enjoyment of myself, my wife, and my children, and I do not see why you servants should not have a share in it, too. Guard it carefully and see that it is not eaten by cats or mice. And under no condition shall the leftovers be thrown to the dogs and cats. What gravy is left in the cooking pot must be saved, and when you clean the pot, be sure to look for possible morsels that may cling to the bottom. Remember," he repeated sententiously, "this is meat."

That was how Little Half Catty bought and made use of the more than half of half a catty on that rare occasion. It was as if he had paid for a piece of unicorn venison, or dragon's liver, or bear's paw. Heaven be praised!

70 📖 The Never-never Land

"THE SONG OF YUTANYUEH"

Huang Choushing
1611 - 1680

» *The following describes a magic land of bliss into which devout Buddhists of accomplished ten virtues may someday be born. Huang Choushing makes seven excerpts from Fayuan Chulin, a book of selections from Buddhist sacred texts, and writes seven poems on them. Only the excerpts are translated, and not the poems. The Chinese Fayuan Chulin is easily obtainable.*

I HAVE HEARD A BUDDHIST MONK speak to me about a place called Chuluchow, and he says, "There one finds food, clothing, shelter, and all necessary things grown from the land without your having to work for them." I often thought of these words and was quite enchanted. Recently, I have found the text of the *Long Aham Classic,** as contained in *Fayuan Chulin*, and gotten a full description of the land. I copy here seven excerpts, and have made poems on them out of sheer delight, disregarding the question whether such a land really exists or not.

The text says: On the north of the Himalayas, there is a land called Yutanyueh.† It is here referred to as Chuluchow. It has an area extending 10,000 *yushun* [a *yushun* being forty li, or about

* "Aham" is the term for denoting Hinayana Buddhism and its sacred texts, in Pali.

† It may possibly suggest Bhutan. "Yutanyueh" is the modern mandarin pronunciation of the name. In the pronunciation of the time of translations of Buddhist classics, the word "Buddha" was a fairly accurate translation of the Hindu word, now pronounced in mandarin as *fotuo*. The ancient pronunciation would be more nearly like *Wutanwat*.

thirteen miles]. There are many mountains and lakes in it, and flowers and fruit trees grow in it. There is a profusion of singing birds. It is surrounded by the Aruta Lake, which is connected with four big rivers. There are no sunken ravines in it, no thistles or prickly plants, no mosquitoes, gnats, or poisonous insects. . . . The ground is soft, rising and falling with your feet. When you want to clear yourself, it opens by itself, and when you have finished, it closes up again by itself.

It grows a kind of rice, which is rich in flavor. It also produces a *mani* pearl, which gives off a hot flame. Put a natural pot over it. The rice will cook itself, and when it is done, the flame goes out automatically.

There is a kind of tree called "leafy arch." The leaves of this tree are arranged like the tiles on a roof and offer a perfect protection from rain. The men and women live under it. . . . When desire comes to a man, he needs only to fix his eyes on a woman and the woman will come to him under the shade of the grove. If it is a father or a mother, with whom satisfaction of desire is out of the question, then the leaves turn outward, permitting light. But if it is not a relative, the tree will bend its arch of leaves over the man and woman, and they can freely enjoy themselves from one to seven days before they part company. . . . Those who have strong desires may have from one to four or five children. There are also monks who feel no desire till the end of their days.

There are other aromatic trees. When it is the season, they grow clothing, or utensils, or food, or beautiful boats. One can go boating. When one goes in bathing in the lake, he takes off his clothes and leaves them on the bank. When he gets to the other side, he picks up more clothes and does not look for the ones he left behind. Then the people go to the aromatic tree, and take musical instruments and sing.

The people of that country have a pregnancy period of only seven or eight days. It may be a boy or a girl, and the baby is left on the streets. Some passer-by will suck his own finger, and put it in the baby's mouth. Sweet milk will flow from the tip of the finger and feed the baby well. After seven days, the baby is already grown up, as tall as the men and women. The boys go to the men, and the girls go to the women.

These men and women have in their previous lives perfected the ten virtues and are born here. They stand thirty-two *chou*.* Their hair is dark brown and almost covers the brows. . . . They are free from all disease. They live exactly one thousand years, not one year more or less. After that, they are reborn in another good place of heaven.

Their land is square, and the inhabitants are also square-faced. . . . They look all alike. . . . When they die, they do not hold funerals and weep. They leave the corpse solemnly in the open places. There is a kind of bird which comes from another region and eats it.

* The original note here says: "A *chou* is one foot eight inches." A *chou* denotes the length from elbow to fingers.

71 ▣ What the Donkey Said

From

MORE GHOST STORIES (SHU YUKUAILU)

Li Fuyen

c. A.D. 830

« *Li Fuyen was a good teller of tales in the ninth century when the short stories of Tang flourished. He has a type of fancy reminiscent of the Arabian Nights. The general theme of transmigration of souls when men are born as animals and animals as men provides a rich ground for imaginative tales. Four of his best tales of this type have been included in my Famous Chinese Short Stories. The story of retribution, based on the cycle of transmigration, is neatly told here in the present story, which is translated for the first time.*

THERE WAS A MERCHANT OF CHANG-AN by the name of Chang Kao who had made a lot of money. He had kept a donkey for years. In August of the year A.D. 817, Chang Kao died, and thirteen days after his death, his wife asked the son, Chang Ho, to bring gifts of food to the monks outside the East City for their service at the funeral. He went on the donkey, but as soon as he had left the alleyway, the donkey refused to go. Chang Ho struck him with a whip and the animal forsooth lay on the ground to show him that he would not go. The young man gave him another crack.

"Why do you beat me?" said the donkey, looking at him.

"Why not? My family paid twenty thousand cash for you. Of course I will beat you if you don't move." After he said it, he

343

suddenly realized that the donkey was talking to him and was greatly astonished.

The donkey continued, "Let me tell you this. Your father bought me for twenty thousand cash. On the other hand, I have been ridden by him for some twenty years already. You don't understand this matter of transmigration of men into animals and animals into men. It goes in a cycle like a wheel. I owed your father a debt for some reason or other, and was therefore transformed into a donkey to be ridden by way of payment. Now that I have paid you back don't you try to take advantage of me. Last night I reckoned the accounts with your father, and all I owe you now is fifteen hundred cash. I owed your father a debt, and therefore he was entitled to ride me. I owe you nothing and you have no right to ride me. If you force me to carry you, I shall also try to force you to carry me. So generation after generation, you will be riding me and I shall be riding you. Where is this all going to end? I owe you fifteen hundred now, right? You try to sell me and see. I am worth ten thousand now, but no one will buy me because I don't owe anybody any money. Tell you what I will do. Bearded Wang, the flour merchant, owes me two thousand. I don't owe him; he owes me and I am going to make him repay that debt. He will buy me for two thousand, and I will give you fifteen hundred and keep five hundred for my own feed. Then my days as donkey are over. You just try and do what I say."

The young man turned back and told his mother the story. She was greatly touched and said to the donkey, "Why don't I let you go free to pasture where you like? I know you are getting old and this life is hard for you. What is fifteen hundred cash? I am willing to cancel the debt. What do you say?"

But the donkey shook its head.

"Then perhaps you want to be repaid for what Bearded Wang owes you?" she asked again.

The donkey nodded its head in approval.

The young man then took it to a broker and said he wanted only fifteen hundred cash for it, but found no buyer. As the donkey was led through the western city, he met a man who wore a heavy beard and paid the price asked for. On being asked what his name was, the buyer said his name was Wang, and his business was selling flour.

It rained for several days after Wang bought it. Chang Ho happened to pass by and learned that the donkey had died. So it seemed that Bearded Wang never had a chance to ride the donkey. He had merely paid his debt.

I was able to learn of this story from a neighbor of Chang Ho who lived to the east of his house. She was a woman from the Li family, wife of Captain Chang Ta of the Palace Guards. I write it down to show how no one gets away with anything, however secret it is kept.

72 📖 Some Dog Stories

From

YUTSU SHINCHIH

Wang Yen
17th century

« *These dog stories, preserved in the collection Yutsu Shinchih edited by Chang Chao with a preface dated 1683, were called in their original title* Our Animal Teachers. *There are always wise souls who believe that the animals have a lot to teach us, and there are always open-minded persons who can see that man is the most degenerate of all animals and that a healthy return to original simplicity of character may be the salvation of mankind. It is in this sense that Wang Yen calls animals not only our teachers but "saint-teachers." This collection consists chiefly of the editor's contemporaries and the author is presumed to have lived in the seventeenth century.*

IN THE TIME OF SUN WU during the Three Kingdoms (third century) there was a Chi Hsinshun who kept a dog, called "Black Dragon." Black Dragon followed him wherever he went. One day Chi was dead drunk and lay down to sleep on a patch of wild grass outside the city. It happened that an officer was out hunting and had caused a fire in the wild tract. Black Dragon, sensing the danger, tried to wake him up and tugged at his gown, but without avail. He saw there was a little creek about thirty yards from the place, went to the creek, and dipped himself in the water. Then he came back and rolled on the grass where his master was still lying in heavy slumber. The dog kept on repeating this operation, running through the smoke and fire, until the little patch of grass was thoroughly wet. The dog was burned himself and died. He had, however, succeeded in saving the master, and when the latter woke up, he saw Black Dragon lying dead by his side, the place all wet and the rest of the patch all burned up. He realized what Black Dragon had done for him and wept bitterly. Out of a sense of gratitude, he petitioned the magistrate, and gave the dog a regular human burial, with a coffin and proper burial gowns. Now there is still a mound at Chinan, called "the Tomb of the Righteous Dog."

YUAN TSAN DIED AS A REVOLUTIONIST. He left a three-year-old orphan, and his amah brought him to the home of one of Yuan's students, by the name of Ti Lingching. This Ti was a rascal and said, "I hear there is a reward for anyone who delivers Yuan's orphan." The amah was furious and protested: "I have come to you with this orphan because you owe debts of gratitude to your master. If you kill this baby to obtain the reward, you will one day die an untimely death. The gods will avenge your master." The child was killed in spite of the amah's protest. Now the child had a big, hairy dog as his friend, and used to ride on the dog while at play. A year after the child died, a big dog suddenly appeared at Ti's home, met him in the yard, and bit him to death. Then he went in and bit Ti's wife also. This was the dog that the child used to play with.

GENERAL CHI CHIUNG of Tang Dynasty used to keep four big hunting dogs who accompanied him on his hunting trips. The general fed them with meat, and noticed that one of them always took a piece in his mouth and ran out to a hidden bush to eat it and would then return. Piqued by curiosity, Chi ordered a servant to follow the dog to the bush. The servant found that the dog had an old, sick mother, thin, emaciated, and diseased. Struck by the dog's conduct, Chi had the mother dog brought home and fed properly, while her son would look on and wag his tail in happiness and gratitude. Thereafter, the dog proved his gratitude by being always the first to catch the game. A year afterward, the mother dog died, and the dog felt upset for days. Later on, when Chi died, the dog watched over his coffin during the entire funeral ceremonies, and when the coffin was let into the ground, the dog scratched the ground madly and died before the grave was completed.

A CERTAIN CHANG OF KUEICHI had to go abroad, leaving in his home only his young wife and a man servant. In time, the two did the logical thing under the circumstances. Chang had a dog by the name of "Black Dragon" who accompanied him abroad. When master and dog returned, the servant and mistress plotted to kill him. A dinner was prepared, and while they sat around the board, pretending to celebrate his return, Chang had discovered the plot and sat silently at the table. He threw a piece of meat to the dog and said, "I have kept you for so many years. Now I am in danger of life. Save me." The dog looked at the meat and then at the servant. Chang slapped his thigh and cried: "Black Dragon!" Thereupon the dog leapt upon the servant, who, taken by surprise, dropped his knife to the ground and fell down, and the dog bit off his genitals. Chang then took the knife and killed the servant. His wife was sent to prison and sentenced to death.

DURING THE REBELLION of Yang Kuangyuan at Chingchow, there was a Mr. Sun living in the city. The food supply was running short in the besieged city, and there was no way of obtaining food from his villa in the country. While the family did not know what to do, they saw their dog lying by the master's side and looking at them wistfully. "Can you go to the villa and fetch food for me?" Sun asked the dog, and the dog wagged his tail as if he understood. At night they attached a bag on the dog's neck with a letter in it and the dog left the city through a water gate. Arriving at his master's villa, the dog kept barking until he was admitted. Learning the message contained in the letter, they sent the dog back with a bag of rice. This was kept up for several months until the siege was called off. For this reason, the whole family was grateful to the dog for saving their lives. When the dog died several years afterward, they buried him in a beautiful spot in the villa.

73 ▣ Sound Movies

From

ANALECTS FORTNIGHTLY

Shu Shehyu
contemporary

« *Shu Shehyu, alias Lao Sheh, was author of* The Rickshaw Boy.
*This sketch first appeared in Analects Fortnightly, a magazine
of humor, to which he was a regular contributor in the 1930's.*

ERH CHIEH, OR MY SECOND SISTER, had never seen a talking picture. But she already had a theory about it, as we all do about the things we haven't seen. The less facts there are, the more theories there must be. Like great men discussing politics, she also indulged in making up a theory about something she did not quite understand. She thought that the "noise pictures" were called by that name because the projecting machine was particularly noisy. Or else, it must be because of the fact that when the "electric men" and "electric women" — by which she meant the stars of the pictures — kissed, a great deal of noise was produced by the public applause. As she really believed in this latter theory, she didn't care much about going to see them, because she used to hide her face behind her fingers when she saw the "electric people" kissing each other on the screen.

But, she was told, there are real talking and singing and laughter in sound pictures. She did not believe it at first, but when all reports confirmed this fact, she began to be curious.

Erh Lao Lao, or the second great-auntie, was also getting curious.

Besides, Erh Chieh had just won a lot of money from cards, and she was going to celebrate. Those invited included the second great-auntie, the third maternal auntie, the fourth maternal sister-auntie, Little Bald-Head, Little Obedience, and Number Four Dog.

As the second great-auntie always went to bed at dusk, it was impossible for them to go to a night performance. It was decided that they should see the two-thirty show and should set out at twelve. This was considered early enough, because after all seeing a movie was only an amusement or an outing, as it were. When she had to meet people at the station, Erh Chieh used to go seven or eight hours ahead of the schedule. When Erh Chieh's husband was leaving for Tientsin last time, she urged him to go to the station three days ahead, because she was afraid he might not get a proper seat.

The point is that, when you leave early, you don't necessarily arrive early; otherwise what is the use of leaving as early as possible? When one agrees to leave by twelve, one is generally just about ready at quarter to one. It took the great-auntie fifteen minutes to find her spectacles; she had them in her inside pocket all the time. Then the third maternal auntie was looking for her buttons, and she had ransacked through four trunks in vain for it, and decided finally to wear a simple dress. Number Four Dog finished his toilet in fifteen minutes, which was pretty good, considering the fact that he used to take over half an hour, and even then the police-man of the street had to give him lessons about washing his face.

Finally they were all outside the door, and were all set to start on the journey, when it was found that Little Bald-Head was missing. Back they came into the house to look for him, but could not establish his whereabouts. They agreed to give up going, because looking for Little-Bald-Head was more important. Everybody began to take off his or her things, and went off in different directions to look for Bald-Head. After a while, Bald-Head appeared by himself; he had gone ahead, and was returning to see why they hadn't started and what had kept them so long. So they began to dress up again. It was a little late, but it didn't really matter; they could go by rickshaws.

The great-auntie, whose opinion was respected on account of her age, used to haggle with the rickshaw coolies on the basis of 120 coppers being equal to one dollar, which obtained in the last years of the Manchu days. She hadn't been out much, and she was consequently inclined to think people were taking advantage of her old age when they told her that a wheat cake cost three coppers. When the rickshaw coolies demanded two or three dimes for the distance of about a mile, she also considered they were taking advantage of her old age. She was going to show them. She would walk. Only when she started, nobody could tell whether her legs were carrying her forward or backward, and she didn't know herself. Apparently, the fourth maternal sister-auntie came to help her, but she really had on high-heeled shoes when she realized she was going to see the movie, and she felt it safer to go with someone. Of course, it was plain to everyone that if either one of them should fall, they would fall together in a heap.

Thus they arrived at the theater, punctually at quarter past three. The performance had already started. Someone was to blame, probably the management. Punctuality in starting programs meant no allowance for human nature and no consideration for old age. It was inhuman. Erh Chieh felt like scolding somebody, but she decided not to show her temper.

They bought tickets, as was the proper thing to do. The moment they were shown in, Little Obedience refused to go in; it was so dark, and in all dark places were hidden red-eyed monsters. The darkness also reminded the great-auntie of night, and night reminded her of going to sleep. She was feeling sleepy and "would rather go home with Little Obedience." So they began to hold a family council, which was quite open to the audience in general. Erh Chieh insisted that the occasion was in honor of the great-auntie, and if she went home, there was no point in their seeing the picture at all. As for Little Obedience, she could buy him some candy and keep him quiet. Furthermore, great-auntie had already one foot in her grave, and if she died without seeing a sound picture, what could she tell the King of Hades, when she was asked? Erh Chieh's persuasion carried effect, and all decided to stay.

There was the question of proceeding down the hall. The fourth maternal auntie held great-aunt by the hand, the third maternal sister-auntie took charge of Little Obedience, while Erh Chieh took care of Number Four Dog, and they proceeded down the dark and treacherous hall with hues and cries very much like Alpine tourists. There were ushers of course, but they wanted to sit in their own preferred manner. This manner was still a mooted question to be decided by a debate open to the public. Were they to sit all in one line? Were they to separate? Were they to sit in front or at the rear? Erh Chieh was quite upset about it, while Number Four Dog was very vociferous and great-auntie was feeling out of breath. The whole audience was forgetting about the picture and their interest centered around this great family. "Sh . . . Sh . . . Sh!" But Erh Chieh could make her voice heard above them all, and was giving brief and clear-cut commands, just to show them she was perfectly at home in society.

When the usher's flashlight — or "electric stick," according to Erh Chieh — was about used up, they made up their mind to sit down anywhere anyhow. But not exactly "anyhow." The question of superiority arose. It seemed entirely proper that great-auntie, being the oldest in age and great in virtue, should sit inside. But great auntie protested out of politeness toward the fourth maternal sister-auntie: she had been married out and she was now "guest" in our family. Erh Chieh was the hostess; the third maternal auntie was after all in the position of a daughter-in-law vis-à-vis the great-auntie; Little Obedience was only a kid. Who was going to disentangle these social and moral relationships for them? It looked as if they were quarreling from the vehemence of their respective humility, until someone among the audience cried out to God. After due noise and courtesy were made, they thought they would all sit down. But . . . they hadn't yet bought candy for Little Obedience. "Candy man!" Erh Chieh shouted rather loud, in fact so loud that the manager rushed in, thinking that the candy man had committed a murder.

When candy had been bought, great-auntie thought of an important thing—she had forgotten to cough. Her cough, however, stirred up the "filial piety" of Erh Chieh, and she fell to discussing the number of days great-auntie had yet to live. Old people like great-auntie don't mind their children discussing their number of days, and were even willing to participate. "The other things I don't care much about," she said, "but I do want a golden nine-lock puzzle. And don't forget about a pair of paper children to accompany me to my grave."

Now, this was a vast and practically endless topic, and was besides of absorbing interest. One thing recalled another, and one event brought up another event. Strange as it may seem, one could talk about family affairs with so much more zest when everybody was in a proper mood, as when in a public theater. In the midst of this interesting talk, the lights were turned on and people began to leave. Erh Chieh called for the seller of melon seeds. One needed to chew melon seeds when discussing family affairs.

The usher came and informed them that the performance was over, and the next one would be at eight o'clock in the evening.

So they had to leave. It was not till great-auntie had gone to bed, that Erh Chieh asked the third maternal aunt, "Come to think of it, what really *is* a sound picture?" After a little pause, auntie replied, "Oh, let it alone. I didn't hear anything, anyway." It was the fourth maternal sister-aunt who proved herself to have been a keen observer. She remarked that foreign devils let out smoke through their nose when they smoke.

"These electric pictures are really wonderfully made. When the smoke comes out through the nose, it looks as if it is real." And they all assented in admiration.

74 ⌾ Tales with Morals

From

SHUEHTAO SHIAOSHU

Chiang Chinchih
c. 1600

《 *The author was a close friend of Yuan Chunglang. (See note for selection 67.)*

ONCE A GENERAL WAS SHOT IN THE HEAD with an arrow in battle, and he quickly ran home to have the arrow pulled out.

He asked a surgeon, which in Chinese is called "an external doctor," to treat him.

The surgeon examined it and, taking a pair of scissors, cut the arrow off as close to the skin as possible, and asked for his fee.

"Please take out the arrow for me, for it is inside my head, and I am going to die of it!" pleaded the general.

"I am an external doctor," replied the surgeon. "What has that got to do with me? I have done my part. You can ask a doctor of internal medicine to attend to the rest of it."

The general did not know what to do.

MORAL: *The authorities today who shirk their responsibilities and pass them on to the next official are of the opinion that the arrow inside should be left to the doctor of internal medicine.*

▣

THERE WAS A QUACK DOCTOR who advertised that he could cure the camel of his hump. Someone brought a camel to him to be cured.

The doctor placed a wooden board on the ground and made the camel lie on it. Then he placed another wooden board on top of the animal and made people go on top and stamp on it as hard as they could.

The camel died of it.

The owner of the camel went to sue him at court for killing the camel.

The camel doctor said: "I am a camel doctor. My business is to make humps straight. It is none of my business whether the animal remains alive."

MORAL: *The magistrates who see to it that the taxes are collected properly, but do not see to it that the people remain alive, are in no way different from the camel doctor.*

▣

THERE WAS ONCE A POOR MAN who picked up a hen's egg. He brought the egg home and said to his wife:

"Look here, I have found a fortune!"

And he showed the egg to his wife, and said:

"This is my fortune, but you have to wait about ten years. I will have a neighbor's hen sit on this egg, and when the chicken grows up, I shall possess a hen. The hen will lay fifteen eggs a month, which means fifteen chickens. In two years' time, we shall have three hundred chickens, for which we shall get ten dollars. With these ten dollars, I will buy five calves, and when these grow up and bear other calves, I shall have twenty-five cows in three years. When these multiply, in another three years we shall have a hundred and fifty cows, which will sell for three hundred dollars. I will loan the three hundred dollars for interest, and in another three years, we shall have at least five hundred dollars. Then I shall spend two thirds of this sum on a house and farm, and one third of it for buying servants and a concubine, and live happily for life."

When his wife heard him mention the word "concubine," she became very angry and smashed the egg to pieces, shouting, "I will not tolerate this seed of all evil!"

The husband was also very angry, and he went to sue his wife at court, the charge being that she had broken up his fortune, and was consequently a bad wife. He asked that the wife be severely punished, and told the magistrate the whole story.

"But," said the magistrate, "your wife stopped you when you had come only to the concubine: you hadn't quite finished telling her what you were going to do yet."

"Indeed, I had finished, Your Honor," said the husband.

"But no," said the magistrate, "your concubine was going to have a son, who would pass the official examinations, become an official, and bring you great honor. Is all this nothing to you? To think that such a huge fortune should be smashed by the fist of a bad woman. She shall be killed!"

"But this was only a discussion; why should I be sentenced to death for it?" protested the wife.

"Your husband's buying a concubine was only a discussion also. Why should you be jealous?"

"That is right, too, Your Honor," said the woman. "But to forestall an evil, you have to nip it in the bud."

The magistrate was delighted and set her free.

MORAL: *To know that a thing does not exist is the best way to forget the desire for it.*

THE SOLICITOR FOR CONTRIBUTIONS

A robber and a monk met a tiger on a mountain path. The robber got ready his bow and arrow to attack the tiger, but that seemed to produce no effect on the tiger, who steadily advanced nearer in spite of the robber's threatening arrow. In that desperate situation, the monk, who held in his hand a book of receipts for soliciting contributions to his temple, threw the book at the tiger and the tiger ran away. Back in his cave, the tiger cub asked its father, "Why are you not afraid of the robber but of the monk?" And the old tiger replied, "Because I could fight with the robber when he came near, but what was I to do if the monk approached me for contributions?"

THE QUACK DOCTOR

One day a quack doctor killed a fat patient. The family of the deceased wanted to sue him, but the affair was finally settled by the doctor undertaking to bury the dead man at his own cost. The quack doctor, however, was very poor himself, and being unable to hire people, he undertook to bury the corpse himself with the help of his wife and two children. The corpse weighed about two hundred pounds, and they had to make frequent stops on the journey. When they bent to pick up the corpse again, the wife remarked to her husband, "My dear husband, next time you go out curing patients, you should pick a thin one."

THE CUCKOO

There was a fool whose wife had a lover. Once he came back at night, and as the lover was trying to leap through the window, he caught one of his shoes. This he put under his pillow thinking that he would use it as evidence and prosecute his wife at court next day. During his sleep, however, his wife secretly exchanged it with one of her husband's own shoes. On waking up next morning, the husband looked carefully at the shoe and finding it to be his own, apologized to his wife, "I am very sorry for last night. I didn't know it was I myself who jumped out of the window."

THE MISER

There was a certain miser who, hearing about the reputation of a greater miser than himself, went to the other miser's home to become his disciple. As usual, he had to bring some present to his new master and brought with him a bowl of water with a piece of paper cut in the form of a fish. The great miser happened to be away from home and his wife received him. "Here is my fish as a humble present from your new pupil," remarked the visitor. The miser's wife received it with thanks and brought up an empty cup and asked him to have tea. After the pupil had pretended to drink tea, the miser's wife again asked him to help himself to the cakes by drawing two circles in the air with her hand. In came the master miser and when he saw his wife drawing two circles, he shouted to her, "What extravagance! You are giving two cakes away! A semicircle should do!"

THE HENPECKED HUSBAND

One day a wife was very angry with her henpecked husband and wanted to torture him with a special instrument for cracking finger bones. There being no such finger-cracker at home, she sent her husband to borrow it from a neighbor. The husband was grumbling all the way as he passed out of the house, considering it as adding insult to injury. "What are you grumbling at?" shouted the wife. The husband was frightened and immediately turned around and said, "I was only saying that we should buy a finger-cracker and keep it at home."

機警

ANCIENT WIT

75 ▣ The Wit of the Ancients

Tsekung, a disciple, asked Confucius, "Do the dead have consciousness?"

"Why don't you wait till you are dead? Then you are bound to know." — *Family Tradition of Confucius.*

Confucius told the following story: Once I was walking in the mountains and saw a woman weeping by a new grave. I asked her what was her grief, and she dried her tears and replied, "We are a family of hunters. My father was eaten by a tiger. My husband was bitten by a tiger and died. And now my son."

"Why don't you move away from this place then?"

"No," replied the woman.

"Why not?"

And the woman replied, "Because there are no taxgatherers here."
— *Family Tradition of Confucius.*

Chiwentse said to Confucius, "I always think thrice before I act." Confucius replied, "To think twice is enough."
— *The Analects.*

Confucius said, "If a man does not say to himself, What shall I do? What shall I do? indeed I do not know what I shall do with such a person." — *The Analects.*

Confucius said, "If a man discovers his mistake and does not correct it, he is committing a second mistake." — *The Analects.*

LAOTSE

Laotse went to visit a sick friend who was very old, by the name of Shang Yung, and they were talking about geriatrics. Laotse wanted to know the secret of his great old age. Shang Yung opened his mouth and asked, "Do you see if my teeth are still left?"

"No," replied Laotse.

"Is my tongue still left?"

"Yes, indeed," replied Laotse.

"Do you get the idea now?"

"I think I know. Gentleness overcomes strength. Isn't that it?"

"Yes," said Shang Yung. "That is all you need to know about the philosophy of life."

— Shen Tao (c. fourth century B.C.) in *Shentse*.

WIT OF CHUANGTSE

Chuangtse once came home from a walk, and his disciples found him wearing a woebegone expression. The latter asked him what had happened, and Chuangtse told the following story:

I was walking in the country and found a woman sitting upon the ground. She was holding a fan in her hand and fanning a fresh grave. I was curious and asked the woman what she was doing, and the woman replied, "I promised my husband never to remarry until his grave was dry. But it rained, and look at this abominable weather these days!" — *Book of Chuangtse*.

WIT OF YEN YING

Yen Ying [a great wit and scholar, sixth century B.C.] was sent as a diplomat to the kingdom of Chu. He was a very short man, and the king of Chu asked him [with the idea of humiliating him], "Are there no better persons in your country to send than you?"

"Of course there are," answered Yen Ying, nettled but calm. "How can you say that, Your Majesty? Why, there are so many able men in our country that when they spread out their long sleeves, they can becloud the sun, and when they perspire, it looks like rainfall."

"Then why do they send you?" asked the king again.

"It is this way. My government sends out diplomats to different countries according to the nature of the country to which they will be attached — the clever ones to clever rulers and stupid ones to stupid rulers. I am about the most stupid in my country. That is why I am sent to you."

Yen Ying was then invited to a dinner by the king. During the dinner, it was arranged to bring two thieves to the king's presence.

"Why are they arrested?" asked the king.

"They have stolen things. They are from the country of Tsi [Yen's country]."

"Why are there so many thieves in your country?" asked the king.

Yen Ying replied, "Have you ever seen the little oranges that are grown north of the Huai River? They are from the same seed as the big oranges south of the Huai. It is the climate. People who are born and live in our country do not steal. But when they come to your country, I don't know why, they do begin to steal. It must be the climate of Chu, I suppose." — *Book of Yentse*.

WIT OF CHI SHIAONAN

Chi Shiaonan was the editor of the great imperial library of rare books and precious editions of Emperor Chienlung (eighteenth century). He was a sound scholar and among the best-read men of his times, and the emperor was very fond of him. His duties made it necessary for him to work inside the palace, in the South Library. One day, it was very hot and Chi stripped himself to the waist. Suddenly the emperor's coming was announced, and he found it impossible to dress himself properly in time. He snatched a jacket and hid himself under the bed. The emperor came in, saw that Chi was not there, said a few words to the assistants, and stood around examining the books. After a stretch of silence, Chi asked from under the bed, "Is the old man gone?"

Chienlung lifted his eyebrows and said, "Chi, come out."

Chi crawled out from under and stood respectfully at attention.

"Now explain yourself. How dare you address me as 'old man'? If you can't explain, you will not get away with this."

"Sire," replied Chi without a thought. "Modern people have no respect for old age. But in classic times 'old man' was the greatest term of respect. It was said of Shipo that he took the best care of the old men of his country, and that was the foundation of the Chou Empire. And Mencius said . . ."

"All right, all right," said Chienlung, and he left with a smile. Chi blew out a puff of relief.

76 ◧ The Person Spoken To

Han Fei
Hanfeitse, ? - 234 B.C.

« The boiling ferment of Chinese thought of different schools had settled down in the third century more or less in favor of a none too idealistic political philosophy of legalism, with a good deal of practical Machiavellian wisdom, such as shown in Han Fei. The strangest transformation from Laotse's philosophy of laissez faire and inaction to a government by stringent laws had been accomplished. Han Fei merged the philosophy of Taoism, the Confucian "restraint" of Shuntse, and the learning of the legalists into one of his own. He was wisely cynical, as seen in the present selection. However, he was made to quaff poison while in jail by a rival politician-scholar, Lisze. The king of Tsin, who was his great admirer, wanted to pardon him but it was too late. His cynicism did not save his life, but he wrote beautifully, in content of thought, in graceful expression, and in clever use of anecdotes. He understood human nature.

The object of his study, "the person spoken to," is the ruler or the prince.

THE DIFFICULTY IN SPEAKING to a person is not that of knowing what to say, nor that of method of argument to make one's meaning clear. Nor does it consist in the difficulty of having the courage to speak one's mind fully and frankly. The difficulty lies in knowing the mind of the person spoken to and fitting one's proper approach to it. If the person spoken to likes to have a name for altruism and idealism and you speak to him about utilitarian profits, he will think you vulgar-minded and keep away from you. On the other hand, if the person spoken to has a good mind for

367

commercial profits and you speak to him about idealism, he will think you an impractical sort of person with whom he will have nothing to do. If the person spoken to likes to appear as a man of principles and is at heart after the profits and you speak to him about principles, he will make a pretense of being close to you but will not take you into his confidence. If you speak to the same person about big profits, he will secretly take your advice but outwardly keep you at a distance. These things one must know.

Often [state] affairs are accomplished in secrecy and spoiled by the news leaking out. You may not be the person who leaks it out, but if you show in your language that you know the secrets, then you are in danger. If a high personage has certain personal faults and you are too frank with your open advice, you are in danger. Before you have earned the confidence of the person spoken to, if you tell him all you think and offer him all your advice, and he goes ahead and follows your advice, he will resent it if he succeeds and become suspicious of you when he fails, and you are in danger. A high personage likes to take credit for what he does and if you spoil it by making it seem your opinion, you are in danger. If he has already done something for which he likes to take credit and you seem to spoil it for him, you are in danger. Try to force him to do what you know he will never do and to stop doing what you know he will never desist from doing, and you are in danger. Therefore, it is said that if you talk to him like an idealistic gentleman, he may think you are being sarcastic, and if you talk to him as if he were interested in small gains or mean advantage, he will think that you are a sly flatterer. If you talk to him about what he loves, he may think you want a favor, and if you talk to him about what he hates, he may think that you are testing or provoking him. If you do not talk enough, he thinks you do not know, and if you talk too much, he will get tired of you. If you bring up a thing casually, he will think you timid, and if you dilate on your big plans and ideas, he may think you raw and insolent. These are the difficulties of speaking to a person which one must know.

There was a rich man of Sung City whose wall fell down after a long rain. His son said to him, "We must repair it at once to prevent burglary." His neighbor said the same thing. That night a burglar really broke into his house and stole a lot of his money. The rich man praised his son for forethought and suspected his neighbor of complicity in the theft. In ancient times, Duke Wu of Cheng wanted to invade the Hu barbarians, and married his daughter to the Hu chieftain. He then asked his staff officers, "I want to start a war of conquest. Whom shall I attack?" Kuanchisze suggested that he attack the Hus. The duke had him killed, saying, "The Hu chieftain is related to me in marriage. You are talking nonsense." The chieftain heard of this and believed in the duke and relaxed his defenses. The duke then invaded the Hus and conquered them. In both these instances, the speaker said nothing wrong, yet the result was disaster in the one case and being under suspicion in the other. It is not difficult to know, but to know what to do with what you know.

In ancient days, Mitseshia [a man] was a favorite of the duke of Wei. There was a law in Wei that whoever made use of the duke's carriage without permission should have his feet amputated. One day Mitse learned that his mother was ill, but it was night and Mitse took the ducal carriage to go and see his mother. The duke heard of this and remarked, "What a good son. He risked having his feet chopped off for the sake of his sick mother." One day Mitse was taking a stroll with the duke in his garden. Mitse tasted a peach which he had plucked from the tree, and finding it very good, offered the uneaten half to the duke. "How he loves me!" remarked the duke. Later when the boy was not so handsome any more and had lost the duke's favor, he said, "He is the one who made unauthorized use of my carriage and who insulted me by giving me the uneaten half of a peach." What the duke now condemned in Mitse's conduct was the same as what he had praised before; the change was in the duke's own love and hatred. Therefore, when a ruler likes a man, his words seem wise and he shows confidence in him; when he dislikes a man, his misdemeanors seem to increase and their relations seem increasingly strained. Therefore, one who wants to speak to a ruler must first abide his time and ascertain whether he is liked or disliked.

A dragon can be ridden. But there is a tuft of ruffled scales under his neck about a foot long. Whoever rubs these scales in the wrong way will be eaten by it. A prince also has his "ruffled scales." Be careful and do not rub them the wrong way.

                  » *After translating this, I feel that such counsel of wisdom is useful even for an employee in a Manhattan bank.*

77 ▣ The Art of Persuasion

« The art of giving advice to a king, especially to dissuade him from a course of conduct, was always a delicate one. The price of failure was instant dismissal or possible death, if the king was so minded. Sometimes it was the task of turning an invading army back to save one's own country. In the time of the War-ring Kingdoms (fifth to third centuries, B.C.), a great class of professional talkers or "persuaders" (shuaikeh, as they were called) grew up, and many a country's destiny was changed by the talkers' wit. But throughout the later periods, the noble art of persuading a king to do what he did not want was always a delicate job.

AGAINST YES MEN

King Wei of Tsi was completely surrounded by courtiers who flattered his vanity and followed his whims. One day, Tsou Chi said to the king:

"Sire, I am not exactly bad-looking. [He was "eight feet" tall.] But in the north city, there is a Mr. Shu, noted for his handsomeness. One day I stood before the mirror and asked my wife, 'Who do you think is handsomer, Mr. Shu or me?' 'Of course you are,' replied my wife. I dared not take her word for it and asked my concubine the same question. 'How can Mr. Shu compare with you?' was her answer. Next morning a guest came and after a while, I asked him the same question, and he replied, 'Mr. Shu cannot compare with you.' The following day, Mr. Shu himself came to see me. I studied him carefully and thought he was much hand-somer than myself. I examined myself in the mirror and was quite convinced that I could not compare with him. So I lay in my bed and thought, My wife praises me because she is partial to me.

371

My concubine praises me because she is afraid of me. My friend praises me because he has something to ask of me.

"Now Tsi is a kingdom of a thousand square li with one hundred twenty cities. All the palace ladies and attendants are partial to you. All the courtiers are afraid of your power. And all the people have something to ask of you. So it seems to me that it is hard for you to hear the truth."

"Well said," replied the king. He then issued an order: "All ministers, officials, and common people who can point out my mistakes shall receive the highest class of rewards. Those who write letters to advise me shall receive the second-class reward. And those who can criticize me and my government at the market place so that it reaches my ears shall receive the third-class reward."

When the order was issued, the king was deluged with a torrent of advice, and the court was crowded with people. This went on for several months. After a year, there was no mistake of the government which had not already been thought of and pointed out by somebody. The neighboring countries Yen, Chao, Han, and Wei heard of what the king had done and came to acknowledge the state of Tsi as their leader. This is called winning the war at home.

— *Chankuotseh.*

YEN CHUO

King Shuan of Tsi met Yen Chuo on the road. He summoned the scholar and the latter said, "Let the king come to me."

The king's assistants were greatly offended at his insolence. "How can you be so rude to the king?" asked the assistants.

"You people do not understand," replied Yen. "That is my way of showing respect to the king."

"How so?"

"If I go up to the king, people may think I want to seek some special favor. If the king comes to me, people will think our king is a patron of scholars."

The king was greatly displeased.

"Tell me," he said to Yen Chuo. "Do you consider a scholar as more important than a king?"

"I do," replied Yen.

"Please explain yourself."

"I can. When Tsin invaded Tsi, the army was issued an order that any soldier who dared to approach within fifty paces of the graveyard of Liushia would be summarily killed. At the same time, it said, 'Whoever captures the head of the king of Tsi shall be made a high minister and given a thousand *yi* [one *yi* equals twenty ounces] of gold.' So the head of a living king is worth less than the grave of a dead scholar."

[The king offered him office, but Yen Chuo declined.]

—*Chankuotseh.*

AGAINST WAR

Duke Wen of the state of Wei was talking with Tien Tsefang when two children, dressed in black and white, appeared as attendants to the duke.

"Are these your children?" asked Tien.

"No," replied the duke. "Their father was killed in the war. I have adopted the orphans."

"I am truly sorry for you," said Tien. "You are taking care of these orphans so that when they grow up and have children, you shall have more orphans to take care of when you send them to war."

From then on, the duke stopped his wars with his neighbors.

—Liu Shiang in *Shuoyuan.*

TUNGFANG SHUO

Tungfang Shuo (c. 161-c. 87 b.c.) was a famous joker of the court of Emperor Han Wuti. The emperor had decided to kill the wet nurse who had nursed him in babyhood, on account of some small matter. The nurse begged Tungfang Shuo to save her life. Tungfang Shuo said to the woman, "His Majesty is cruel-hearted and a very stubborn person. If someone tries to intervene, it will make matters worse and hasten your death. You do this. When you are about to be taken away, you look at me with your pleading eyes, and I shall find a way to save you."

The nurse did as she was told, and kept on looking at Tungfang Shuo when the guards were taking her away. Tungfang Shuo shouted to her, "Go on! Don't be silly. His Majesty is a grown-up person now. Do you think he will remember that you nursed him with your own milk?"

The emperor was touched and released the woman.

— *Shiching Tsachi.*

PROHIBITION

In the time of the ruler of Shu, Shienchu (third century A.D.), there was a prohibition on wine on account of a drought, in order to show economy and appease the gods. There were men who were arrested for having vats and distillery apparatus in their houses, punishable in the same terms as those actually caught making illegal liquor. Chien Yung was driving in the country with the ruler when they saw a young man.

"Have that man arrested," cried Chien Yung.

"What has he done?" asked the ruler in puzzlement.

"He is going to commit adultery."

"How do you know?"

"He has the organs of adultery, just as the brewers have their vats."

The ruler broke into a loud laugh and ordered that the men be released. — *Shiching Tsachi.*

78 🈷 Parables of Chuangtse

From

BOOK OF CHUANGTSE

Chuangtse
c. 335 - c. 275 B.C.

« *The phenomenon of Chuangtse, who lived 2,200 years ago, has not been repeated in China's history. Quite apart from the depth of his thought and his command of the Chinese language never yet equaled in Chinese literature, Chuangtse shows a freedom and ease in creating fables and anecdotes about saints, fish, and turtles, and exhibited such a freshness of thought, which all the greatest Chinese writers like Su Tungpo, Po Chuyi, and Liu Tsungyuan were not able to match. This man had reached a freedom of spirit and understanding of the universe and human life which made this sudden freedom and laughter possible.*

The following consists of selections with a flashing humor. These are things he tossed off very often in the midst of discussion of the deepest problems of philosophy. The structure of chapters in Chuangtse is extremely loose. All the selections here except the first three are found in the famous chapter "Autumn Floods" in his collected writings. (See also selections 11, 12, 75, 92, and 93.)

THE BUTCHER'S KNIFE

Prince Huei's cook was cutting up a bullock. Every blow of his hand, every heave of his shoulders, every tread of his foot, every thrust of his knee, every *whshh* of rent flesh, every *chhk* of the chopper, was in perfect rhythm — like the dance of the "Mulberry Grove," like the harmonious chords of "Ching Shou."

"Well done!" cried the prince. "Yours is skill indeed!"

375

"Sire," replied the cook, laying down his chopper, "I have always devoted myself to Tao, which is higher than mere skill. When I first began to cut up bullocks, I saw before me whole bullocks. After three years' practice, I saw no more whole animals. And now I work with my mind and not with my eye. My mind works along without the control of the senses. Falling back upon eternal principles, I glide through such great joints or cavities as there may be, according to the natural constitution of the animal. I do not even touch the convolutions of muscle and tendon, still less attempt to cut through large bones.

"A good cook changes his chopper once a year — because he cuts. An ordinary cook, once a month — because he hacks. But I have had this chopper nineteen years, and although I have cut up many thousand bullocks, its edge is as if fresh from the whetstone. For at the joints there are always interstices, and the edge of a chopper being without thickness, it remains only to insert that which is without thickness into such an interstice. Indeed there is plenty of room for the blade to move about. It is thus that I have kept my chopper for nineteen years as though fresh from the whetstone.

"Nevertheless, when I come upon a knotty part which is difficult to tackle, I am all caution. Fixing my eye on it, I stay my hand and gently apply my blade, until with a *hwah* the part yields like earth crumbling to the ground. Then I take out my chopper and stand up, and look around, and pause with an air of triumph. Then wiping my chopper, I put it carefully away."

"Bravo!" cried the prince. "From the words of this cook I have learned how to take care of my life."

FINAL INSTRUCTIONS

Chuangtse was about to die, and his disciples wanted to give him a sumptuous funeral.

"I regard the heaven and earth as my coffin and outer coffin, the sun and the moon as a pair of jade gifts, and the constellations as my burial jewels. And the whole creation shall come to my funeral. Will it not be a grand funeral? What more should I want?"

"We are afraid that vulture crows will come and eat our master," said the disciples.

"Above the ground, I shall be eaten by the vultures, and underground, I shall be eaten by the ants. Why rob the one to give it to the other? Why are you so partial [to the ants]?" Chuangtse replied.

THE WALRUS AND THE CENTIPEDE

The walrus* envies the centipede; the centipede envies the snake; the snake envies the wind; the wind envies the eye; and the eye envies the mind. The walrus said to the centipede, "I hop about on one leg, but not very successfully. How do you manage all those legs you have?"

"I don't manage them," replied the centipede. "Have you never seen saliva? When it is ejected, the big drops are the size of pearls, the small ones like mist. At random they fall, in countless numbers. So, too, does my natural mechanism move, without my knowing how I do it."

The centipede said to the snake, "With all my legs I do not move as fast as you with none. How is that?"

"One's natural mechanism," replied the snake, "is not a thing to be changed. What need have I for legs?"

The snake said to the wind, "I wriggle about by moving my spine, as if I had legs. Now you seem to be without form, and yet you come blustering down from the North Sea to bluster away to the South Sea. How do you do it?"

"'Tis true," replied the wind, "that I bluster as you say. But anyone who sticks his finger or his foot into me, excels me. On the other hand, I can tear away huge trees and destroy large buildings. This power is given only to me. Out of many minor defeats I win

* *Kuei,* a mythical, one-legged animal.

the big victory. And to win a big victory is given only to the sages."

THE FROG AND THE TURTLE

Prince Mou leaned over the table and sighed. Then he looked up to heaven and laughed, saying, "Have you never heard of the frog in the shallow well? The frog said to the turtle of the Eastern Sea, 'What a great time I am having! I hop to the rail around the well, and retire to rest in the hollow of some broken bricks. Swimming, I float on my armpits, resting my jaws just above the water. Plunging into the mud, I bury my feet up to the foot arch, and not one of the cockles, crabs, or tadpoles I see around me are my match. Besides, to occupy such a pool all alone and possess a shallow well is to be as happy as anyone can be. Why do you not come and pay me a visit?'

"Now before the turtle of the Eastern Sea had got its left leg down, its right knee had already stuck fast, and it shrank back and begged to be excused. It then told the frog about the sea, saying, 'A thousand li would not measure its breadth, nor a thousand fathoms its depth. In the days of the Great Yu, there were nine years of flood out of ten; but this did not add to its bulk. In the days of Tang, there were seven years of drought out of eight; but this did not make its shores recede. Not to be affected by the passing of time, and not to be affected by increase or decrease of water — such is the great happiness of the Eastern Sea.' At this the frog of the shallow well was considerably astonished, and felt very small, like one lost. . . .

WALKING GAIT OF HANTAN

[Wei Mou was giving advice to Kungsun Lung.] "Have you never heard how a youth of Shouling went to study the walking

gait at Hantan?* Before he could learn the Hantan gait, he had
forgotten his own way of walking, and crawled back home on all
fours. If you do not go away now, you will forget what you have
and lose your own professional knowledge."

Kungsun Lung's jaw hung open, his tongue clave to his palate,
and he slunk away.

CHUANGTSE FISHING

Chuangtse was fishing on the Pu River when the prince of
Chu sent two high officials to see him and said, "Our prince desires
to burden you with the administration of the Chu state."

Chuangtse went on fishing without turning his head and said,
"I have heard that in Chu there is a sacred tortoise which died
when it was three thousand [years] old. The prince keeps this
tortoise carefully enclosed in a chest in his ancestral temple. Now
would this tortoise rather be dead and have its remains venerated,
or would it rather be alive and wagging its tail in the mud?"

"It would rather be alive," replied the two officials, "and wagging
its tail in the mud."

"Begone!" cried Chuangtse. "I too will wag my tail in the mud."

CHUANGTSE AND HUEITSE

Hueitse was prime minister in the Liang state, and
Chuangtse was on his way to see him.

Someone remarked, "Chuangtse has come. I think he has a mind
to be minister in your place."

Thereupon Hueitse was afraid, and searched all over the country
for three days and three nights to find him.

Chuangtse went to see him, and said, "In the south there is a

* Capital of Chao, famous for its dancers and prostitutes in Chuangtse's times.

bird. It is a kind of phoenix. When it starts from the South Sea to fly to the North Sea, it would not alight except on the *wu tung* tree. It eats nothing but the fruit of the bamboo, drinks nothing but the purest spring water. An owl which had gotten the rotten carcass of a rat looked up as the phoenix flew by, and screeched. Are you not screeching at me over your kingdom of Liang?"

HOW DO YOU KNOW?

Chuangtse and Hueitse had strolled onto the bridge over the Hao when the former observed, "See how the small fish are darting about! That is the happiness of the fish."

"You are not a fish yourself," said Hueitse; "how can you know the happiness of the fish?"

"And you not being I," retorted Chuangtse, "how can you know that I do not know?"

"If I, not being you, cannot know what you know," urged Hueitse, "it follows that you, not being a fish, cannot know the happiness of the fish."

"Let us go back to your original question," said Chuangtse. "You asked me how I knew the happiness of the fish. Your very question shows that you knew that I knew. I knew it [from my own feelings] on this bridge."

79 ▣ Parables of Liehtse

From

BOOK OF LIEHTSE

Liehtse
4th century B.C.?

« Very little is known of the personal life of Liehtse, reputed to be able to ride the winds. Chuangtse referred to him several times in his works. The book of Liehtse is rich in fables, compiled by Taoists.

THE CONCEALED DEER

There was a woodcutter in Cheng who came across a frightened deer in the country and shot and killed it. Afraid that other people might see it, he hid it in a grove and covered it up with chopped wood and branches, and was greatly delighted. Soon afterward, however, he forgot where he had hid the deer, and believed it must have all happened in a dream. As a dream, he told it to everybody in the streets. Among the listeners there was one who heard the story of his dream and went to search for the concealed deer and found it. He brought the deer home and told his wife, "There is a woodcutter who dreamed he had killed a deer and forgot where he hid it, and here I have found it. He is really a dreamer."

"You must have dreamed yourself that you saw a woodcutter who had killed a deer. Do you really believe that there was a real woodcutter? But now you have really got a deer, so your dream must have been a true one," said his wife.

God and apologized to him, saying, "We did not know that you were a man of God, and have cheated you. We did not know that you were a divine saint and have abused you. Do you regard us as fools, or do you consider us blind or deaf? Please explain to us your secret doctrine."

"I have no secret doctrine," replied the farmer. "Even my mind does not know how I have done it. However, there is a point which I will tell you. When you two were stopping at my house, I heard you talking about the power of the Fan family, saying that they could make or ruin a man and make a rich man poor and a poor man rich. And I had no doubts in mind, but sincerely believed you. That was why I was willing to come such a long distance. And I thought all that you people said was sincere. I was only worried that I might not have enough faith in me and might not do all that was in my power. I was not conscious where my body was and what was good and what was bad for me. I had only this sincere mind, and matter could not go against it. Now that I know you people are cheating me, my mind is full of suspicions and I have to be constantly on the lookout. When I think of how I escaped being burned or drowned in the water, I am still trembling and excited. How dare I go near the fire or water now?"

From that time on, the followers of Fan dared not abuse beggars or horse doctors they met on the way, but always came down from their carriage and bowed to them. When Tsai Wo heard the story, he told Confucius about it, and Confucius said, "Don't you know? The absolutely sincere man can influence matter, his power can move heaven and earth and influence the spirits, and he can go through the universe without meeting any obstruction, not to speak of going through fire and water and such common dangers. Shang-chiu Kai was able to overcome matter even when he was being cheated; how much more when you and I are both sincere? Remember it, young man."

80 ◳ The Old Man at the Fort

From

HUAINANTSE
Liu An
C. 178 - 122 B.C.

« *Liu An was prince of Huainan; hence the name of his book,
Huainantse, by which he is generally known. He was a Taoist,
and was reputed to have ascended to heaven in broad daylight.*

THERE WAS AN OLD MAN at a frontier fort in the north
who understood Taoism. One day he lost his horse, which wandered into the land of the Hu tribesmen. His neighbors came to
condole with him, and the man said, "How do you know that
this is bad luck?"

After a few months, the horse returned with some fine horses
of the Hu breed, and the people congratulated him. The old man
said, "How do you know that this is good luck?"

He then became very prosperous with so many horses. The son
one day broke his legs riding, and all the people came to condole
with him again. The old man said, "How do you know that this
is bad luck?"

One day the Hu tribesmen invaded the frontier fort. All the
young men fought with arrows to defend it, and nine tenths of
them were killed. Because the son was a cripple, both father and
son escaped unharmed.

Therefore, good luck changes into bad, and bad luck changes
into good. The workings of events are beyond comprehension.

81 ▣ Something To Weep About

From

BOOK OF MENCIUS
Mencius
372 - 289 B.C.

THERE WAS ONCE A MAN in Tsi state who had a wife and a concubine. Whenever this man went out, he always had meats and wines, and when his wife asked him who he had dined with, [he said] it was always with wealthy and noble friends. So the wife said to the concubine: "Whenever our good man goes out, he always dines on meats and wines, and when we ask him who he has dined with, it is always with 'wealthy and noble friends.' But we never see any of his noble friends come to our house. I am going to watch him and see where he goes."

She got up early and followed her good man where he went. In the whole city, no one talked with him. Finally he went to the Eastern Outer City, and begged of the people who were offering sacrifices [at the temples] to give him the leftovers, and being not yet satisfied, he went on to beg of other people. This was the way he filled himself. The wife returned and told the concubine: "A good man is a person we rely on for life. But our good man behaves like this." The two women began railing against their husband, and were weeping in the courtyard. The man, knowing nothing about all this, came back in his usual suave manner, and boasted as usual. From the gentleman's point of view, the people who seek for power and glory and wealth and whom their wives and concubines do not have to be ashamed of and weep for are very few indeed.

82 ▣ Truth Is Harder To See than the Sun

From

COMPLETE WORKS OF SU TUNGPO

Su Tungpo
1036 - 1101

THERE WAS A MAN BORN BLIND. He had never seen the sun and asked about it of people who could see. Someone told him, "The sun's shape is like a brass tray." The blind man struck the brass tray and heard its sound. Later when he heard the sound of a bell, he thought it was the sun. Again someone told him, "The sunlight is like that of a candle," and the blind man felt the candle, and thought that was the sun's shape. Later he felt a [big] key and thought it was a sun. The sun is quite different from a bell or a key, but the blind man cannot tell their difference because he has never seen the sun. The truth [Tao] is harder to see than the sun, and when people do not know it, they are exactly like the blind man. Even if you do your best to explain by analogies and examples, it still appears like the analogy of the brass tray and the candle. From what is said of the brass tray, one imagines a bell, and from what is said about a candle, one imagines a key. In this way, one gets ever further and further away from the truth. Those who speak about Tao sometimes give it a name according to what they happen to see, or imagine what it is like without seeing it. These are mistakes in the effort to understand Tao.

83 ▣ The Ferryman's Wisdom

From

PROSE WORKS OF CHOU YUNG

Chou Yung
1619 - 1679

« *Like many great painters during the Ming Dynasty, Chou Yung
was one of the many poets whose disappointment at the Manchu conquest of China made them seek their escape, and find
their salvation, in poetry and painting. It was said that "his
painting was better than his prose, his poems better than his
paintings, and his calligraphy better than his poems." He refused
to accept office in the government.*

IN THE WINTER OF 1650, I was going into the city of
Chiaochuan from the Little Harbor, accompanied by a boy carrying a big load of books, tied with a cord and strengthened with a
few pieces of board.

It was toward sunset and the country was covered with haze.
We were about a mile from the city.

"Will we be in time to get into the city before the gates are
closed?" I asked the ferryman.

"You will if you go slowly. But if you run, you will miss it,"
replied the ferryman, casting a look at the boy.

But we walked as fast as possible. About halfway, the boy fell
down. The cord broke and the books fell on the ground. The
boy sat crying. By the time we had retied the package and reached
the city gate, it was already closed.

I thought of that ferryman. He had wisdom.

84 ▣ The Beggar's Philosophy

From

COLLECTED WORKS (YUANTSE)

Yuan Chieh

A.D. 723 - 772

« *Although Yuan Chieh fought and won battles and made a good
administrator pacifying the southern tribesmen, he called himself "Carefree Scholar," "Romantic Squire," and later "Super-
fluous Old Man."*

IN 748, I WAS LIVING AT THE CAPITAL and had a beggar
for a friend. Someone was embarrassed by my conduct and asked
me why I did so. I said:

"In ancient times, when there were no gentlemen friends in the
village, a scholar befriended the clouds and mountains. When
there were no gentlemen friends in the neighborhood, he made
friends with the pines and bamboos. When there were no gentlemen friends in the house to talk with, he amused himself with
wine and music. But when he went to a strange city, he sought the
gentlemen's company. This beggar, I have discovered, is quite a
cultivated gentleman. In fact, I am honored by his friendship."

My friend was amazed and asked me to explain.

I told him the beggar's words, as follows:

You ask me why I carry a cane and a pot to beg for people's
leftovers and discarded clothing? The explanation is quite simple.
I want to merge with the city crowd and be regarded as a man like
all of them. People don't like you if you pretend that you are

queer or different. I beg because I am poor. There is no shame in it. Some people think it is a shame, but of course this is pure prejudice. We all beg. People all around me beg every day, and beg more shamelessly. Some beg for official posts, some for marriage to a family of some social standing. Have you ever seen their faces when they beg? Some beg the servants of the influential families to help them; some beg the doorkeeper or the maids in order to get in, with sweat on their brows. The poor beg the rich and the rich beg the poor; the powerful beg the common men and the common men beg the powerful for assistance and favors. Prisoners beg to have their sentences commuted and sick men beg to be permitted to live a little longer. And many, mind you, can't even get what they beg and pray for. How many men beg their wives at home? How many beg at the temple? How many beg their own servants at a certain crisis to do them a little favor?

One must go along with the crowd and do what the others do. You should really copy my example and learn a little of the beggar's language and the beggar's shamelessness. That is the way to be tolerated and liked in this world. Don't you try to be different from the world and be persecuted for it.

85 因 On City Noises

Sha Changpai
c. 1671

THERE ARE NOISES OF THE FORESTS, of the jungles, and of the cities. When birds, beasts, and men get together, one always hears a booming, boiling confusion of noises. Sometimes one listens to the cries of animals and songs of birds in the forests and imagines that these cries and songs are pure expressions of joy without a purpose. By the analogy of human noises in the city, however, one must conclude that they have a very definite purpose, either to show off what they have got, or to cry for what they haven't, for the satisfaction of some immediate primitive desires.

The climate of Peking is dry, and the city noises carry a long way. The peddlers' cries are heard everywhere, on the avenues, in the alleys, and in the most remote areas. The peddlers carry their wares and thread the streets where homes are to sell what the housewives may want to buy. There are thousands of them, in rain or shine, morning and night. These noises are noises of men who have something to sell and want to sell it. It would be unreasonable to assume that the noises of men are for the satisfaction of some needs and those of animals are not. I think of these cries as cries of men who cry aloud and appeal to the public that they have something to sell in order that they may make a living thereby, and who continue to do so till the end of their days.

This noise of the city is therefore symbolic of all human activities and professions. All mankind tries to sell something. Those who have power sell power and those who have influence sell influence. Artists, writers, officials, bureaucrats, and women sell their art, their writing, their favors, their cunning and thought and personal charms to obtain what they want. They all try to show off what they have got, and cry for what they haven't, for the satisfaction of some immediate desires. There are even whispers in the middle of the night, and caucuses behind closed doors, on unmentionable topics and inaudible to the world outside, the words without noise, the song without words, for the satisfaction of some immediate needs, which speak nevertheless louder than the bells and drums of the city. The function of these noiseless noises is the same as that of peddlers' cries, but the contents are not always so honorable.

Alas! only the phoenix can command the harmony of the birds' songs, only the unicorn can bring order to the cries of animals, and only the sages can bring about the satisfaction of men's needs so that the voice of men shall be a voice of peace and happiness, not a voice of turmoil and discontent. It is not right that men should escape to the mountains and live as hermits to enjoy the songs of birds and cries of animals, thus placing men below the animal creation.

FOOLS TO THIS WORLD

86 ▣ The Emperor's Friend

From

LATER HISTORY OF HAN (HOU HANSHU)

Fan Hua
A.D. 398 - 445

« *It is difficult to overestimate the importance attached to power and government office in the psychology of Chinese scholars. The most common sentiments one runs across in Chinese scholars' compositions are: (1) the compassion for a remarkable, poetic talent who died in poverty, expressed in a way so that the poet's harsh fate is identified with thousands of undistinguished and untalented scholars, and (2) gratitude to a high official or a ruler who appreciated such good talents, expressed as something of critical importance in one's life. This is understandable because the scholars were the ruling class, and "success" in life was conceived as success in passing the imperial examinations with a government degree, which was the gateway to an official career. Scholars may be classified into those who tried all their lives to pass the examinations and could not, those who became the average-run officials, those who took service to the country seriously and often chanced dismissal from office to live a life of retirement, rarely those who were good men themselves and met good rulers, and finally, those who spurned office and the emoluments and "honor" and preferred to live the carefree life of the common man.*

Naturally, the last class was the most admired. Of this class, Yen Tseling is probably the most pronounced example. The fishing terrace of Yen Tseling on the beautiful Fuchunkiang River above Hangchow is one of the historic sites. Yen was a friend of the emperor when his imperial Han House was wiped out by a usurper for sixteen years, who later restored the dynasty and became Han Kuangwu (reigned, A.D. 25–57).

YEN KUANG'S SOCIAL NAME was Tseling; his other name was Chun. He was a native of Yuyao in Kueichi. He was a classmate of Emperor Kuangwu in their youth when Yen was already noted for his brilliance. When Kuangwu ascended the throne, Yen changed his name and disappeared. The emperor constantly thought of him and ordered that he be found, with the help of his portrait and descriptions. Someone in Tsi reported seeing a man who agreed with the description. The emperor ordered that a carriage be sent with black and pale brown silk gowns to welcome him. Only after the third request did he consent to come to the headquarters of the North Army. He was treated royally and a messenger arrived with a letter from Minister Hou Pa, who was an old friend of Yen. The messenger expressed the regret that Hou was not able to come personally owing to important government business, and the message was couched in the most humble terms. When night fell, the messenger still could not persuade him. Yen then dictated a letter of reply to Hou, saying, "I am happy for you that you now occupy one of the highest posts in the government. Guide His Majesty to walk in the path of love and righteousness and the people will thank you. Flatter him and pamper his whims and there will be chaos."*

When the emperor saw the letter as submitted by Hou Pa, he smiled and said, "He is still the same rebel." He ordered a carriage and went personally that very day to see his old friend. Yen would not even get up from his bed. The emperor came to his bed and felt his belly with his own hand and said, "Oh, Tseling. Why don't you come and assist me?"

Yen kept his eyes closed without giving a reply. After a while, he opened his eyes and studied the emperor and said, quoting some ancient retired scholars, "Every man must be allowed to do what he really wants."

* According to Huangfu Mi's *Biographies of Retired Scholars*, Yen was pictured as insolent in manners. He refused to write the letter with his own hand. When the messenger (Hou's son) asked Yen to add a few more words, Yen curtly replied, "Are you buying vegetables?"

"Well," said the emperor in disappointment, "even I cannot persuade you."

Later, the emperor sent for Yen to visit him at the palace as a friend. He remained there for several days and they talked of old times.

"Do you see any change in me?" the emperor asked.

"Your Majesty has grown a little fatter," Yen replied.

And when they slept in the same couch, in his sleep Yen put his leg across the emperor's stomach.

The next day, the astronomer reported that a guest star had crossed the emperor's constellation. The emperor smiled and said, "This is nothing. I was sleeping in the same bed with my old friend."

The emperor offered him the office of an imperial censor-advisor, but Yen declined. He retired to live as a farmer on Fuchun Mountain. The place where he fished in the river was later named after him as "Tseling Rapids."

In the seventeenth year of the emperor's reign, he was again asked to assume office and again declined. He died at his home at the age of eighty. The emperor mourned him with great sorrow and gave his family grants of a million cash and a thousand sacks of grain.

87 回 Letter Declining Marriage to a Princess

From

WENCHIH (A COLLECTION OF ESSAYS)

Anonymous

« *I have put together here three "odd" letters (selections 87, 88, and 89), written by people who are considered "odd" in this world. The author of this piece is unknown, but it refers to the custom of many royal families' choosing a scholar for a son-in-law at the end of the Eastern Chin Period, and therefore probably belongs to the beginning of the fifth century A.D.*

I have received your royal communication that it is proposed to give Princess Linhai to your humble servant in marriage. While I feel exceptionally honored, I must frankly state my reasons for my hesitation in accepting such a rare honor.

I am a common person from a poor family. Seen from every angle, I must consider myself unworthy of such a match. Though I have enough to support a poor family and am of age, I often wonder why I am still unmarried. No matchmaker has come to my door and no wealthy family has ever considered me as a prospective son-in-law. I am aware that in recent years, many princesses have married into common families, and now that such a humble and unattractive person as myself has been selected, I am afraid that so it will be. This union with the Royal House may be a great honor for my clan and family, but I hardly think I can call it fortunate for myself. I hope Your Royal Highness will bear with me and try to understand the reasons.

Since the Chin Dynasty began, there have been many brilliant scholars selected to marry princesses. I need only recall that both Wang Tun and Huan Wen were henpecked by their titled wives; Chen Chang escaped by pretending insanity, and Tseching by burning his feet to acquire a limp. Wang Yen lay in snow at the palace gate to beg for release from the contract and Ho Yu jumped into a well, etc. All these were brilliant scholars, but they were unused to bending themselves before the conventions and stringencies of court life. They could not complain to the court or talk about it and mostly suffered in silence.

For one marrying a lady of royal birth, the restrictions are worse than one may suffer from a commoner's wife, and the lady's orders have the character of a royal command. It is natural for a man to entertain his common friends and to come and go from his house as he pleases. However, when one is royally connected, his friends will stop coming to see him, and he does not have the liberty to invite whom he likes when he wants to. He is thus forsaken by his friends and his relatives. The royal servants will be watching every move in the home and report, while the eunuchs will be expecting gratuities and favors every time they come. The lady's maids will proffer her advice to be severe with her husband, and nuns and women servants will compete in gaining her favors. Now these royal servants and eunuchs are mostly dull, stupid persons, with untutored minds and given to carrying gossip. The lady's maids rely on their past connections and are generally interested in intrigue, while the nuns and women servants are so knowing about what to do and what not to do that it makes you want to stop talking to them. Then there will be people to see and receive, and astrologers, fortunetellers, and priestesses about the house. And yet one must consider oneself head of the house, responsible for everything that happens, including the finances. Besides, one has not the liberty to call on old friends or relatives. Your hands and feet are tired. If you want to go out, you are asked why, and if you don't, you are gradually estranged from your friends. Mornings, you must be at home, to be ready on call, and if you go out, you must be back before sundown. Thus one never sees the night life, or comes home greeted by the morning stars.

In addition to all this, everything one does and every word one says are immediately reported by the busy servants. Even sitting down at dinner, one is surrounded by a platoon of watching women. If some of the maids are prettily dressed, the husband is at once suspected of being in love. Or if someone present is not properly dressed, he is reprimanded for disrespect. The taking of a concubine should not necessarily mean that one is tired of his wife; no slight to the wife is intended. Now one must stop all this and be solely and unequivocally devoted to her ladyship. One is liable to be called "uncouth," or else charged with being "disrespectful" to her high position. Then it must also be remembered that in family affairs the husband is always regarded as the head. Hence, when there is need among the relatives, people will come always to the husband for loans to ease up a tight situation. Some may have lost at the gambling table, and others may want to keep up appearances, and all this may be quite true. Now suddenly everything you say is regarded with fear and taken for some royal commandment. You are not a human being any more. All kinds of misunderstandings arise from this and people may even joke about you behind your back.

But there is even a weightier consideration. Everyone likes to have lots of children, but the sharp powers of jealous womanhood often make this impossible. You may have observed that people who marry princesses often die without progeny. I fear not so much for the inconveniences which may happen to myself, but for the dire fate of extinction awaiting my branch of the family. Many husbands of princesses have had to face it, but they would rather die than bring this to the attention of the court. Hence I have been rather explicit, not only for my own sake, but also for the sake of those suffering husbands in the hope that the matter will receive your royal attention.

I pray therefore that Your Royal Highness will grant my request and excuse me from the fateful step, so that we people of humble birth may lead a normal happy home life. But if this request is refused, I shall have no other recourse but to go mad and disappear or jump into the sea.

88 ▣ Letter on the Secret of Getting Along

Letter to

LIU YICHANG

Tsung Chen
1535 - 1560

« This is a famous satire on politics. Although the author died at
the age of thirty-five, he ranked among the "five poets" of his
day and, which may not appear from the letter itself, held good
official positions.

I am happy to receive a letter from you from a thousand
miles away. I would be very happy to hear news about you even
without the beautiful gifts which you sent me. I do not know how
to thank you. The sentiments of the letter indicate that you, as my
elder, have not forgotten me and know that I have been thinking
of you quite often.

As for what you say about "getting along with superiors and inferiors" and showing "competence at the job," I do want to say
something. I know my incompetence already, but am even more
conscious of the difficulty of getting along with people.

How do people try to get along these days? Day and night a man
in the government would go on horseback and call on the influential people. He reaches the house of an important minister and sees
the concierge. The concierge purposely makes it difficult for him to
get an interview with the high personage. So he uses honeyed words

and exercises his charms like a woman on the concierge, and gives him a tip. While the concierge goes in with his card, he is not asked to go in and is kept waiting. He stands at the stables with the horses and drivers, suffering the awful stench, but he would not think of going away even if he was suffering from cold or hunger or intense heat.

About dusk, the man who took his tip comes out and reports that His Excellency is tired and will not see any more guests today. Will he come tomorrow? That night he takes a nap in a sitting position without undressing and gets up as soon as he hears the cock-a-doodle-doo. He washes up, dashes over on horseback, and knocks at the gate.

"Who is it?" asks the concierge angrily.

"It is I, the caller who was here yesterday."

"Are you out of your mind?" asks the concierge more angrily still. "How do you expect His Excellency to get up so early to receive guests?"

The man swallows the insult and pleads, "Anyway I am here already. Won't you please let me in?"

The concierge gets another tip and he opens the gate and lets him stand at the stables.

If he is lucky, the high personage will send for him. He shuffles forward across the yard with his head properly bent.

"Come in," says the host.

He bends and bows, and purposely stays in that position an extra second. When he straightens himself, he hands over to His Excellency his "longevity gift"* of money. The host refuses to take it, but he insists, and the host insists on not receiving it, and he insists again on his taking it. Finally the host sees no other way than to ask his secretary to receive it. The caller bows again, and again purposely stays in that position an extra second. When he straightens himself up again, he leaves with five or six more bows.

When he leaves the reception room, he informs the concierge,

* A euphemism for a bribe.

"You see His Excellency wants to see me. Next time I come, you must not stand in the way." The concierge makes a respectful bow to him in return.

Greatly delighted, he takes his departure. When meeting some friends on the way, he cracks his whip and informs them, "I just came from His Excellency's home. I was received royally, most royally." He exaggerates a little. The friends begin to believe that he was royally received and to respect him. The high personage would drop a remark casually: "So-and-so is a good man. I have a good opinion of him." His hearers would agree with him and join in the praise of that person.

This is what you call "getting along with superiors and inferiors." Do you think that I could do it?

I am afraid that I must inform you that since last New Year's Eve when I dropped a formal card, I have not tried to see that high personage for a whole year. When I passed his house, I shut my eyes, covered my ears, and dashed past as if someone was chasing me away. This is my stubborn nature, and the reason I can never succeed in pleasing my superior officials. And the worst about it is that I don't care. I have often said to myself, "I will do what is right in my position and leave the rest to fate." I am afraid that when you read this letter, you will consider me incorrigible.

89 回 Letter Severing Friendship

Letter to

SHAN CHUYUAN

Chi Kang
A.D. 223 - 262

« *Chinese Romanticism was at its height in the third and fourth centuries* A.D. *Confucianism had state protection and patronage during the Han Dynasty, roughly to the end of the second century, but it had in the end produced politically, not a government of saints and sages, but of autocratic women and eunuchs. When the Han empresses said they ruled, they really ruled as if the empire was their private property, and the eunuchs were their henchmen. Hence the reaction toward Taoism in the following centuries. This Romanticism took the form of philosophical detachment from politics, unconventional living, and a great deal of drunkenness.*

Chi Kang and Shan Chuyuan (Shan Tao, A.D. *205–283) were great friends. They were among the "Seven Friends of the Bamboo Grove." All of them were Taoists by belief and temperament, more interested in preserving their self or their soul, than in saving the world. Chi Kang in particular was a great believer in Laotse, Chuangtse, and in practicing the various arts for prolonging life.*

This period of Chinese history is generally called the period of "pure conversation" with the horsehair flyswatter gracefully waved during a conversation like a fan, as the symbol. From my observation, this "pure conversation" was chiefly like the French salon of the eighteenth century, interested in wit and le bon mot and précieuses remarks, such as an apt quotation applied to common subjects, or distinction between some abstract moral qualities. I have found very little real wit in it.

As will be seen from the selection, insects really had a lot to do with this conversation, and not the flies alone. They were really returning to nature. Lice received inordinate attention among the conversationalists and in their records.

The occasion for the letter was that Shan Chuyuan, being a minister of civil service, had recommended the writer to take his place. Deletions have been made to save space.

Dear Chuyuan:

I hear that you proposed to recommend me to take your place. You do not really know me. You stand for a lot of things which I cannot stand. When I heard that you were promoted, I was sorry for you. . . .

I lived very much to myself as a child, and used to offend my mother's brother. I did not study the [Confucian] classics and am by nature lazy to the bones. I often go without washing my face for fifteen days, and unless I itch a great deal, I just do not wash. Even when I am pressed to go to the toilet, I would rather delay it by not getting up and letting it turn inside a little. Besides, I have been used to living my life in my own way and cannot stand the forms of social intercourse. My friends are used to it and ignore it. And then the reading of Laotse and Chuangtse makes me yearn for freedom, caring less and less for power and position and more and more for true simplicity. We see that animals are best trained when young; when they are broken after they are grown-up, they chafe at the reins and prance and buck and heave. They may be dressed with a golden harness and fed the finest of foods, yet continue to dream of the tall grass and the deep forests.

I consider that there are seven things in a life in the government which I cannot stand, and two things which I am bound to do which will be considered improper. Among the unbearable things comes the first: to be asked to get up for office when my nature is to lie in bed late. Secondly, I love to walk about and sing in the countryside, or go fishing, and I cannot do this with government servants watching me. I shan't dare to make an incorrect move. Thirdly, I love to sit while swinging my legs and scratch myself when bitten by lice on my body. How am I going to do this, wearing the official cap and gown and paying respects to my superiors? Fourthly, I hate correspondence. I cannot in conscience leave it unanswered; yet at best I shall make only interrupted efforts. Fifthly, I never care for attending funerals, which nevertheless are regarded by society as very important. I may offend people by not attending, and some may feel inclined toward revenge for a supposed insult. But I cannot help myself. If I try and pretend and go through the ceremonial weeping, eventually I cannot do a good job of it and shall be blamed for it. Sixthly, I hate to mix up with the common, uncultivated people. I shall have to associate with these and go through the noise and confusion and babble of a public dinner. Seventhly, I am impatient of business duties, and all the worries and responsibilities that go with an office. Besides all these, I am usually free with my criticism of Confucius and Mencius and their ideal kings. There are other things in this life to attend to. Clearly this will not be permitted by so-called "high" society. Then it is my habit to say what I think, and this again will bring me into trouble.

For these nine grave reasons, I consider myself unfit to go into government. Besides, I strongly believe in the methods of prolonging life recommended by the Taoists, such as eating spiked millet and deer bamboo (*Polygonatum falcatum*). And I love to live in the country and look at the fish and listen to the birds. These things I certainly cannot do when I am burdened with an office. Friends should try to understand one another's individual nature. Human nature is something which cannot be forced. . . . I have been recently interested in the art of prolonging life, and trying to get rid of the ambitions of fame and power and the desires of the senses, in order to let my mind roam about in nothingness. I place the highest value on inaction. Even without the aforementioned nine considerations, I simply do not covet what you regard as worth while. . . . I figure that at the worst, I shall die poor. Don't you try to get me involved, with the risk of being punished for violating some government regulations. . . .

[He goes into his family details.] You are bothering me only because you think you want to enlist some good men for the service of the government. . . . There are others much more able than myself. My only distinction is that I do not care for these things. What I really crave is to be left alone and live my remaining years in peace. I am not trying to be singular. But if you persist and want to drag me into the government, and perhaps even force me to do it, I shall go insane, I am sure. I cannot believe that you have such a bad grudge against me as to wish this on me.

I have explained myself. And this is to say good-by.

Chi Kang

90   ▣ Mi Fei, the Eccentric Genius

Preface to

COLLECTION OF MI FEI'S
SUNDRY SCRIPTS

Chen Chiju
1558 - 1639

« Genius borders on insanity. Mi Fei (1051–1107), one of the greatest landscape painters of all China's history, already won the name of "Mi the Crazy One" in his lifetime. He once asked Su Tungpo, "People call me crazy. What do you think?" Tungpo replied, "I follow the majority." While Tungpo painted bamboos and rocks in the foreground, with powerful strokes for the bamboo leaves and sparse contours for the rocks, leaving the background a blank, Mi Fei developed his special landscapes of distant views of snow and haze and mountain peaks and sparse winter branches. Tungpo came to know him quite late, especially in the last year of his life, Mi being a much younger man, and then gave him unreserved recognition. He was also a great connoisseur and devoted collector and spared no effort in trying to see valuable art treasures. Later he painted for the emperor and was given the extraordinary privilege of seeing the emperor's private collections.

Mi Fei earned the name of being crazy because he had a craze for beautiful rocks, so much so that when falling in love with a special piece of rock of unusual rugged strength of lines in Wuwei, where he was magistrate, he dressed up in his formal cap and gown and knelt down before the rock and called it "father-in-law." Once he received a stone of a special luster from a monk and slept embracing the stone for three days. He also coveted the emperor's own inkstone which he saw while commissioned to do a painting, and said to the emperor, "This inkstone has been contaminated by my unworthy hands, and is no longer fit for Your Majesty." The emperor, Huitsung, himself a great painter, smiled and gave it to him. Otherwise he was a very courteous and unassuming person. When one says that genius borders on insanity, it means, in Mi Fei's case at least, only that genius implies an intense love for the object of his devotion which other people cannot understand.

This essay makes the distinction between true genius and mere eccentricity, serving I think a useful warning to people who are merely eccentric without genius. Chen Chiju (better known as Chen Meikung) was a great collector of rare scripts and published an important library of rare books. (For note on Chen Chiju, see selection 47.)

WHEN I READ The Anecdotes of Mi the Crazy One by Lu Yujen, I was dissatisfied at its incompleteness and thought I should try to make it complete someday. The collectors of Chiangtung often take down whatever Mi Fei wrote on his or other people's paintings. Fan Changkang, who is a very well-read man, has collected these and arranged them in a book called Chihlin [Collection of Sundry Scripts], and has asked me for a preface.

I think there were many charming people in history, but only Mi Fei was known for his eccentricity. The point is that such a name is not easily earned. Behind it there must be a great "expansive spirit" [of Mencius]. Modern people often like to defy conventions and call themselves "emancipated" by being sloppy and disorderly, making Mi the Crazy One a cover for their eccentric tricks.

But is it easy to be "eccentric" like Mi Fei? In the first place, he was a highly cultivated man. He based his calligraphy on the foundation of Wang, father and son, and later was influenced by Yen Pingyuan [Chenching]. And he cut and he hewed before he developed his own style. His landscapes were built on the solid foundation of [Tung] Chuyuan. He did not write much, poems or prose, but what he did was surcharged with power and depth. In the second place, he was not isolated but had the friendship of many great scholars and painters like Huang Shanku, Tsin Shaoyu, Shueh Wenchu, Li Lungmien, Liu Ching, and Wang Chinching, who all loved his company. He was thus able to discuss art and literature and history with these men and wrote his comments on paintings in their presence. In the third place, he had exceptional opportunity to see the best, from the manuscripts of Wang, Shieh, Ku, and Lu to the original works of Wang Mochieh [Wang Wei]. His own collection almost rivaled a royal private collection, and he lived at the Paochin, Chingming, and Haiyu Temples. In the fourth place, he loved order and cleanliness to the point of a fetish. He went so far as to wash his ceremonial gown after attending sacrifices with the emperor at the temple, for which he was dismissed from his office. This came from his extreme inability to stand dirt of any kind. In the fifth place, he did not follow the fashions of his times but dressed simply, lived quietly, and did not talk much, nor did he follow the usual social rules. In the sixth place, he was not a flatterer or a snob. He was commissioned by imperial order to write a copy of *Huangtingching* and paint a screen for the emperor's use. The way he laid his brush compelled the admiration of the emperor, who granted him a gift of wines, fruit, and stationery and held the door screen for him to pass. But he dared ask the emperor for the inkstone which he loved. In the seventh place, his eccentricity was not a pose, for in his correspondence when he came to the signature where he wrote [in the usual form] "Fei makes his bow," he really stood erect and made a bow [to the absent correspondent].

Indeed Mi the Crazy One was unique in his times. . . . He died in his office with the Huaiyang Army. The day before he died, he burned all his works, arranged his coffin in the hall, lighted an incense on it, and sat erect in it. When the time came, he put his palms together and drew his last breath.* It seems that there was not a speck of material concerns in his mind. Perhaps he was what

---

* His last words were: "I came from the Land of Fragrance; to the Land of Fragrance now I return," the words of a Buddhist.

the disciples of Confucius would call "an ancient eccentric." In the time of Confucius, the "eccentric one of Chu" was Chiehyu; in the time of the Neo-Confucianists, the "eccentric one of Chu" was Mi Fei. Many can try to copy his eccentricity, but not many possess that gift of the expansive spirit.

91   Why I Became a Monk

From

THE LAST TESTAMENT
(TO HIS MONASTIC BROTHERS)

Li Chuowu
c. 1525 - c. 1605

« *Li Chuowu was one of the most original minds of the sixteenth century. In history, in interpretation of the classics, and in discussions of Buddhism, he made important contributions which were original and shocking to others. He was among the first to appreciate the novels as literature. But most important of all, he was a Buddhist and an outspoken critic of Confucianism, for which he was persecuted to death. Of a very strong independent nature, he could never get along with his associates in the government. Once, on a summer day, he shaved his head and kept only his beard in order to keep cool, for which he was dismissed from a magistrate's office. Greatly respected for his scholarship, he was always invited by friends to stay with them. He loved to sweep floors as a matter of cleanliness, and used up brooms faster than his servants could make them. It was said that for this reason he could not stand women. He sent his wife and daughters home a thousand miles away in Fukien while he remained up north and never married again. On the other hand, his Buddhist view made him accept women among his hearers when he lectured on Buddhism. Eventually, some ten years after he wrote this Last Testament to his monastic brothers at the age of seventy, he was officially accused of attacking Confucianism (which meant no more than that he had independent views of it) and was put in jail. While in jail awaiting sentence, he borrowed a razor and slashed his own throat, and died two days later.*

413

This Last Testament *is a great document running to about 15,000 words. He left instructions to his Buddhist disciples to keep the rules of the faith and not disgrace it. Running in it was a strong personal feeling like the tone of the Epistles of St. Paul to the churches of Asia Minor. I give here only two excerpts, one being his exhortations to his monastic brothers and the other giving his reason for becoming a monk.*

1. EXHORTATIONS

When I die, do not send news of my death to my family. For I regarded myself as dead to the family already when I shaved my head and entered this monastery, and wished my family to regard me as dead already. . . . In other words, my death does not begin today, and since my death may not be regarded as happening today, why wait until my pagoda grave is sealed and then regard me as dead? So you should continue to live even as when I am with you. You should be careful with your speech and your actions, and even more so after my death, that people may say, "The monks of Lunghu Temple really keep the faith, and are worthy to be the associates of Chuowu (myself)." This is the way to please me. Do not grieve because you do not see me any more, because although my body is no longer with you, my spirit is with you whenever you open my books. When you read my books, you shall see my mind and spirit even a thousand times more clearly than even if I were daily with you. Besides, I have this *Last Testament*, which is my agreement with you. Keep these rules of the monastery, and you shall feel as if Old Man Chuowu were living face to face with you, looking at you and pointing at you with my own fingers. For I am so close to you as you are close to me. So grieve not and regard not only the skeleton which shall be all that is left of me as representing me. This I wish you to remember. . . .

You shall keep watch over my pagoda and live according to the rules of the church. So long as Chou Yushan lives, he will take care of you and protect you. Do not be afraid. Liu lives near the city, and he is a true follower of mine, as much as Yang Fengli and the others. Sister Mei Tanjan is born with a woman's body, but in many ways she is ahead of the brothers in her faith. She has taken the holy path and has a firm understanding of the truth and I am not worried. Although she has not formally taken me as her master, it is because she knows that I do not wish to be taken as anyone's master. But she often sent a messenger over a dozen miles to ask me about the doctrines, and I did my best to reply to her questions. She regards me silently as her master, so even though I do not have a single disciple in this world, I could not refuse to answer her questions. In our correspondence, she addresses me as "master" and I also address her as "master." Thus I have not truly broken the rule not to be taken as anyone's master. Is it not strange that she calls me "master" and I call her "master"?

The others I address as "bodhisattvas" who still live in their homes, whereas Sister Tanjan has shaved her head. There are bodhisattvas living in rich homes who receive many visits from their friends and relatives, wherefore they do not have the time and leisure to come together and discuss their religion. They study their sutras at home and often send to ask pertinent questions. These lay sisters cannot therefore be accused of wanting to communicate with me because of my name, and even if lay brothers were to do so, they would be reckoned among the enlightened. They come to me only because they are desperately struggling with the problem of life and death and must ask questions of the temple. You must treat them with respect, for they are bodhisattvas with a female body. There will be some gossip among their relatives, out of love or jealousy. You should be deaf to such rumors and devote your minds entirely to the problem of your salvation. If those who stay at home are steadfast in their search for truth, how much more should you devote yourself to prayer, who are not bothered with the worldly affairs? . . .

2. WHY I BECAME A MONK

You say sometimes among yourselves that since you have left the world, you are better than those who remain with their families. I have also left the world, but wherein am I better than the others? I left because there really was no other way out. I did not enter the monastery because I had thought that this was a good thing to do, nor because I thought that this was the only way to lead a religious life. Can one not do so at home?

It is my nature that I am impatient of having anyone control my life. The moment man is born into this world, he is controlled by others. Leave alone the period of childhood and of elementary school; even after one is grown-up and in college, he is under the control of parents and teachers and the master examiners. In the government service, he is under the control of his superiors, and when he resigns to return to his home village, he is again under the control of the district and county magistrates and his parents and grandparents. . . . That is why I refused to return home and wandered all about the country. It is true, I have a great desire to find a friend who knows my heart, but most probably I shall never find one. But I am sincere in this one thing: my innermost craving to achieve absolute freedom and not be controlled by others, and therefore I refuse to accept office or go home. I have not said this to anyone before because it would be difficult for people to believe. . . .

Someone may ask, why do I have to do it here at Macheng, and why did I not do it in my own village? Alas! you would not know the trouble I had before I could bring the razor to my head! When Teng [the magistrate] saw me cut off my hair, he shed tears and told me what his mother said: "I could not eat for a whole day when I heard this unexpected news. You must make him grow his hair again. If you can, I shall regard you as a truly good magistrate and a truly good son to me." Indeed it was not easy for me to become a monk. . . . Do not regard entering a monastery as a good thing and lightly receive alms and contributions from the people.

My throat tightens when I write these words. Alas! I ran into so many troubles in my life and went through such sufferings because I wanted to be just myself. All the ink of the universe will not suffice to record what I suffered. . . .

CODA

I have written the Six Sections in this agreement with you, and in the last section, where I pour out my troubles, you see that I have not tried to spare myself. I have begged you not to weep over me at my death, but here once more I have written so sadly, for I could not help myself. I want you not to feel sorrowful, yet I want you also to feel this sorrow in my heart. For this is true sorrow and true sorrow cannot be stopped. Who can stop it?

« Li Chuowu was a "character," and there is no question but that he was a mild psychopath in his stubbornness and inability to get along with others. He could not stand the average run of men and could not tolerate the officious, the haughty, and the hypocrites. Still he had a great mind, and was ruthlessly honest with himself. Below is a translation of his most extraordinary portrait of himself.

SELF-WRITTEN EPITAPH

He was narrow and impatient in his character, haughty in his manners, vulgar in his language, and eccentric in his mind. He had very few friends, but when he met people he put on a cordial expression. He loved to criticize others' faults, and disliked what was good in them. In his hatred of people, he severed his connections with them and continued for life to think of ways to hurt them. A lover of animal comforts, he called himself "Poyi" and "Shuchi" [great hermits]; made of the most common stuff, he declared that he was full of truth and virtue. He would not give a cent to a fellow man under the cover of imitating Yushin [a retired saint farmer], and would not lift a finger to help others in the name of Yang Chu [the philosopher of egotism]. His actions did not match his words, and he could not get along with anybody.

Therefore all the people of the village hated him. Tsekung asked Confucius, "What would you think if all the people hated a person?" and Confucius said, "That would not be enough." It is enough for me.*

* Confucius's reply was that it was not enough that all the people of the village liked or disliked a person for a test of a man's character. The true test of a good man was that he was liked by all the good people of the village and hated by the bad.

座
悟

WISDOM

92 ▣ The Tao of God and the Tao of Man

From

BOOK OF CHUANGTSE

Chuangtse
c. 335 - c. 275 B.C.

« *Chuangtse was the great exponent of Taoism after Laotse. I have selected here his discussions of the Tao of God and the Tao of man, distinguishing between the ideal and the practical, the religious level and the level of human affairs. This best sums up the Taoist point of view in a practical way. All except the last excerpt come from the chapter in his collected writings called "The Great Supreme," the most religious in feeling of Chuangtse's writings. That it is deeply religious will become self-evident. For religion is essentially a reverence for life. (See also the author's wit in selections 11, 12, 75, and 78.)*

TO LOSE ONESELF IN TAO

THE TRUE MEN OF OLD did not know what it was to love life or to hate death. They did not rejoice in birth, nor strive to put off dissolution. Unconcerned they came and unconcerned they went. That was all. They did not forget whence it was they had sprung, neither did they seek to inquire their return thither. Cheerfully they accepted life, waiting patiently for their restoration [the end]. This is what is called not to lead the heart astray from Tao, and not to supplement the natural by human means. Such a one may be called a true man.

421

Such men are free in mind and calm in demeanor, with high foreheads. Sometimes disconsolate like autumn, and sometimes warm like spring, their joys and sorrows are in direct touch with the four seasons, in harmony with all creation, and none know the limit thereof. . . .

For what they cared for was ONE and what they did not care for was ONE also. That which they regarded as ONE was ONE, and that which they did not regard as ONE was ONE likewise. In that which was ONE, they were of God; in that which was not ONE, they were of man. And so between the human and the divine no conflict ensued. This was to be a true man.

Life and death are a part of destiny. Their sequence, like day and night, is of God, beyond the interference of man. These all lie in the inevitable nature of things. He simply looks upon God as his father; if he loves him with what is born of the body, shall he not love him also with that which is greater than the body? A man looks upon a ruler of men as one superior to himself; if he is willing to sacrifice his body [for his ruler], shall he not then offer his pure [spirit] also?

When the pond dries up and the fishes are left upon the dry ground, rather than leave them to moisten each other with their damp and spittle, it would be far better to let them forget themselves in their native rivers and lakes. And it would be better than praising Yao and blaming Chieh to forget both [the good and bad] and lose oneself in Tao.

The Great [universe] gives me this form, this toil in manhood, this repose in old age, this rest in death. And surely that which is such a kind arbiter of my life is the best arbiter of my death.

A boat may be hidden in a creek, or concealed in a bog, which is generally considered safe. But at midnight a strong man may come and carry it away on his back. Those dull of understanding do not perceive that however you conceal small things in larger ones, there will always be a chance of losing them. But if you entrust that which belongs to the universe to the whole universe, from it there will be no escape. For this is the great law of things.

To have been cast in this human form is to us already a source of joy. How much greater joy beyond our conception to know that that which is now in human form may undergo countless transitions, with only the infinite to look forward to? Therefore it is that the sage rejoices in that which can never be lost, but endures always. For if we emulate those who can accept graciously long age or short life and the vicissitudes of events, how much more should we emulate that which informs all creation on which all changing phenomena depend? . . . — *"The Great Supreme."*

THE FOUR FRIENDS

Four men; Tsesze, Tseyu, Tseli, and Tselai, were conversing together, saying, "Whoever can make Not-being the head, Life the backbone, and Death the tail, and whoever realizes that death and life and being and non-being are of one body, that man shall be admitted to friendship with us." The four looked at each other and smiled, and completely understanding one another, became friends accordingly.

By and by, Tseyu fell ill, and Tsesze went to see him. "Verily the creator is great!" said the sick man. "See how He has doubled me up." His back was so hunched that his viscera were at the top of his body. His cheeks were level with his navel, and his shoulders were higher than his neck. His neck bone pointed up toward the sky. The whole economy of his organism was deranged, but his mind was calm as ever. He dragged himself to a well, and said, "Alas, that God should have doubled me up like this!"

"Do you dislike it?" asked Tsesze.

"No, why should I?" replied Tseyu. "If my left arm should become a cock, I should be able to herald the dawn with it. If my right arm should become a sling, I should be able to shoot down a bird to broil with it. If my buttocks should become wheels, and my spirit become a horse, I should be able to ride in it — what need would I have of a chariot? I obtained life because it was my time, and I am now parting with it in accordance with Tao. Content with the coming of things in their time and living in accord with

424 » THE IMPORTANCE OF UNDERSTANDING

Tao, joy and sorrow touch me not. This is, according to the ancients, to be freed from bondage. Those who cannot be freed from bondage are so because they are bound by the trammels of material existence. But man has ever given away before God; why, then, should I dislike it?"

By and by, Tselai fell ill, and lay gasping for breath, while his family stood weeping around. Tseli went to see him, and cried to the wife and children: "Go away! You are impeding his dissolution." Then, leaning against the door, he said, "Verily, God is great! I wonder what He will make of you now, and whither He will send you. Do you think he will make you into a rat's liver or into an insect leg?"

"A son," answered Tselai, "must go whithersoever his parents bid him, east, west, north, or south. *Yin* and *yang* are no other than a man's parents. If *yin* and *yang* bid me die quickly, and I demur, then the fault is mine, not theirs. The Great [universe] gives me this form, this toil in manhood, this repose in old age, this rest in death. Surely that which is such a kind arbiter of my life is the best arbiter of my death.

"Suppose that the boiling metal in a smelting pot were to bubble up and say, 'Make of me a Moyeh [famous sword]!' I think the master caster would reject that metal as uncanny. And if simply because I am cast into a human form, I were to say, 'Only a man! only a man!' I think the creator too would reject me as uncanny. If I regard the universe as the smelting pot, and the creator as the Master Caster, how should I worry wherever I am sent?" Then he sunk into a peaceful sleep and waked up very much alive.

— *"The Great Supreme."*

THE BEST ON EARTH, THE MEANEST IN HEAVEN

"But if such is the case," said Tsekung, "which world [the corporeal or the spiritual] would you follow?"

"I am one condemned by God," replied Confucius. "Nevertheless, I will share with you [what I know]."

"May I ask what is your method?" asked Tsekung.

"Fishes live their full life in water. Men live their full life in Tao," replied Confucius. "Those that live their full life in water thrive in ponds. Those that live their full life in Tao achieve realization of their nature in inaction. Hence the saying, 'Fish lose themselves [are happy] in water; man loses himself [is happy] in Tao.' "

"May I ask," said Tsekung, "about [those] strange people?"

"[Those] strange people," replied Confucius, "are strange in the eyes of man, but normal in the eyes of God. Hence the saying that the meanest thing in heaven would be the best on earth; and the best on earth, the meanest in heaven."

— *"The Great Supreme."*

THE TAO OF GOD AND THE TAO OF MAN

For to have a territory is to have something great. He who has something great must not regard the material things as material things. Only by not regarding material things as material things can one be the lord of things. The principle of looking at material things as not real things is not confined to mere government of the empire. Such a one may wander at will between the six limits of space or travel over the Nine Continents, unhampered and free. This is to be the Unique One. The Unique One is the highest among man. . . .

What then is Tao? There is the Tao of God, and there is the Tao of man. Honor through inaction comes from the Tao of God: entanglement through action comes from the Tao of man. The Tao of God is fundamental: the Tao of man is accidental. The distance which separates them is great. Let us all take heed thereto!

— *"On Tolerance."*

"HORSES' HOOFS"

Chuangtse
C. 335 - C. 275 B.C.

« *This essay is one of the most devastating attacks on civilization and Confucianism. But one should not forget Chuangtse's positive dictum that the aim of government and philosophy should be to "let the people live out the even tenor of their lives and that "all creation shall be able to fulfill their instincts of life [the laws of their nature]."*

HORSES HAVE HOOFS to carry them over frost and snow, and hair to protect them from wind and cold. They eat grass and drink water, and fling up their tails and gallop. Such is the real nature of horses. Ceremonial halls and big dwellings are of no use to them.

One day Polo* appeared, saying, "I am good at managing horses." So he burned their hair and clipped them, and pared their hoofs and branded them. He put halters around their necks and shackles around their legs and numbered them according to their stables. The result was that two or three in every ten died. Then he kept them hungry and thirsty, trotting them and galloping them, and taught them to run in formations, with the misery of the tasseled bridle in front and the fear of the knotted whip behind, until more than half of them died.

The potter says, "I am good at managing clay. If I want it round, I use compasses; if rectangular, a square." The carpenter says, "I am

* Sun Yang, 658–619 B.C., famous horse trainer.

good at managing wood. If I want it curved, I use an arc; if straight, a line." But on what grounds can we think that the nature of clay and wood desires this application of compasses and square, and arc and line? Nevertheless, every age extols Polo for his skill in training horses, and potters and carpenters for their skill with clay and wood. Those who manage [govern] the affairs of the empire make the same mistake.

I think one who knows how to govern the empire should not do so. For the people have certain natural instincts — to weave and clothe themselves, to till the fields and feed themselves. This is their common character, in which all share. Such instincts may be called "heaven-born." So in the days of perfect nature, men were quiet in their movements and serene in their looks. At that time, there were no paths over mountains, no boats or bridges over waters. All things were produced, each in its natural district. Birds and beasts multiplied; trees and shrubs thrived. Thus it was that birds and beasts could be led by the hand, and one could climb up and peep into the magpie's nest. For in the days of perfect nature, man lived together with birds and beasts, and there was no distinction of their kind. Who could know of the distinctions between gentlemen and common people? Being all equally without knowledge, their virtue could not go astray. Being all equally without desires, they were in a state of natural integrity. In this state of natural integrity, the people did not lose their [original] nature.

And then when sages appeared, crawling for charity and limping with duty, doubt and confusion entered men's minds. They said they must make merry by means of music and enforce distinctions by means of ceremony, and the empire became divided against itself. Were the uncarved wood not cut up, who could make sacrificial vessels? Were white jade left uncut, who could make the regalia of courts? Were Tao and virtue not destroyed, what use would there be for charity and duty? Were men's natural instincts not lost, what need would there be for music and ceremonies? Were the five colors not confused, who would need decorations? Were the five notes not confused, who would adopt the six pitch-

to others is greater. If the injury committed is greater, the man is considered to be worse and the punishment is greater.

If a man now goes into someone's stables and steals his horses or cattle, he is considered to be still worse than the stealer of chicken and pigs and dogs. Why? Because the injury done is greater, he does more harm to others, and his crime is still greater.

To go further, if a man kills an innocent man, takes away his clothing and his spear and sword, the offense is still greater than that of stealing horses and cattle. Why? Because the more harm he does to others, the worse he is considered to be and the greater the crime.

All educated men condemn such actions and call them wrong. But the same persons do not realize that a war of aggression against another country is wrong, but instead praise it and give it their support. They consider that it is right to do so. Can these people be said to know the difference between right and wrong?

It is considered wrong to kill one person, and the crime is punished for one murder. Following this reasoning, the crime of committing ten murders is ten times worse than that of killing one man, and the murderer's crime is ten times greater. To kill one hundred persons would be a hundred times worse and the crime is multiplied a hundredfold.

All educated men condemn such murders and call them wrong. But the same persons do not realize that a war of aggression against another country is wrong, but instead praise it and give it their support. They consider that it is right to do so. They are really not conscious that it is wrong, for they write about such wars of aggression in their history books. If they knew that it was wrong, they would not have done so.

If a man calls something which is a little black "black," but calls deep black "white," then it may be said of him that he does not know the difference between black and white. If a man tastes something slightly bitter and calls it "bitter," but calls what is very bitter "sweet," he, too, may be said not to know the difference between sweetness and bitterness.

Now if a man condemns a small wrong as "wrong," but does not consider the great wrong of aggression against a neighbor, but gives it praise and support, how can such a man be said to know the difference between right and wrong?

It is therefore seen that the educated men of this world do not know the difference between right and wrong.

95 ▣ The Sages and Ourselves

From

BOOK OF MENCIUS

Mencius

372 - 289 B.C.

« *Mencius was regarded next only to Confucius, so much so that Confucianism is commonly spoken of as "the teachings of Confucius and Mencius" — and this in spite of the fact that he was not an immediate disciple. The following selection shows his teaching on the "original goodness of man."*

KUNGFUTSE SAID, "Kaotse says that the original human nature is neither good nor bad. Some people say that human nature can be either good or bad; therefore when the Emperors Wen and Wu were in power, the people loved virtue, and when the Emperors Yu and Li were in power, the people loved violence. Again other people say that some natures are good, while other natures are bad, and that therefore even under the rule of Emperor Yao, there was a bad man Shiang, and even with a bad father, Kusou, there was produced a good son, Shun. There were the good princes Chi and Pikan with such a bad man as Chou for their uncle and king. Now if you say that human nature is good, then are all those people wrong?"

"If you let them follow their original nature," replied Mencius, "then they are all good. That is why I say human nature is good. If men become evil, that is not the fault of their original endowment. The sense of mercy is found in all men; the sense of shame is found in all men; the sense of respect is found in all men; the sense of right and wrong is found in all men. The sense of mercy is what we call charity. The sense of shame is what we call righteousness. The sense of respect is what we call propriety. The sense of right and wrong is what we call moral consciousness. Charity, righteousness, propriety, and moral consciousness are not something that are drilled into us; we have them originally with us, but often forget about them. Therefore it is said, 'Seek and you will find it, neglect and you will lose it.' ". . .

Mencius said, "In years of prosperity, most of the young people are well behaved, and in bad years, most of the young people turn to violence. This is not due to a difference in their natural endowments, but because something has happened to lead their hearts astray. Take, for instance, the growing of wheat. You sow the seeds and till the field. The different plants are planted at the same time and grow from the same piece of land, and soon they sprout beautifully from the earth. When the time for harvest comes, they all ripen. There is a difference between the different stalks of wheat, which is due to the difference in the soil, in the moisture from the rain and the dew, and to differences in human care. Therefore, all who belong to the same species are essentially alike. Why should you doubt that this holds true also of human beings? The sages belong to the same species as ourselves. As Lungtse has said, 'A man who proceeds to make a pair of shoes without knowing the feet measurements will at least not end up by making a wicker basket.' Shoes are alike because the people's feet are alike. There is a common taste for flavor in our mouths. Yiya [a famous *chef*] is but one who has discovered our common taste for food. If, for instance, one man's taste for flavors should differ from that of another man, as the taste of dogs and horses, who belong to a different species, differs from the human taste, then why should the whole world follow the judgment of Yiya in regard to flavor? Since in the matter of flavor the whole world regards Yiya as the ultimate standard, we must admit that our tastes for flavors are alike. The same thing is true of our ears. In the matter of sounds, the whole world regards Master Kuang as the ultimate standard, and we must admit that our ears are alike. The same thing is true of our eyes. In regard to Tsetu, the whole world considers him a handsome man, and whoever cannot see his handsomeness may be said to have no eyes. Therefore I say there is a common love for flavors in our mouths, a common sense for sounds in our ears, and a common sense for beauty in our eyes. Why then do we refuse to admit that there is something common in our souls also? What is that thing that we have in common in our souls? It is reason and a sense of right. The sage is the man who has first discovered what is common to men's souls. Therefore, reason and the sense of right please our minds as beef and mutton and pork please our palates."

96 ▣ Farmers Are Best

Letter to

BROTHER MO, FROM "FAMILY LETTERS"

Cheng Panchiao
1693 - 1765

« *The warm feeling for the common people and the poor and a hatred of official snobbery are the two things which come out most strongly in the writings of this poet and painter. He was also usually regarded as "odd" among his own generation. (See further note in selection 49.)*

I received a letter from home on the twenty-sixth of the tenth month, and was delighted to learn that we got 2,500 bushels from the new fields at the autumn harvest. From now on I can afford to be a farmer during the remainder of my days. We must have all sorts of things made — mortars, grinding stones, sieves, bamboo pans, big and small brooms, and rice measures of all kinds. The women of the family shall lead the maids in housework and all learn to pound rice, shake grains, and work with their hands and feet. It will give an atmosphere of living on land and bringing up children there. On a cold, icy day, when poor relatives come to our door, first give them a big bowl of toasted [boiled] rice, which, helped out with a small dish of pickled ginger, is the best means of warming up the aged and the poor. In our leisure days, we can eat cakes of broken rice and cook "muddle congee," and eat it, sinking our head into the bowl held between the hands. On a frosty or snowy morning, this makes the whole body warm. Alas! I hope to be a farmer until the end of my days!

I think the best class of people in the world are the farmers. Scholars should be considered the last of the four classes.* The most well-to-do farmers have a hundred *mu* [about sixteen acres], the second seventy or eighty *mu*, and the next fifty or sixty *mu*. They all toil and labor to feed the rest of the world. Were it not for the farmers, we should all starve. We scholars are considered one class higher than the farmers because we are supposed to be good sons at home and courteous abroad, and maintain the ancient tradition of culture; in case of success, we can serve and benefit the people, and in case of failure, we can cultivate our personal lives as an example to the world. But this is no longer true. As soon as a person takes a book in hand, he is thinking of how to pass the examinations and become a *chujen* or *chinshih*, how to become an official and get rich and build fine houses and buy large property. It is all wrong from the very start, and the further one goes, the more wicked one becomes. It will all come to a bad end. Those who are not successful at the examinations are still worse; they prey upon the people of the village, with a small head and thievish eyes. True, there are many who hold firm to their principles, and there are everywhere some who set the highest standards for themselves. But the good suffer on account of the bad, with the result that we have to shut up. The moment we open our mouths, people will say, "All you scholars know how to talk. As soon as you become officials, you will not be saying the same things." That is why we have to keep quiet and accept the insults.

* Cheng here reverses the traditional Chinese classification which is in the following order: scholars, farmers, artisans, and businessmen.

97 ▣ Kingship

Huang Tsungshi
1610 - 1695

« Huang Tsungshi (alias Huang Lichow) was one of the serious historians and thinkers of the seventeenth century. After a period of youthful involvement in politics, in which he showed unusual courage among the radicals, he escaped by luck and, after the overthrow of the Ming Dynasty by the Manchus, devoted his life to pure scholarship, admired by many disciples, refusing all offers to receive government appointment by the great Manchu emperor, Kangshi.

IN PREHISTORIC TIMES, every man labored for himself and for his private interests, and there was no one to think of the public good or fight a common evil of society. Then the kings arose who worked for the public good and not the good of their own selves. They fought what was evil to the community as a whole and neglected what might not be good for their own selves. Thus kings were people who worked a thousand times harder than the people, without benefit to themselves. This was hardly an enviable position. Therefore, there were those who worked for the public benefit and never wanted to be called kings, like Shuyu and Wukuang, and other rulers who worked for the public benefit as kings and then handed over their power to others, like Yao and Shun; again others who were made kings and were forced to remain kings, like Yu. It was human nature, whether ancient or modern, not to relish such a position.

The kings of later times were different. They concentrated the power of government in themselves, and having done so, thought it

437

even allowable to take all the profits of the land for themselves and throw all that was disagreeable and onerous upon others, so that the people were not able to work for their own benefits or their own good, while the profits of the land became the private property of one family. At first, the kings felt embarrassed, but later they lost such embarrassment. The land and the people then belonged to one ruling house, the exclusive right and privilege to be handed down to their children and their children's children. The First Emperor of Han betrayed this way of thinking when he said to a scholar, "Do you think my success at my *profession* is greater or lesser than yours?" Being a king *was* a profession, like all others carried on for benefit.

The difference lies in this: in ancient times, the people were the masters, and the kings the guests, and the object of the kings' labors was the people. Now it is the kings who are the masters and the people the guests, and there is not one corner of the earth where the people can live peacefully their own lives, all because of the rulers. Therefore, when someone aspires to be a king, he does not mind sacrificing the lives of millions and taking away children from their parents in order to work for his "private property." Without the slightest qualm of conscience, he says to himself, "I am building up this ruling house for my children." And when he has attained to kingship, he does not mind grinding out the bones and marrow of the people and breaking up families to labor and to serve that he alone may enjoy all the luxury and amusements of an easy living. Without a qualm of conscience, he says again to himself, "I am entitled to the earnings of my property, am I not?"

Kings have thus become the great enemy of the people. For if there were no kings, people would be able to work for their own benefit and their own living. Alas! is this the purpose for which kings exist?

In ancient times, the people loved their kings like their father and compared them to Heaven. That was well deserved. Now the people regard their kings as their enemy and call them "That lonely person." That is well deserved, too. There are narrow-minded scholars who still say that the cardinal relationship between king and subject is eternal, to the extent they doubt the propriety of Tang and Wu in overthrowing their overlord tyrants Chieh and Chou, and are inclined to discredit the story of those patriots like Poyi and Shuchi who refused to serve a conqueror. It would seem to them that the lacerated flesh and bones of the millions of people were worth less than the mouse's head of a foreigner. Could it be that they truly believe that the whole world exists for the particular benefit of one person and one family in the heart of the Creator?

Therefore King Wu [who rose to overthrow a tyrant] was a sage. Mencius [who regarded it as right under certain circumstances for the people to regard their ruler as enemy] spoke the words of a sage. The kings of later times wish to wrap up kingship in the sacred cloak of a phrase "like father and like Heaven" behind which the people are not allowed to peer. Such rulers hold the views of Mencius as most inconvenient to themselves and would like to dethrone Mencius* from his place of worship. The narrow-minded scholars are to blame for leading them to think this way.

However, if it was possible for a king to maintain his private property forever and ever, one could understand the selfish motive which prompted such action. Since the king thought of the land as his own property, it was equally natural for some other people to desire to gain control of that same piece of property. The king could place all his property in an iron safe and have it heavily padlocked. But after all, there was only one man or family that wished to guard it, and many who wanted to get at it. In a few generations, and sometimes within the king's own lifetime, the blood of the king's own children flowed! People used to wish that they might never be born in a royal family, and the king Yitsung said once to his young princess, "Why were you doomed to be born

* Mencius has always been regarded as cofounder of Confucianism with Confucius. One always speaks of Kung-Meng (or Confucius-Mencius).

in my family?" What a bitter confession of remorse! Is this not enough to cool off the ambition of someone who starts out to found a dynasty?

Therefore, if the functions of king and ministers are clearly understood, no one would want to occupy the position of power, as in the case of Shuyu and Wukuang in ancient times. If the functions of king and subject are not clearly understood, everybody would have the right to wish the throne. It may be difficult to understand the proper functions of king and subject, but it should not be difficult to weigh the advantages and disadvantages between temporary glory and a lasting disaster.

98 〖回〗 On the Importance of Partiality

Kung Tsechen
1792 - 1841

« Among the scholars of the nineteenth century, Kung Tsechen
(Ting-an) was an outstanding one. He had an independent
mind, and a terseness of style which is classic. A prodigy when a
child, he grew up under the aegis of a learned grandfather, and
had an extraordinary knowledge of subjects in remote fields.
There is a story that when in Peking, he fell in love with the
mistress of a Manchu prince, fled in danger, and was assassinated
on the way south. The mistress was also dismissed from the
prince's household. It is said that in writing and thought, he
"formed a school of his own," which means he was an original
thinker.

THERE WAS A HIGH MINISTER who was approached by a
certain official and offered a bribe. The next morning he made this
known at the court, exposing his friend, and thus obtained pub-
licity for his integrity. The fellow officials said to one another, "Mr.
So-and-So is impartial; he puts the public interest first."

Kungtse [the author] heard of this and discussed this matter of
partiality and impartiality with his friends.

"What is partiality? How did it arise?" I was asked.

Kungtse replied as follows:

In astronomy, there is the intercalary month to regulate the
year's length, and there are the cold breeze in summer and the
warm sun in winter to equalize the imbalances. In the earth, there
is unevenness in the soil of rich fields and sandy farms. So the
heavens and the earth are partial to something. The sun and the

441

moon do not shine into a lady's bedchamber, but allow for some privacy. The great kings and emperors proclaim a holiday and go to their ancestral temples to worship, a great occasion which is formally recorded in the court annals. After all, what is all this solemn occasion for except the prayerful thought that God may "protect my children and grandchildren and preserve my country from its enemies." Why was God asked to preserve his own country and not someone else's country, and protect his own children and grandchildren, and not someone else's children?

What touches people more than the stories of great patriots who suffered for their country, or good sons who sorrowed for their parents, and widows who raised the orphans to keep up the family line and glorify the family? Such acts are approved by the sages, praised by all generations, sung about in poetry, and celebrated in history. Why did the loyal ministers show their loyalty to their own kings and not to other kings? Why were good sons devoted to their own parents and not to other people's parents? Why do widows and chaste wives reserve their bodies for their own husbands; why do they refuse to sell their bodies to the general public?

Besides, there was the last king of Yen who gave away his kingdom and royal dynasty of eight hundred years to Tsechih [a usurper]. There was the last emperor of Han, who did not love his own imperial house and without a blink surrendered to Tung Shien [usurper] the royal power, which the First Emperor labored so hard to establish, and the imperial family kept up for four hundred years. These two rulers seem to be entirely impartial. It would seem that these two persons put the public interest above their own interests to an extent unequaled by all the sage rulers of the past. Did not Mencius say that "if everybody will love his own parents and honor the family elders, the world will be at peace?" Was not Mencius a "partialist?" . . .

There is a proper need for privacy. Foxes and birds copulate in the open before the public without shame. Human beings require that privacy be respected through the provision of rooms and curtains and beds. To the animals, there is no thought and no idea of relatives, and they satisfy their love in a free domain without restrictions. They have no idea of father-and-son relationship, much less of private friends. In men, however, there is always a feeling of closeness or remoteness of a particular person, of intimate associations and frequent dinners together and exchange of confidences.

Were one to carry through the principle of absolute impartiality, would it be a world of human beings or of beasts? . . .

99 ▣ Do Ghosts Exist?

From

LUNHENG (A COLLECTION OF ESSAYS)

Wang Chung
A.D. 27 - C. 100

« *Wang Chung was an independent critic, unattached to any school of philosophy, who liked to think things out for himself. This made him an essayist of the Montaigne type. He started to write his essays chiefly after he was sixty and these embodied his mature reflections on life.*

PEOPLE SAY that a dead man's ghost has consciousness and can do harm to people. By the general analogy of animals, a dead man does not become a ghost and is incapable of doing harm to people. How does one prove this? Man is an animal, and an animal is also an animal. If an animal does not become a ghost when it is dead, how should man become a ghost? . . .

Life in man depends upon his spirit, and this spirit is extinguished when he dies. Man's spirit [*ch'i*, or energy] comes from his blood, and when man's blood runs out after he dies, the spirit or energy is exhausted. Then the body decomposes and becomes dust. What would the spirit depend on to become a ghost? We sometimes compare a deaf or blind man to ordinary vegetation which cannot see or hear. Now when the spirit leaves a man, it is something more serious than the mere loss of vision or hearing. . . .

Since the universe began, millions of people have died at different ages. The number of living people today is much smaller than those who have died in the past. If, therefore, the dead be-

444

come ghosts, then we should meet a ghost at every step. When a man sees ghosts at his deathbed, he should see millions of them filling all the streets, alleys, hallways and courtyards, and not see just one or two ghosts. . . .

It is in the nature of things that a new fire can be started, but there is not an extinguished fire which starts burning again. New human beings are born, but it is impossible to have a dead man come alive again. If it were possible to restart an already extinguished fire, then I might be inclined to accept the supposition that dead men might receive shape and form again. By the analogy of the extinguished fire, it is clear that dead men cannot come alive again as ghosts.

What we mean by ghosts is that they are the spirits of dead men. But if this is correct, then when one sees a ghost, he should see the naked spirit alone, and not dressed in a gown and girdle. For the clothing is not made of spirit; when it is buried, it decomposes along with the dead man's body. It is unreasonable to assume that it remains for the ghost to wear it. It is possible to argue that a man's spirit depends upon his blood energy, and that this blood energy goes with the decomposing body but the spirit survives it to become a ghost. But clearly a man's clothing, which is made of cotton or silk, is not infused with that blood energy the way a body is. How then shall the clothing retain its shape and form? Therefore, if we admit that when one sees a ghost's clothing it comes from one's imagination, so we must also say that when one sees the form of a ghost, it comes also from one's imagination. Therefore that which is imagined is not the spirit of a dead man. . . .

Form comes from association with the spirit, but the spirit also becomes conscious by association with material form. As there is no fire which burns by itself, so how shall there be a conscious spirit without a body? When people talk and do things by the side of a person who is asleep, the man who is asleep is not aware of it. Likewise when people do good or bad things in the presence of a coffin, the dead cannot be aware of it. If, therefore, a man who is merely asleep with his bodily form intact cannot be aware of what is taking place, how shall it be possible when the bodily form is already decomposed?

When a man is hit and hurt by someone, he makes a complaint to the officer and tells people about it because he has consciousness. Sometimes a man is murdered and no one knows who was the murderer, or sometimes one even does not know the whereabouts of the corpus delicti. If the dead victim had consciousness, he would certainly be angry with the murderer and would consequently be able to make a complaint to the authorities and give them the name of the murderer; or he would be able to go home and tell his family where his body is. Since the dead does not do that, we can conclude that he has no consciousness. . . .

A man in good health has a collected mind, but when he falls ill, his mind becomes confused because his spirit has been disturbed. Death is, as it were, the extreme of sickness. If a man's mind is already confused and incoherent when he is sick, it must be still more so when he is dead. When the spirit is disturbed, the mind loses its power of recognition; it must be still more true when the spirit is dispersed. A man dies as a fire is extinguished. An extinguished fire does not give out light, and a dead man cannot have consciousness. The two cases are strictly comparable. . . .

If a man cannot become a ghost, the dead cannot harm people. How does one prove this? A man's strength comes from his nourishment, and when he is strong, he can commit violence. A sick man, however, cannot drink and eat as usual; he becomes steadily weaker until he dies. Now when a man is very ill, he cannot even denounce or shout at his enemy in the room, or prevent a thief from stealing his things. This is because he is in a weakened condition. Death is the extreme of such a weakened condition. How then shall a ghost do harm to men? A man may dream that he has wounded or killed a man, and the next day he wakes and sees his own body and the body of the one he dreamed of having killed and cannot find any wounds. Now dreams come from the spirit. If the spirit in a dream can not do real harm to people, how can the spirit of a dead man do so? . . .

100 ▩ A Thought on Immortality

"THOUGHT ON SELF-RELIANCE"
"TSELI SHUO"

Chang Shihyuan
1755 - 1824

ALL LIVING THINGS in this universe die. Among the plants, birds, beasts, and insects, some are born in the morning and die at eve, some have a life span of a year, and some last ten, or hundred, or a thousand years. But they all die. The difference is merely one of length of time.

The same is true of man. When he is living, he labors and occupies himself with something and worries and plans as if he were going to live forever. But when his spirit is dispersed and he dies, he cannot even grow enough flesh to cover his white bones. Death comes to him exactly as it comes to the plants and birds and beasts and insects.

A gentleman is aware of this fact. He therefore does not regard life and death as depending upon the existence or nonexistence of bodily form, but rather upon the growth or decay of his spirit of life. When a man is perfectly well in his body but his vital spirit is gone, he may well be regarded as dead. If, however, one's life spirit is developed to find expression in principles of truth and justice or in literature, it becomes then a part of the great stream of life of this universe. He is then freed from this dependence on a material body.

We find in the classics and history the ancient wise men who died long ago but whose light shines through the ages like the stars and the sun. I may truly say that these men are still living with us.

Therefore, whether man is mortal or immortal depends entirely upon the man himself. However, all men die and few there are indeed who have become immortal. A scholar should make up his mind and rely on himself.

禅
悟

ZEN

101 ▣ Selection from the *Lankavatra Sutra*

« Buddhism was certainly known in China in the first century of the Christian era. From the third century on, there was a great influx of Buddhist monks and literature to China. Bodhidharma, the Father of the Shan Sect in China, came from India in the beginning of the sixth century. Shan (in Japanese, Zen), the effort of human mind to grasp the ultimate, undifferentiated and unconditioned reality behind appearances by a flash of intuition, found a fertile soil in China. In a peculiar sense, Shan was essentially a product of Buddha's metaphysics joined to Chinese Taoist mysticism and humor.

The Lankavatra Sutra and the Surangama Sutra are favorite readings of the Shan Buddhists. These, while religious, are essentially treatises of philosophy and metaphysics, dealing with the problems of the sense perceptions and knowledge of reality, clearing away false perceptions, and leading step by step to the highest samadhi, or enlightenment. As reading goes, they are exceptionally fine and clear, and the Surangama especially is, in its method of exposition and clarity, like Plato's dialogues. This explains the high prestige of Buddhism among the Chinese scholars. Only the most crassly uninformed will think of the body of Buddhist teachings as a mass of superstitions.

The Lankavatra (also spelled "Lankavatara") gives a systematic exposition of the entire Buddhist theory of knowledge and of reality, which is the realm of Kant's Ding-an-sich, unconditioned by a priori categories of reason, and described in Buddhist terms as chenju or "suchness." "Lanka" is the name of the mount in Ceylon where the Buddha developed the lectures. Both the Surangama and the Lankavatra are considered to have been written in the first century in Sanskrit. There are three existing translations in Chinese, done in Sung, Yuan, and Tang dynasties, the earliest by Dharmaraksha, done in 420, having been lost. The present translation is by Professor Suzuki and Dwight Goddard and appeared in A Buddhist Bible.

By the egolessness of things is meant that the elements that make up the aggregates of personality and its objective world being characterised by the nature of maya and destitute of anything that can be called ego-substance are therefore un-born and have no self-nature. How can *things* be said to have an ego-soul? By the egolessness of persons is meant that in the aggregates that make up personality there is no ego-substance, nor anything that is like ego-substance nor that belongs to it. The mind-system, which is the most characteristic mark of personality, originated in ignorance, discrimination, desire and deed; and its activities are perpetuated by perceiving, grasping and becoming attached to objects as if they were real. The memory of these discriminations, desires, attachments and deeds is stored in Universal Mind since beginningless time, and is still being accumulated where it conditions the appearance of personality and its environment and brings about constant change and destruction from moment to moment. The manifestations are like a river, a seed, a lamp, a cloud, the wind; Universal Mind in its voraciousness to store up everything is like a monkey never at rest, like a fly ever in search of food and without partiality, like a fire that is never satisfied, like a water-lifting machine that goes on rolling. Universal Mind as defiled by habit-energy is like a magician that causes phantom things and people to appear and move about. A thorough understanding of these things is necessary to an understanding of the egolessness of persons.

There are four kinds of Knowledge: Appearance-knowledge, Relative-knowledge, Perfect-knowledge, and Transcendental Intelligence. Appearance-knowledge belongs to the ignorant and simple-minded who are addicted to the notion of being and non-being, and who are frightened at the thought of being un-born. It is produced by the concordance of the triple combination and attaches itself to the multiplicities of objects; it is characterised by attainability and accumulation; it is subject to birth and destruction. Appearance-knowledge belongs to word-mongers who revel in discriminations, assertions and negations.

Relative-knowledge belongs to the mind-world of the philosophers. It rises from the mind's ability to consider the relations which appearances bear to each other and to the mind considering them; it rises from the mind's ability to arrange, combine and analyse these relations by its powers of discursive logic and imagination, by reason of which it is able to peer into the meaning and significance of things.

Perfect-knowledge belongs to the world of the Bodhisattvas who recognise that all things are but manifestations of mind; who clearly understand the emptiness, the un-bornness, the egolessness of all things; and who have entered into an understanding of the Five Dharmas, the twofold egolessness, and into the truth of imagelessness. Perfect-knowledge differentiates the Bodhisattva stages, and is the pathway and the entrance into the exalted state of self-realisation of Noble Wisdom.

Perfect-knowledge [jnana] belongs to the Bodhisattvas who are entirely free from the dualisms of being and non-being, no-birth and no-annihilation, all assertions and negations, and who, by reason of self-realisation, have gained an insight into the truths of egolessness and imagelessness. They no longer discriminate the world as subject to causation: they regard the causation that rules the world as something like the fabled city of the Gandharvas. To them the world is like a vision and a dream, it is like the birth and death of a barren-woman's child; to them there is nothing evolving and nothing disappearing.

The wise who cherish Perfect-knowledge, may be divided into three classes: disciples, masters and Arhats. Common disciples are separated from masters as common disciples continue to cherish the notion of individuality and generality; masters rise from common disciples when, forsaking the error of individuality and generality, they still cling to the notion of an ego-soul by reason of which they go off by themselves into retirement and solitude.

Arhats rise when the error of all discrimination is realised. Error being discriminated by the wise turns into Truth by virtue of the "turning-about" that takes place within the deepest consciousness. Mind, thus emancipated, enters into perfect self-realisation of Noble Wisdom.

But, Mahamati, if you *assert* that there is such a thing as Noble Wisdom, it no longer holds good, because anything of which something is asserted thereby partakes of the nature of being and is thus characterised with the quality of birth. The very assertion: "All things are un-born" destroys the truthfulness of it. The same is true of the statements: "All things are empty," and "All things have no self-nature,"— both are untenable when put in the form of assertions. But when it is pointed out that all things are like a dream and a vision, it means that in one way things are perceived, and in another way they are not perceived; that is, in ignorance they are perceived but in Perfect-knowledge they are not perceived. All assertions and negations being thought-constructions are un-born. Even the assertion that Universal Mind and Noble Wisdom are Ultimate Reality, is thought construction and, therefore, is un-born. As "things" there is no Universal Mind, there is no Noble Wisdom, there is no Ultimate Reality. The insight of the wise who move about in the realm of imagelessness and its solitude is pure. That is, for the wise all "things" are wiped away and even the state of imagelessness ceases to exist.

102   Selection from the *Surangama Sutra*

« *Buddha doubted the cognitive reasoning which Descartes never did and jumped Kant's categories of a priori reasoning to arrive at the intuitive grasp of unconditioned reality. The Surangama Sutra has been a great favorite with Chinese scholars who are Taoistically bent in mind. Su Tungpo loved it, and Chang Chao's (see selection 2) favorites are Chuangtse, Su Tungpo, and the Surangama. Reading it always gives me a feeling similar to the one I get when reading Plato's dialogues. It is presented in a very readable English form in the translation by Wai-tao, in* A Buddhist Bible, *edited by Dwight Goddard as a work of love.*

The selection is merely intended to give the reader a taste of the style of this masterpiece, and the interesting technique of exposition by Buddha. Long extracts are available in my Wisdom of China and India.

THEN THE LORD BUDDHA SAID: — Ananda, I want to question you; please listen carefully. You have just said that, at the time your faith in me was awakened, it was due to seeing the thirty-two marks of excellence. Let me ask you: What was it that gave you the sensation of seeing? What was it that experienced the sensation? And who was it that experienced the feeling of being pleased?

Ananda replied: — My Lord! At the time I experienced the sensation of being pleased, it was both through my eyes and my mind. When my eyes saw my Lord's excellencies, my mind immediately experienced a feeling of being pleased. It was then that I made up my mind to become thy disciple so that I might be delivered from the cycle of deaths and rebirths.

The Lord said: — From what you have just said, Ananda, your feeling of being pleased originated in your eyes and mind. But if you do not know where lies the perception of sight and where the activities of the mind originate, you will never be able to subjugate your worldly attachments and contaminations. It is like a king whose city was pestered by robbers and who tried to put an end to the thieving but was unsuccessful because he could not locate the secret hiding place of the robbers. So it is in the lives of human beings who are always being troubled by worldly attachments and contaminations, causing their perception of sight to become inverted and unreliable and seducing their thoughts and causing them to wander about ignorantly and uncontrolled. Ananda, let me ask you? Referring to your eyes and mind, do you know their secret hiding place?

Ananda replied: — Noble Lord! In all the ten different orders of life, the eyes are in the front of the face, as are my Lord's clear lotus eyes, and mine also. The same is true of the other sense organs, they are on the surface of the body, but the mind is hidden within the body.

The Lord Buddha interrupted: — Ananda, you are now sitting in the Lecture Hall, are you not? And when you are looking out to the Jetavana Grove, can you tell me where the hall and the grove are situated?

Certainly, my Lord. This quiet and splendid Lecture Hall and the Jetavana Grove are both situated in Anathapindika's beautiful park.

Now, Ananda, what do you see first, the people in this hall or the park outside?

I first see my Lord, then I see the noble audience, and other things in turn, and only afterward do I see the grove and the lovely park outside.

True, Ananda! Now tell me, while you are looking outside at the grove and park, what is it that enables you to distinguish the different views that your eyes see?

Noble Lord! It is because the windows and doors of the lecture hall are open wide. That is why I can see the distant views from inside the hall.

Then the Blessed Lord, in view of the great audience, reached out his golden hand and softly stroked Ananda's head, at the same time speaking to both him and the great assembly, saying: —

There is a particular Samadhi called The Highest Samadhi, which was the Lord Buddha's Crowning Experience, and by it he attained a perfect realisation of all manifestations and transformations. It was a wonderful door that opened to the mysterious Path that all the Tathagatas of all the ten quarters of all the universes have followed. It is of this Highest Samadhi that I am going to speak. Listen very carefully.

Then Ananda and the great audience bowed to the ground in deep adoration and then resumed their seats and waited humbly for the Master's solemn teaching.

The Lord Buddha then addressed Ananda and the great assembly, saying: —

Ananda, you have just said that from the inside of the lecture hall you can look out to the grove and the distant park because the windows and doors are open wide. It is possible that there are some within this very audience that only see these outside things and who are unable to see the Lord Tathagata within.

Ananda interrupted: — But my Lord, how can it be that anyone in this hall who can see the grove and streams without can fail to see the Lord within?

It does seem absurd, Ananda, but it is just that way with you. You say that your mind exists within your body and that it is quite clear of all obstructions, but if this clear mind really exists within your body, then you ought to see the inside of your body first of all. But there are no sentient beings who can do this, that is, see both the inside and outside of their bodies. Though they may not see all the inside things — such as the heart, stomach, liver, kidneys, etc. — but at least they ought to see the growth of the finger-nails, the lengthening of the hair, the knotting of the sinews, the throbbing of the pulse. If the mind is within the body, why does it not see these things? But if the mind is within the body and can not see the things within, how can it see the things without the body? So you must see that what you have said about the perceiving mind, abiding within the body, is untrue.

With a respectful bow, Ananda said to the Lord: — Listening to the words of my Lord, I begin to realise that my mind, after all, may be outside my body. It may be like a lamp. If the lamp is within the room, it will certainly illumine the room first and then shining through the open door and windows will illumine the yard outside. If it was like that, why is it that one seeing only outside objects does not see the things within? It must be that the mind is like a lamp placed outside of a room, for then it would be dark within. If one can clearly understand what his mind is, he would no longer be puzzled, but would have the same intelligence and understanding that the Buddhas have. Would it not be so, my Lord?

The Lord replied: — Ananda, this morning all of the Bhikshus followed me to the city of Sravasti begging for food in regular order and afterwards all returned to this Grove. I was fasting at the time, but the others ate the food. What think you, Ananda? If only one of the Bhikshus ate the food, would the others be satisfied of their hunger?

Ananda replied: — No, my Lord, and why? Because, although all of these Bhikshus are Arhats, yet their physical bodies are individually separated. How could it be, that one Bhikshu eating, could satisfy the hunger of all?

The Lord Buddha replied: — Ananda if your perceiving, understanding mind is really outside your body, then what the mind perceives could not be felt by the body, and what the body feels could not be perceived by the mind. Look at my hand, Ananda. When your eyes are looking at it, does your mind make any discriminations about it?

Yes, my Lord, it makes discriminations.

The Lord continued: — But if your mind and body are in mutual correspondence, how can it possibly be said that the mind exists outside the body? Therefore, Ananda, you ought to know that what you have just said about the mind existing outside the body is impossible. . . .

« This kind of exposition goes on for another ten or twenty thousand words.

EPIGRAMS AND PROVERBS

103 📖 Thoughts and Epigrams

« It would be easy and fascinating to compile a book of unusual quotations, but this is hardly the place for it. I have put down here important thoughts and statements by various thinkers and philosophers of the past as they came to my mind, helped out with some references. I have kept away from Laotse largely because he is available in many books of mine, although he was the best epigram maker of all China. Readers can be referred to either my translation in Wisdom of Laotse or to any other translation, notably one by Witter Bynner, and an excellent one by Arthur Waley. The whole book of Laotse consists of epigrams. Compared with him or with Chuangtse, Confucius seems slow-witted.

All thoughts come in flashes. They should stand by themselves. When they are expanded, they lose some of the force of the original thoughts.

I consider the following as a rather random collection, and not a comprehensive one.

The Universe

DID HEAVEN EVER TALK? The four seasons go their rounds and things are produced. When did Heaven talk? — Confucius.

What is God-given is called nature; to follow that nature is called Tao [the Way, Truth]; to cultivate the tao is called culture. —Tsesze (grandson of Confucius).

To come to an understanding of the universe from being one's true self is the way of nature; to realize one's true self from an understanding of the universe is the way of culture. Whoever is his true self has an understanding of the universe; whoever has a true understanding of the universe realizes his true self. — Tsesze.

461

The way of the great learning consists in keeping clear the [originally] clear character [of men]. — Tsesze.

The function of the mind is thinking and the knowledge of truth depends upon the exercise of this function of thinking. First establish the main principles, and the small details cannot get away. — Mencius, cofounder of Confucianism.

All things come from somewhere, but you cannot see their root; all things appear from somewhere, but you cannot see the door. — Chuangtse (see introductory note, selection 78).

The Great [universe] gives me this form, this toil in manhood, this repose in old age, this rest in death. Surely that which is such a kind arbiter of my life is the best arbiter of my death. — Chuangtse.

Fishes live their full life in water. Men live their full life in Tao. — Chuangtse.

Fishes forget themselves in water. Men [should] forget themselves in Tao. — Chuangtse.

How do I know that love of life is not an illusion after all? How do I know but that he who dreads death is not as a child who has lost his way and does not know his way home? — Chuangtse.

Those who dream of the banquet, wake to lamentation and sorrow. Those who dream of lamentation and sorrow, wake to join the hunt. — Chuangtse.

He [the enlightened one] simply looks upon God as his father; if he loves him with what is born of the body, shall he not love him also with that which is greater than the body? — Chuangtse (see selection 92).

Only by not regarding material things as material things can one be the lord of things. — *Chuangtse.*

Truth is infinite, but human intelligence is finite. To pursue the infinite with the finite is a dangerous occupation. — *Chuangtse.*

Above the physical forms is the Tao; within the physical forms are the functioning things. One should look at it this way: The Tao is also functioning things; functioning things are also Tao. — *Cheng Mingtao (Neo-Confucianist, twelfth century).*

The primeval force is like a tree. It grows a trunk and branches, and twigs and flowers and leaves. It grows on and on. By the time it grows a fruit, there is contained in it the principle which makes it grow on and on. And it will so grow, and become once more the primeval force [*taichi*] and there is no stopping it. — *Chu Shi (the greatest Neo-Confucianist, twelfth century).*

Yin and Yang

One yin [female principle] and one yang [male principle] make up the Tao. — *Yi Chuan, (Commentary on Book of Changes), attributed to Confucius.*

The primeval unity [*taiyi*] gives birth to the two polarities [*liangyi*]; the two polarities give birth to yin and yang. — *Lushih Chunchiu. (Lu lived in the third century B.C. He could be the real father of the builder of the Great Wall because he purposely planned to present his mistress, already pregnant, to the monarch of Tsin. The book was compiled by scholars living under his patronage.)*

There is no Tao without yin and yang. Therefore the two polarities of yin and yang are the Tao itself. Yin and yang are forces

[chi], within physics; the Tao is metaphysics. — Cheng Yichuan (Neo-Confucianist, twelfth century).

The primeval force [taichi] contains within itself potential and kinetic forces. One cannot separate the potential and the kinetic. — Chu Shi.

The mind is the universal reason [li] itself. — Lu Shiangshan (Idealist philosopher, twelfth century).

Li [universal reason, or laws governing things] exists inside chi [force]. Force does not exist without li [laws]. Force exists in space. Space is not empty without force. The two are one and the same. — Wang Chuanshan (great exponent of the force theory, 1619–1692).

Human Life

The king of Chu lost a precious bow and looked for it for days. After a while he gave up and said, "What does it matter? A man of Chu lost it and a man of Chu has found it." When Confucius heard it, he said, he should have left out the word "Chu."

Admit that you do not know what you do not know — that is knowledge. — Confucius.

Sometimes I lose myself in some spell of work and neglect my meals, sometimes feel so happy and forget my worries, and am not aware that old age is coming on. — Confucius.

Don't be slow to correct a mistake. — Confucius.

Do not worry that people do not know you. Worry that you may not be worth knowing.— Confucius.

He who hoards much loses much. — Laotse.

There is no beauty even in victory. He who calls it beautiful loves slaughter. — *Laotse.*

Suppose a criminal should be killed. Who dares to kill him? — *Laotse.*

Heaven protects with love those it would not see destroyed. — *Laotse.*

Food and sex are the two great desires of man. — *Confucius.*

When young, beware of the desire to fight. When in manhood, beware of sex. When one has grown old, beware of the desire for possession. — *Confucius.*

A good physician's son often dies of disease. — *Mencius.*

A good maker of shields worries only that the man may be hurt. A good maker of bows and arrows worries only that the man may not be hurt. — *Mencius.*

I love fish, but I also love bear's paw. If I cannot have both, I will forget the fish and take the bear's paw. I love life and I also love righteousness. If I cannot have both, I will sacrifice life and do what is right. — *Mencius.*

When God wants a man to do great things, He first starves his body, belabors his muscles, makes him go through hardships and privations, and frustrates what he sets out to do. — *Mencius.*

A great man is one who has not lost the heart of a child. — *Mencius.*

There is quite a difference between "I can't do it" and "I won't do it." Usually it is the latter. — *Mencius.*

Rule a big country as you would fry minnows. Leave them alone in the pan. — *Laotse.*

I have lived fifty years to know the mistakes of the forty-nine. — *Chupoyu (a friend of Confucius).*

I cannot bend my waist [and kowtow] for the sake of five bushels of rice [official salary]. — *Tao Yuanming (poet, A.D. 372–427).*

The gentleman grows upward; the uncultivated man grows downward. — *Confucius.*

Every man can be a sage. — *Mencius.*

Break the regulations, rather kill an innocent man. — *Tsochuan (probably sixth century B.C.).*

God hears through the ears of my people and sees through the eyes of my people. — *Book of History.*

> Steal a hook,
>   And you are called a crook.
> Steal a kingdom,
>   And you are called a duke.
>   — *Chuangtse.*

The gentleman fears God's will, fears the great men, fears the words of the sages. The rascal fears nothing. — *Mencius.*

Not blind, she is my fiancée; blind, she is also my fiancée. — *Liu Tingshih (eleventh century — he married a girl who became blind after engagement, and lived happily ever after).*

Treat him well. He is also somebody's son. — *Tao Yuanming (instruction to his boys when sending a poor boy to help them with the farm).*

These are the poems and prose writings I wish to preserve. Whoever adds to them, I shall come as a ghost and break his skull. — *Cheng Panchiao (preface to his own selected works, after destroying what he considered of no permanent value; see introductory notes, selections 49 and 96).*

It is difficult to be muddle-headed, and difficult to be intelligent. It is even more difficult to graduate from intelligence into muddle-headedness. — *Cheng Panchiao.*

Beware of the man who has no hobbies. If he is not sincere in loving what he loves, he is also probably not sincere in hating what he professes to hate. — *Yuan Chunglang (see introductory note, selection 67).*

I would rather owe the world a debt than have the world owe me a debt. — *Tsao Tsao (usurper, of the period of the Three Kingdoms, pictured as a typical unscrupulous or treacherous person, but extremely intelligent).*

You are cooking beans by burning beanstalks. Don't you feel at all that they come from the same root? — *Tsao Tsechien (son of Tsao Tsao, who made this successful appeal when he was about to be killed by his brother; in spite of the bad reputation of Tsao Tsao, his was a family of great talents).*

There are no bad men in this world. — *Su Tungpo (see introductory notes, selections 37 and 64).*

In God's eyes, there is no rejected person. — *Laotse.*

So the people have no rice to eat. Why don't they eat meat? — *said by a stupid, profligate, ancient king during a famine. (He lost his throne.)*

Eggs have hair. — *Hueitse (contemporary of Chuangtse and a sophist; eggs have hair potentially in the chicken embryo).*

Everybody dies. How he dies is important. Sometimes a death has the weight of the Taishan Mountain; sometimes it is lighter than a feather. — *Szema Chien (see introductory notes, selections 38 and 39).*

The more classical the tune, the less people there are who can join you. — *Sung Yu (poet, c. 290–c. 223 B.C., in answer to the king who asked him why he was unpopular).*

Between husband and wife, there are other things perhaps more serious than the husband painting his wife's eyebrows. — *Chang Chang (?–48 B.C., answering the charge of which he had been accused before the emperor).*

Eat pickled turnips with yellow beans. It gives the taste of walnut. — *last words of Chin Shengtan (see selection 3), contained in a sealed letter to his family as he went to his execution, as a joke upon the magistrate. (His execution was a gross miscarriage of justice because Chin had joined in protest against overtaxation of the farmers.)*

When lips are cut, the teeth are exposed. — *Tsochuan (said by a scholar trying to persuade an invader to spare his country as buffer state).*

When a bird is dying, its cry is pitiful. When a man is dying, his words are good. — *ancient proverb.*

I prefer the vulgar people to the snobs. — *Confucius.*

» *Confucius is wrong. There is no choice between the two. Snobs without money are vulgarians, and vulgarians with money are snobs.*

From

KUEIYUYUAN CHUTAN

Shu Shuehmou

1522 - 1593

« *This man, who was a Minister of Ceremonies, was against the whole idea of "orthodoxy" and "orthodox tradition" in the Confucian School, believing that the scholars stood to benefit by such rigid codification of Confucius's lively thoughts and teachings. In particular he was against the Neo-Confucianist School — known popularly as taoshueh, similar in connotation to the word "Puritans" in English — believing that it led to great hypocrisy.*

THE DISASTERS OF FIRE AND FLOOD and bandits usually strike the poor people first. The wasting diseases of emaciation usually strike at the powerful and the rich.

The best of high officials always ended up with a piece of ugly writing which sent them back to the country — an impeachment. The worst of men always obtained a beautiful piece of writing at the end of their days — a eulogy on a tombstone.

If a man has read a great number of books, and does not think things through, he is only a bookcase. One may read through the entire Buddhist Tripitaka, but if he has not a pure heart, he can end up only as a wooden figure.

Be careful not to open your mind to a man of few words. Be equally careful when you meet a man who pushes himself and wants to win your friendship.

A man on his deathbed will yet give detailed instructions, even though he has not much. A retired official will gabble about his days at the capital, even though he no longer holds the official rank.

A man is physically stronger than a woman, but against an aggressive wife his hands are limp. Parents like to maintain their dignity before children, but when they have a disobedient son, they usually shut up.

The world regards those who look down upon money as fools. That is why bribery is rampant. Similarly people who are not accommodating are regarded as "slow stuff" [tardy in getting promotion], and that is why the court is full of yes men.

Clean, fresh writing is like polished sandalwood where the wood grain shows its natural beauty. On the other hand, the writings of the hosts of imitators are like lacquer ware, which shine on the outside but do not wear well.

Do right and do it alone. Commit something wrong and you will need a gang to work with. That is why even a burglar posts someone to watch for him.

There are times when a poor scholar is forced to beg something of his friends, but he will do it with dignity. Even the sages died, but they died with a lasting fame.

When a wife feels unhappy and the husband shares her unhappiness, her unhappiness will vanish. But when a wife gets into a rage, it won't do for the husband also to get into a rage.

It is said that an unscrupulous man can end up as a cabinet minister and the man who has done him a good turn then receives his boomerang. It is also said that an official who owes debts to others must be an honest official. If so, the man who loans him money will feel very sorry to see him lose his job.

If a man quickly gets rich shortly after he gets an office, he cannot amount to much. But if he stays in an office for years and still is not rich, he does not amount to much, either.

A man often talks big to impress people but is a coward at heart.

A hypocrite often makes a pretense of sterling honesty but reminds me of a courtesan who refuses to taste food at dinners and then goes home and gorges herself.

An official may solidly turn down big bribes but nibble at little gifts of carpets or coats. That is because the mouse has its own caution in stealing food. Or a man may be honest at first and then grab something really worth while. That resembles a tiger's crouch before the spring.

A police officer may catch thieves with one hand and receive booty with the other. A man may join in condemning adultery but love to take a peep at the adulteress.

Law may be too strict, or too lax. But strict enforcement of law is like screwing the strings too tight, which still produce some music. A general state of lawlessness is like having the strings too loose, when there is no sound at all.

Do not ask your children's opinions when you want to retire, especially the younger children. And do not ask your wife when you want to take a concubine, especially a lately married one.

Man loves woman like one thirsty asking for a drink. Woman loves man like one in a hot climate seeking for a cool place. Therefore the latter stays longer.

A stupid son is worse than a profligate son because there is no hope of a change. A muddle-headed official is worse than a dishonest one because he drags others down with him.

A well-read man often gives opinions from his reading and airs them as his own.

A man whose face changes color at the sight of ten dollars should not be made a mayor. One whose face changes color at the sight of a hundred dollars should not lead an army.

Better try to build up a company of friends when you have money than try to win disciples by your lofty teachings.

Better feed people than bait them with words.

A miser can amass a considerable fortune, but let something happen and he will be like a crushed rat on the streets. A big-hearted man can also go broke, but something happens and he still stays as alive as a centipede who has lost some legs.

A person who likes to drop names can fool the innocent, but not the people with a better background.

Snobbery can be worse among the rich than among the poor. The hatred among brothers is sometimes worse than that among friends.

When you see a man whose eyes are dull and fixed, you can be sure that his mind is gone. When you see a man who is obsequious, look out.

A rash temper can conceal secret greed. A servile, ingratiating appearance helps to conceal emptiness of mind.

Eating and sex follow instincts in which men and animals are alike. Beyond these, in things outside instincts, the truth must be learned through some hard thinking.

If a rich man associates with the poor, he gets a good name. When a poor man associates with the rich, he gets money.

Humility is a virtue, but too much of it bespeaks cunning. Too much silence in a man also indicates a designing mind.

Praise a man at his back and not to his face, and he will really appreciate it when he hears about it.

Wealth and power do not come to a high-minded scholar because he never cares for them and does not run after them. They do come to an aggressive man because he goes to it like an army fighting with its back to a river.

« About one third of the book has been translated.

105 ▣ Wish I Had Heard It from an Elder

From

AN TEH CHANG CHEH YEN

Chen Chiju
1558 - 1639

« *(See introductory note, selection 47.)*

A *shiutsai* [college graduate], like a virgin, is afraid of people. When he enters the government service, he has to feed people, like a daughter-in-law. When he finally retires in old age, he likes to give people advice, like a mother-in-law.

There are two sentences that can constitute the art of government: Act in a crisis with calm, and act during a calm by thinking ahead of a crisis.

In judging people, judge a common man by where he stands in the important things, but judge a great man by watching what he does in the little things.

Sit quietly for a moment and you realize how you have been foolishly running about. Learn to keep your mouth shut and you realize how you have talked too much. Avoid getting involved in too many things and you realize that you have been wasting your time in unnecessary things. Close your door and you realize that you have been mixed up with too many kinds of people. Have few desires and you realize why you have had so many ills. Be human and you realize that you have been too critical of others.

A member of the gentry always talks about "saving face and keeping regulations." That is what keeps him so busy and occupied. But face and regulations are external things.

How do I know what is good? Anything I do which is appreciated by people is good. How do I know what is bad? Anything I do which makes people disgusted is bad.

Man conquers heaven. When his mind is set and the vital energy moves, neither fate nor oracles have any power over him.

When there is no news to talk about, the world is in a good way.

A vulgar man always looks for favors and forgets them when he has got what he wants. A gentleman hesitates a great deal before he accepts a favor and then he always remembers it.

Medicine is for saving life, but in the hands of quacks can kill people. Soldiers are for killing people, but in the hands of wise rulers, can save people's lives.

The unbalanced youth who are critical of the older people often die young. This is natural. Since they are critical of the old, why should God let them grow old?

Wang Shaoho says, Confucius warned against love of fighting, love of sex, and love of possession. But these three things are exactly what we share with the animals. Is that why we must be careful?

He who always says that he is right never thinks.

In war, think always of how to save lives.

Forgive your servants when they offend you. Do not forgive them when they offend others.

A man is difficult to know. But a man who is too easy to know is not much worth knowing.

A man who saves up good words as one saves up pennies will eventually be rich mentally.

Do unto others as you would have others do unto you. But better not expect others to do unto you what you would do unto them.

One must try to be good, but not goody-goody. One must be realistic in understanding the world's ways, but idealistic in one's own motives and action.

Confucianists and Buddhists quarrel and dispute with each other because the Confucianists do not read Buddhist books and the Buddhists do not read Confucianist books. Both are talking about what they do not know.

A reader must learn to stand typographical mistakes as one must learn to stand the ruffians in a market place.

A wealthy man brings few tears to his deathbed because the children are too much occupied with thoughts of the will. A poor man brings many years to his deathbed because the children love him and have nothing else to think about.

An elderly man does not lightly criticize someone who is really superior.

Beware of a man who is always doubtful when he hears something good about a man, but is quick to believe something bad.

106 ▣ Talks with a Monk

From

YENTSI YUSHIH

Chen Chiju
1558 - 1639

READ A FEW MORE BOOKS and talk a little less.

There are people who are completely illiterate but are poets, who cannot say a single *gatha* [prayer-formula] but are religious, who cannot touch a drop but appreciate wine, and who do not know a thing about rocks but have the sense of painters. They are born that way.

I do not know who wrote this "More-and-Less Song." It runs as follows: Drink less wine, eat more rice. Take less meat, eat more vegetables. Shut your eyes more, open your mouth less. Comb your hair more, take less baths. Live alone more, mix in company less. Collect more books, keep less jades. Stand more insults, take less fame. Do more good works, think less of government honors. Repeat not an advantage, and count less on good luck.

Su Tseyu [Su Tungpo's brother] loved to say, "Being often ill is good for studying Taoism. Having many sorrows is good for understanding Buddhism."

Seafood is not salty although it comes from the sea.

There is a formula for enjoying living in the mountains: no trees planted in rows, no rocks without moss, no worries in the mind, no flurries in the house.

When I get an ancient edition, I have it copied; after it is copied, I have it checked; after checking, have it set up, after setup, have it checked again; after checking, have it printed; and after printing, have it checked again. Even with such care, there are two or three per cent typographical errors. In this matter, where the eyes face something directly and closely, there are mistakes. How much less credence should we place upon gossip carried by word of mouth?

The White-skeleton Vision Method [Buddhist]. First imagine that your right toe is infected and has a festering sore; gradually it spreads to the ankle, and then the knee and the waist. The same thing happens to your left leg. Gradually the disease spreads from the waist, the belly, then up the chest, and gradually covers the neck and the head. Your whole body will have decayed and only a white skeleton remains. You should then look at this white skeleton piece by piece, and every piece, carefully, steadily, and long. Then you ask yourself, "Who is this white skeleton, and who is the person looking at the white skeleton? You separate your self from the body and regard them as two different things. Then you gradually see the white skeleton move away from your body, first ten feet, then fifty feet, then a hundred feet, then miles. You feel that this white skeleton does not belong to you at all. Keep this image in mind and you will come to think of your self as different from the bodily frame. We borrow, as it were, this frame to live in merely like a guest, and refuse to believe that it will last forever for us to live in. In this way, we can come to look upon life and death as the same thing.

« What a cruel thought, and what a sad one! Buddhists have taught people to banish their sex desires by looking upon a beautiful young woman and reflecting that she is only a mass of fairly stable bones and not so stable flesh. One can fool oneself, but what ugly thoughts!

When you look at a good piece of calligraphy, see it as if you had suddenly met a stranger. Do not scrutinize his ears, eyes, and particular features, but look at his laughter, his expression, and the living spirit of the man.

Mr. Fu says, "Loosen your belt and do not knit your brows, and you will feel much better whatever happens."

« *I have translated at random a small portion selected from the book. There is much in it which has to do with artistic appreciation, similar to Quiet Dream Shadows (selection 2) and which needs not be duplicated. The process of selection for translation is largely a matter of the meeting of the minds of the author and the translator. Sometimes, in reading a line, the minds meet and the English translation comes easily and naturally. Sometimes one has to search for the proper expression, and then it will most likely be belabored. Sometimes one tries, fails, and just gives up.*

There is a whole jungle of such books of reflections in the Paoyentang collection, edited by the present author (better known as Chen Meikung), and in other collections. Chen Meikung himself produced about ten volumes of such notes. I hope I have selected the best in the above two books.

A great many other books contain moralizations or platitudes, of the making of which there is no end. Shut up a Chinese scholar for a few months or a year in prison, and he is sure to come up with a book of moralizations.

107 📖 Proverbs

« The following are Chinese popular proverbs, supplied largely by
my wife, partly translated by my daughter Adet, and supplemented by what I can ransack out of my head. Some proverbs
are not easy to translate: firstly, because they depend on a rhyme
effect which is necessarily lost, and the rhyme is what makes
them stick easily in memory; secondly, because the aptness of
imagery, which often depends on local color, may be lost. All
roundabout explanations kill it. The reader is also referred to
"One Hundred Proverbs" in my Wisdom of China and India,
which, however, are literary epigrams rather than folk proverbs.

THE BEST WAY of not being found out is not doing it.

You cannot do a thing without four persons knowing it. Heaven
knows, the earth knows, you know, and I know.

Who has not something on his conscience is not jumpy when
someone makes a midnight knock on the door.

The sky over my head and the earth beneath my feet — a man's
pride of independence.

A severe law-enforcement officer produces thieves.

A child has ears and no mouth. (He should not interrupt or
answer back.)

Eat until you are old. Learn until you are old. (It is never too
old to learn.)

You cannot teach an old dog new tricks. (Incorrigible.)

Choose and choose, and marry a goose. (Of girls who are too choosy in picking husbands.)

They fight at the headboard of the bed and make up at the foot of the bed. (Young couples always make up after a quarrel.)

The best judge cannot settle domestic quarrels.

Eat from inside the rice bowl and talk outside it. (Of disloyal members of the family.)

Pull someone's fist to strike the stone lion. (Let someone pull the chestnut out of the fire.)

Sit and eat, and you eat a mountain away. (There must be an income.)

Time flies like a shuttle [in a loom].

Marry a chicken, follow a chicken. Marry a dog, follow a dog. (A wife always follows her husband.)

Do not give a comb to a monk, nor a fine comb to a nun. (Useless gift.)

The tiger flees through the front door; the wolf comes in through the back.

Riding a tiger, one cannot go on and one cannot dismount.

The moon is not always round, the flowers do not always bloom, and men do not always have a happy reunion.

A mile-long mat awning [for a great feast of celebration] must sooner or later be taken down.

The chicken thief is now posing as an alderman. He has not stolen a chicken for three days.

Kill a chicken as a warning to a monkey. (As a lesson to other offenders.)

Dogs do not bark at a frequent caller. (A too frequent caller is left alone by his host.)

Pierce two hawks with an arrow. (Kill two birds with one stone.)

In shooting a tiger or catching a bandit, depend on your own brother.

Across the ditch, one finishes the dish. (One always eats more at a friend's house because of change of flavor.)

A mother cow licks at its calf. (Mother love is irrepressible.)

In writing, one's own is best; in women, some one else's wife.

The elbow bends inward. (It is natural to think first of one's own family.)

An old man has crossed more bridges than a young man has crossed streets. (Listen to those with experience.)

A bad pilot blames the crooked river.

Peace in heaven, peace on earth, no peace in human heart. When there is peace in the human heart, there is peace in the world. (Tien *ping*, ti *ping*, jen shin pu *ping*. Jen shin *ping ping*, tienshia tai *ping*.)

When the water level rises, the boat rises with it. (All friends and relatives benefit when someone gets an official promotion.)

Do not rub the scales under a dragon's neck. (Do not twist a lion's tail.)

Playing classical music before a cow. (Casting pearls before swine.)

A dog's mouth does not produce an elephant's ivory. (Of people who are abusive.)

Throw things at a mouse and you break the vase. (Of unwise measures.)

Leave a chicken in the care of a wild cat. (Of misplaced trust.)

Eat fish and be afraid of fishy smell. (Of one about to commit something wrong and is afraid of shame; also of hypocrisy.)

Restring a musical instrument. (Of a man who remarries.)

All men are husbands. (Of promiscuous women.)

Wait till his eyebrows are scorched. (Make no preparation until immediate danger comes.)

A mother-in-law's smiles are like the April sun. (Undependable.)

You discover the pine's sturdiness in winter. (A gentleman's strength is shown in a crisis.)

Sweep the snow before your own doorsteps, and ignore the frost on your neighbor's roof. (Mind your own business.)

The bedbug says the louse stinks. (The pot calls the kettle black.)

Foxes of the same hole. (Birds of a feather flock together.)

A stork in a poultry yard. (A compliment to an outstanding person.)

A celestial steed prances in the clouds. (A great spirit in freedom.)

Do not be a horse and cattle for your children and grandchildren; they have their own luck. (Do not be a slave for them.)

Kill a chicken with a beef butcher's chopper. (Unnecessary expenditure of effort.)

With money you can make the devil work the mill for you. ("Working the mill" is done by men or animals going round and round a millstone in the center, back-breaking work.)

Money talks to the gods.

Money can give orders to devils.

Money is gone at a gambling table. Man is gone at the battlefield.

Money is courage.

So long as the green hill remains, do not worry about lack of fuel. (Keep the property.)

He neglects burning incense in times of peace and hugs the Buddha's leg in times of need.

The monks give a feast to the Goddess of Mercy [or to Buddha].

(Of many hosts who, in inviting the guest of honor, invite themselves to a feast.)

Many monks and little congee. (Too many mouths to feed.)

You can't catch a tiger cub unless you go to the tiger's lair.

Blind man riding a blind horse.

A big tree gives a large shade. (A rich man helps many relatives.)

When the trunk is steady, let the top branches wave in the wind. (A virtuous woman cannot be seduced with flirtations.)

A tree wants quiet, but the wind will not let it. (From an ancient reference, describing one's regret that when one has the chance to provide comforts for one's parents, the parents are already dead.)

When the tree falls, the monkeys are scattered. (Rats abandon a sinking ship.)

A tree depends upon the root. A man depends upon the heart.

Hear the pig's cries at the butcher's at midnight, and you know what the battlefield is like.

Good iron is not made into nails; good men are not made into soldiers.

Good bamboo produces good bamboo shoots. (Good children come from good parents.)

Bad bamboo shoots from good bamboo. (Bad children from good parents.)

Such a father, such a son. (A compliment on the good son of a distinguished father.)

Have a son and everything is all right.

Predestined enemy. (*Yuanchia*: lovers who quarrel and make up, make up and quarrel, but cannot get away from one another.)

Good man, good man, a really good bad man. (Of a hypocrite.)

A good fighter flees from the moment's danger. (He who fights and runs away lives to fight another day.)

A good horse does not graze at the owner's front door.

Of all thirty-six ways, escape is the best way.

Yield to him, yield to him. After a few years, just look at him. (Let him take advantage. He will get his due in time.)

You can deceive your superiors, but not your inferiors.

A cunning fox has three holes.

A rabbit crying at a fox's funeral. (Crocodile tears.)

Kill the hunting dog when the rabbits are all killed off. (Of an emperor who killed his ablest generals after his conquest of empire.)

The fox shows its tail. (Secret evil intention is out.)

A fox does not know its tail stinks, and a snail does not know its tail crinkles. (A man does not see his own weakness.)

A wolf may travel a thousand miles but still loves meat. (His predatory nature does not change.)

The dog is the loyal minister; the cat is the selfish politician.

A dog trying to catch mice, none of his business.

Attach a dog's tail to an ermine. (Poor addition to something beautiful.)

Add legs to a painting of a snake. (Uncalled-for addition.)

One pinprick draws blood. (Of masterful satire; criticism that hits the nail on the head.)

A golden brooch fallen into a well. (Looking for a needle in a haystack; all a matter of luck.)

A good house changes a man's spirit; good nourishment changes a man's constitution.

Nothing is difficult to a man who has persistence.

Water drowns a good swimmer more often than a bad one.

The poor man grows lice on his body; the rich man grows sores. (There is an idea that a rich man is more prone to disease.)

Hide the disease from your doctor. (A man tries to conceal his disgraceful affairs and will not take advice.)

It is easy to live like a poor man, difficult to pretend to be rich.

The young girl likes beauty, her mother likes money [in suitors].

The son is always in the mother's heart, but the mother is not always in the son's heart.

Water flows downward, not upward. (Do not expect gratitude from children.)

You forget how you were fed by your parents; just wait till you feed your children.

Having children is a blessing, but less children, less worry.

The man who has does not understand the man who hasn't.

Three cents money, three cents goods. (You get what you pay for.)

In the last analysis, wool comes from the sheep. (All financial schemes for revenue must take money from the taxpayer.)

Money cannot buy off gossip behind your back.

Friends of wine and meat, and a married couple of rice and fuel. (Utilitarian friendship and marriage.)

A wife who ate coarse meals with you is never driven away from home. (A wife who has slaved and endured hard times with her husband cannot be divorced, by law and by public opinion, after the husband gets rich.)

A man who has children worries for his children. A man who has no children enjoys real peace.

Money cannot buy your heart's wish.

Money cannot buy "I wish I knew."

Pay your debt and you can borrow a thousand times. Fail to repay, and once is too much.

Talk of the devil and the devil appears.

If money could buy off the road to hell, you would not see funerals at rich men's homes.

Do not buy land at a river's bend; do not marry another living man's wife.

Don't lie to your friends and don't tell the truth to your wife [or husband].

Seeing the saddle makes one think of the horse. You love a house and also the raven on its roof. (Love me, love my dog.)

One dog barks at a shadow; a hundred dogs bark at the noise of barking. (Public stirred by an unfounded rumor.)

Beware of the bureaucrat, not of the high official. (Based on an untranslatable pun. Watch out for the man who handles the red tape.)

When you see a ghost, do not be afraid and the ghost will disappear.

Disaster comes out of the mouth, not into it. (One should be careful with one's words and not offend the great and powerful.)

Close brothers, clear accounts. (Do not mix up business with a family relationship.)

One who rides in the sedan chair is a man; one who carries it is also a man. ("Is a man" means "must be treated with human dignity.")

A gentleman does not mind learning from one less learned than himself.

Do a hasty thing slowly. (Make haste slowly.)

A bullfrog hopes to eat swan's meat. (A vain wish.)

A hungry dog waits for a piece of liver bone. (A vain wish.)

Looking at the sun from the bottom of a well. (Narrow vision.)

You cannot carve on rotten wood. (Lazy minds cannot be taught.)

When you drink water, think of its source.

Discipline your own children, not others'.

Better rely on your own strength than your parents' health.

Lovely face, luckless fate.

A lazy seamstress takes long stitches.

Hasty stitches make a loose garment.

Learn more; then you know how much more you need to learn.

Neither a home nor a country can be without a head.

Drink less and talk less.

Unpolished jade does not shine; an uneducated man cannot fit a post.

Within the four seas, all men are brothers.

A gentleman blames himself; a foolish man blames others.

Other villages are pretty, but none is like one's own.

You cannot straddle two boats without falling.

What is difficult at the beginning becomes easy at the end, and bitter turns into sweet.

Do not condone a small evil; do not pass by a small request for charity.

He who does not learn a craft spoils his whole life.

Words can heal a wound; they can also cut like a knife.

A leopard's skin survives the animal. A reputation survives the man.

No matter where you spread salt, it will be salty; no matter where you pour vinegar, it will taste sour.

The few cannot win against the many; the weak cannot fight against the strong.

Easy to go to work with many, but easier to share a meal with a few.

He who flatters me can also ruin me.

Shake one branch and ten branches will shake with it.

The softer the mud, the deeper one digs. (The gentle and submissive are always preyed upon.)

Do not spare a little expense when doing a big thing.

A mouthful of Omitabhas [used somewhat like "hallelujahs"], a bellyful of malice.

One word can save a nation; one word can also destroy a nation.

Leave a little humanity between you, and it will be easier when you next meet.

Fame will not crown a lazy man's head.

Choose your neighborhood; select your friends.

Money will make up for heroism, wine for courage.

Industry makes up for stupidity.

When water is too clear, there are no fish. A man in a hurry has no wisdom.

The avarice of man is like a snake trying to swallow an elephant.

When two tigers fight, one will be hurt.

Kindness is the basis of all good; avarice the source of all evil.

In a corner, a dog will jump over a wall. Caught in a scrape, a man's wit will think of a way out.

Rough kitchenware will take a lot of knocks.

The wisest man will make a slip. The most stupid man will have one bright good idea.

An inch of time is like an inch of gold, but an inch of gold will not buy an inch of time.

If you are poor, you are lonely even in a city. If you are rich, you will have callers even in the deep mountains.

Do not take advantage of the poor; do not rely on the rich.

Those who despise money will eventually sponge on their friends.

When you have too many lice, you don't feel the itch; when you have too many debts, you stop worrying.

Children do not see their mother's ugly face; a dog will guard its master's hovel.

Wisdom does not depend on age; a man of a hundred may be full of empty talk.

A parent who is long sick in bed is often ignored by even the most filial of sons.

Your wife and children wear like your own clothes. Your brothers are your hands and feet.

If there is discord among brothers, others will take advantage of it.

One husband, one wife. One horse, one saddle.

One heart cannot serve two.

A good man does not beat his wife. A good dog does not bite chickens.

Words over a pillow may be lost once, but not twice.

One rotten pear spoils the whole basket.

Fires and floods have no preference for persons.

Mending the fence after the sheep has escaped. (Locking the barn door after the horse is stolen.)

When you go out, look at the sky. When you enter a house, watch the faces.

A needle is not sharp at both ends.

When you are managing a household, you learn the price of fuel and rice; when you have children, then you appreciate your parents.

Getting up early in the morning is like gaining an extra day.

Fortune comes not in pairs. Misfortunes never arrive singly.

On a tree, some of the fruits are sweet, some sour. From the same womb, some of the children are dumb, some smart.

Good articles do not sell cheaply.

The forefathers plant a bamboo; their children enjoy its shade.

Rivers can be channeled and mountains moved; the hardest is to change the ways of a man.

Meeting a person face to face is better than hearsay.

A single strand of silk will not make thread. A single tree will not form a forest.

古文小品译美目录

ABOUT THE AUTHOR

Lin Yutang's family name is Lin. Nevertheless when people call him "Mr. Yutang," he rather likes it because it is so Chinese. In a nation of ten million Changs and ten million Wangs, naturally such a custom developed. But "Mr. Lin" would also be correct. Born of a Presbyterian minister in 1895 in an inland village on the southeast coast of Fukien, he considers his upbringing in a village in deep mountains had a permanent influence on his character.

He took his degrees from St. John's (Shanghai), Harvard, and Leipzig. He considers he got all his English before coming to Harvard. In the Widener Library he first found himself, first came alive; never saw a Harvard-Yale football match. He was a teacher at Tsinghua University, Peking, in 1916-19; married and went abroad with his wife to study, 1919; studied in the School of Comparative Literature under Bliss Perry and Irving Babbitt at Harvard in 1919-1920; worked with the Y.M.C.A. for Chinese laborers at Le Creusot, France, to support himself, 1920-1921; studied at Jena and Leipzig, 1921-23; was professor of English at Peking National University, 1923-26; and Dean of Women's Normal College, 1926; was chased out of Peking by the Dog-Meat General in 1926, blacklisted among the radical professors; became Dean of Arts in Amoy University, 1926; joined the Wuhan Nationalist Government as a secretary to the Foreign Ministry at Hankow in first half of 1927; "liked the Revolution but got tired of the revolutionists." Since the summer of 1927, he has devoted his time entirely to authorship. He was editor of the literary fortnightlies, *Lunyu, Jenshienshih,* and *Yuchoufeng,* 1929-35 in Shanghai. Now the only important things to him are his books and his family, including two grandchildren, Niuniu and Didi.

This book was set in
Perpetua and Electra types,
printed, and bound by
The Haddon Craftsmen.
Typography by
Andor Braun.